D0443721

Social Accountability
in Communication

Social Accountability in Communication

Richard Buttny

SAGE Publications
London · Newbury Park · New Delhi

SAGE Publications Ltd
6 Bonhill Street
London EC2A 4PU

SAGE Publications Inc
2455 Teller Road
Newbury Park, California 91320

SAGE Publications India Pvt Ltd
32, M-Block Market
Greater Kailash – I
New Delhi 110 048

British Library Cataloguing in Publication data

Buttny, Richard
   Social Accountability in Communication
   I. Title
   302.2

   ISBN 0-8039-8306-9
   ISBN 0-8039-8307-7 pbk

Library of Congress catalog card number 93–84861

Typeset by Type Study, Scarborough
Printed in Great Britain by Biddles Ltd, Guildford, Surrey

For Mom and Dad,
William and Peggy Buttny

Contents

Foreword

by Marvin B. Scott

In this Foreword I would like to glance backward at the birth of 'Accounts.' In March of 1967 Stanford Lyman and I submitted a manuscript to the *American Journal of Sociology*, and on May 4 we received our rejection notice. The anonymous reviewer wrote, and I quote from the original:

> This is a serious paper on an original topic, revealing broad knowledge of the literature and introducing a suggestive new concept. All this argues for publication. . . . Nevertheless, I have reservations about this paper. It does not seem to get anywhere; it does not clarify a new area of social interaction as its beginning promises to do.

The reviewer was right in the sense that the promise of 'a new area of social interaction' was not to be fulfilled in that paper, but had to wait almost three decades before Richard Buttny put it all together in the present work.

What the reviewer undervalued was the suggestive idea that the study of social order may be fruitfully explored through the analysis of talk, and more especially talk that restores fractured sociation. The following year, the 'Accounts' manuscript was published unchanged in the *American Sociological Review*. Sociology, along with philosophy, was taking a 'linguistic turn.'

The ideas behind 'Accounts' were already in the air in the late 1950s when I was completing my undergraduate Communications major and Philosophy minor at the University of Illinois. On the one side, the serious talk was of Kenneth Burke, especially his *Grammar of Motives* and *Permanence and Change*, with the emphasis on the notion that an understanding of communicative interaction involved knowing the 'vocabularies of motives' in use; on the other, the excitement was with Wittgenstein's later philosophy, especially as it was employed by his disciple J.L. Austin, who guest-lectured on campus and led me to his essay, 'A plea for excuses.' During the same serendipitous year, C. Wright Mills spoke at the Champaign-Urbana campus. As a reporter on the campus daily, I was sent to cover his talk, and in preparation read all his works, and was struck that one chapter in his *Character and Social Structure* was entirely devoted to Burke's idea of 'vocabulary of motives.' Sociology, it seemed, was the field in which one could empirically explore the conceptual notion that would later be called 'accounts.'

The term 'accounts' was the label first employed by Harvey Sacks, who formed a circle in Berkeley of fellow students who were writing their doctoral dissertations under Erving Goffman – Sacks, Emmanuel Schegloff, David Sudnow, Sherri Cavan, and myself. A typical weekly session (which was held at Sacks' apartment) consisted of each person reporting on his or her work, submitting it in effect to Sacks' ethnomethodological critique. My dissertation was on horse racing, and in my report I described material from a chapter I was writing on a distinctive pattern of talk (involving 'excuses' and 'justifications') that characterized certain race track regulars. When I completed my description, Sacks said that my topic had been on 'accounts.' He went on to say that the 'restoration talk' that I had described was only one kind of 'accounting practice,' and the study of such practices was the core concern of 'ethnomethodology.'

When I submitted to Goffman my dissertation chapter on 'Race track accounts,' he rejected it on the grounds that I was losing focus on the subject of social organization. He added, in passing, that 'accounts' was not one of his concepts and he smelled Harvey, who had taken on the status of a rival as a source of influence on Goffman's circle of students.

Thus it was not until my collaboration with Stanford Lyman that the concept was permitted to flower. Lyman and I had already collaborated on an influential paper on 'Territoriality,' and we regarded the 'Accounts' paper as part of *A Sociology of the Absurd*, a collection of essays, which, taken together, was meant to provide a general framework for an 'adequate description' of social interaction.

The meta-narrative of the 'absurd', along with all narratives, has been deconstructed under postmodern scrutiny. Nevertheless, the concept of 'accounts' has demonstrated its continual fruitfulness for the exploration of a significant dimension of social life. The seemingly inexhaustible possibilities that this concept furnishes are suggested in the marvelous consolidation and application Buttny provides in this work.

Hunter College
City University of New York

Acknowledgments

I am struck by how many different voices from colleagues and friends as well as from my readings appeared in writing these pages. Folks helpful to me at different stages along the way were: John Adams, Charles Antaki, Louie Campbell, Vern Cronen, Paul Drew, Tom Isbell, Arthur Jensen, Jim Katz, Jack Lannamann, Sam Lawrence, Sheila McNamee, Bud Morris, Barnett Pearce, Lee Upton and Rod Watson – I am grateful. Also, I owe thanks for the editorial assistance from Rita Schlegel. I am especially indebted for the inspiration from the many walks with Shilo and the many talks with Jodi Cohen.

This book is an outgrowth of journal articles and book chapters I have written and co-authored on accounts and social accountability over the past few years. Chapters 1, 3, 4, 9, and 10 were written originally for this manuscript. Chapter 2 is a nearly complete revision of 'Accounts and the accountability of social action' (1993) in B. Dervin and U. Hariharan (eds), *Progress in Communication Sciences,* Vol. 11, Ablex Press. Chapter 5 is a synthesis of two prior works on therapeutic discourse: 'Blame–accounts sequences in therapy: the negotiation of relational meanings' in *Semiotica*, 78 (1990), and 'The uses of goals in therapy' (with Jodi R. Cohen) in K. Tracy (ed.), *Understanding Face-to-Face Interaction*, Erlbaum Press (1991). Chapter 7 is a slightly revised version of 'The problem of communicating Zen understanding: a microanalysis of teacher–student interviews in a North American Zen monastery' (with Thomas L. Isbell) in *Human Studies*, 14 (1991). Chapter 8 is a revised version of 'Discourse direction and power: diverging strategies during a welfare interview' (with J. Louis Campbell III) in S. Thomas and W.A. Evans (eds), *Culture and Communication*, Vol. 4, Ablex Press (1990).

I was within and without, simultaneously enchanted
and repelled by the inexhaustible variety of life.

F. Scott Fitzgerald

1

Introduction and Preview: Social Accountability and the Practical Necessity for Accounts

[Human] conduct . . . is a drama of met and failed expectations, a morality play with consequences for the actors that has a parallel motivational commentary that both actors and critics may and do use to justify, explain, exculpate, license, excuse, and, in general, account for the drama and their part in it. (Mangham and Overington, 1990: 335)

This epigram captures a central function of human speech – the ability to account for one's actions so to change, mitigate, or modify others' assessments. To be accountable to others arises from the condition that persons can be held responsible or answerable for their actions. In practically any social situation the necessity for accounts can emerge: from offering an excuse for arriving late for an appointment, to labeling one's intentions as 'just teasing,' to graciously declining a dinner invitation, to explaining a betrayal to a friend, to defending one's actions in a courtroom. Accounts can be identified in ordinary language by the familiar terms: excuses, apologies, justifications, defenses, explanations, narratives, and the like.

Accounts involve talk designed to recast the pejorative significance of action, or one's responsibility for it, and thereby transform others' negative evaluations. This *transformative function* is the most distinctive feature of accounts as a *discursive practice*. Accounts, of course, are not invariably successful in changing others' critical assessments. The ultimate resolution of the problematic incident may demand further accountability practices – apologies, explanations, arguments, or restitution. Here I want to underscore the power of speech in reinterpreting persons' conduct.

In this chapter I paint in broad strokes a picture of the processes of accounting and social accountability in everyday life and conclude with a preview of the forthcoming chapters.

The Social Accountability of Action

Everyday actions may be said to be done well or poorly, to succeed or fail, to be competent or incompetent, and as a consequence, as meriting varying degrees of praise or blame. Blame, and the critical judgments underpinning it, reflect our ontological condition as moral beings: persons can be held accountable by others for breaches of social and moral[1] orders (Harré, 1979). This distinctively human capacity to be blamed and to be held responsible for actions creates the practical necessity for the communication of accounts. Speech activities such as: calling another to account through accusations, criticisms, or questions; the responses to these – justifications, excuses, or defenses; and the resolution or continuation of this accounting will be identified by the general notion of 'the social accountability of action.'

Persons are self-interpreting creatures of their own and others' actions. The linguistic capacity for persons to give commentaries about their actions, to explain themselves, or to narrate dramatic episodes in their lives, points to the rhetorical character of speech in the resolution of problematic events (Harré and Secord, 1973). Consider, for example, the biblical rendering of the mythical first accounts episode:[2]

> And the Lord God called unto Adam, and said unto him, Where art thou?
> And he said, I heard thy voice in the garden, and I was afraid, because I was naked, and I hid myself.
> And He said, Who told thee that thou wast naked? Hast thou eaten of the tree, whereof I commanded thee that thou shouldest not eat?
> And the man said, The woman who thou givest to be with me, she gave me of the tree, and I did eat.
> And the Lord God said unto the woman, What is this that thou hast done?
> And the woman said, The serpent beguiled me and I did eat.
> (Genesis 3: 9–13)

Both Adam and Eve admit that they ate from the forbidden tree, but they do not just leave it at that because the reasons for or causes of the trouble may alter the accuser's understanding of the act or their part in it. Adam and Eve each account by portraying their transgressions as influenced by another agent.

This primordial type of excuse, 'He/she/it made me do it,' points to the *underlying conditions* or *assumptions* of action which can be drawn on to construct our accounts. For instance, free choice is presumed to be a necessary condition for responsibility, so if a person can convincingly avow that he/she did not act freely, then the burden of responsibility cannot hold. Account-givers commonly draw on such conditions for actions in their accounts as a way to reframe the incident or their responsibility for it. Accounts offer a valuable site for uncovering a culture's taken-for-granted assumptions and folk logic of right action.

In this biblical text Adam's sin makes him self-aware of his nakedness and leads him to hide from the Lord. 'Hiding,' whether physically or metaphorically through concealing, may be seen as attempting to avoid accountability: '[I]n Judeo-Christian mythology, human history proper begins with the awareness of Adam and Eve that they are observable' (Sacks cited in Heath, 1988: 143). To be observable to others is to be accountable to them. Verbal accounting may be seen as revealing oneself to another. But, accounts can conceal as well as reveal, for example, half-truths and veiled claims. Hiding, of course, is considered a childish way of dealing with accountability; the person who runs away (literally or figuratively) from moments of accountability can suffer from presumption of guilt. Adult status demands more sophisticated ways of hiding, concealing, or obfuscating. As Goffman observes, 'The goodness or badness of an account must, of course, be distinguished from its trueness or falseness. True accounts are often good, but false accounts are sometimes better' (Goffman, 1971: 112).

On Being Socially Accountable

A person can be held accountable for pejorative, offensive, or unusual actions because he/she is a member of a larger moral community governed by shared codes of conduct, norms, and legal rules (Blatz, 1972). Deviations from social or moral orders may lead to a variety of responses from others, such as: (a) invoking legal sanctions and institutional authority, (b) verbal rebuke, accusation, or criticism, (c) questioning, prompting, or calling for accounts, (d) waiting for the offender to initiate an explanation, or (e) letting it pass, or overlooking the offense. How actions are perceived, become labeled, and responsibility ascribed are crucial processes in situations of accountability.

Human conduct can be said to fail in various ways. The type and severity of the failure will have differing implications for accountability and the kinds of accounts required to repair the breach. Moral communities distinguish different kinds of failures. As a beginning point consider these analytical distinctions of failure and their associated implications for accountability (Feinberg, 1970: 126–7): (1) instances of defective skill or ability; (2) insufficient care or effort; (3) improper intentions, for example, cheating.

Being held accountable for failure reflects certain assumptions about human action. For instance, (1) persons who have not yet acquired a requisite competence or ability (the novice, children, the developmentally disabled) cannot be seriously blamed for their errors. Such lack of skill or ability has reflexive implications regarding the individual's status or category of personhood – as a not yet competent member or adult. The acquisition of such statuses carries with it a corresponding level of accountability for acceptable performance in that status. Persons seen to be competent who yet make errors in performance can be held accountable. Repeated errors can even lead auditors to question the performer's competence. For instance, it is expected that a running back in North American football will occasionally fumble the ball, but runners who repeatedly fumble will soon be on the bench. But the running back who does not play hard will be seen as more culpable than fumbling. This is an instance of Feinberg's second type of failure, 'improper care or effort.' The important difference between these two categories is the amount of control that one can be said to have over one's actions. One who does not show sufficient care or effort does not fail due to lack of ability, as with the novice, but due to lack of concern. Persons are believed to have more control over their will than over their abilities.

The most serious kind of failure involves (3), 'improper intentions.' It may be impossible to succeed at all one's activities, but it is possible to have proper or good intentions. Intentions, like the second category of 'effort,' are thought to be more in one's control than 'ability.' Persons are taken to be more responsible for what they can control. Failures due to a lack of ability reflect the actor's competence, but failures due to improper intentions reflect the actor's moral character.

How failures and offenses emerge in social interaction will be an important issue throughout this work. How an action, event, or state-of-affairs gets identified and labeled will have consequences for the necessity and shape of the respondent's accounts. The reflexive implications of failure can create a problematic situation for the actor. For the action itself not only can be said to fail (in one of the ways distinguished above), but the action can reflect upon the person who performed the action. That is, ascriptions of failure can be made of the *person* as well as of the *action* (Harré and Secord, 1973). Repeatedly arriving late for appointments can lead to the person-ascription of being absent-minded, busy, selfish, and the like. Person-ascription of failure is more serious than action-attribution in that the former is a consequence of repeated violations as well as taken to be more incorrigible: 'Involved are the notions that he who fails to guide himself by a particular rule has done so at best because of a *momentary lapse*, at worst because of *faulty character*' (Goffman, 1971: 99; emphasis added).

Accounts as a Re-presentation of Action
Having outlined how conduct can be said to fail, offend others or discredit the actor, I turn to how actors can respond to such problematic

circumstances. One of the driving interests in the research on social accountability stems from the issue of the social constructions of meanings and how actors negotiate such ascriptions.

As individual actors, we usually know more about the conditions, circumstances, and constraints on our actions than others do. These 'conditions,' when conveyed in accounts, combined with shared knowledge, can transform the significance of the event. The event can be 'seen differently' by reconfiguring the event's underlying conditions, or previously unknown or unappreciated circumstances. This transformative power of speech shows that events remain open to (re)interpretation because the significance of a 'particular event' depends on a web of interrelated events, actions, social actors, motives, and so on – a change in one of these parts may effect a change in the whole (Buttny, 1985).

For instance, we may all observe a person physically strike another, but what action did we see? As the 'action-motion distinction' underscores, the social or moral significance of an event cannot be adequately described solely by reference to bodily motions: the movement of the arm, the clenching of the fist, the defense postures, even the specification of spatial–temporal coordinates (Burke, 1966). To know *what actions* occurred we need to know about things like the actors' intentions, relational history, background knowledge, contextual antecedents, background circumstances, and the like which comprise an episode within a social drama.

Frequently the above-mentioned dimensions of action (intentions, background knowledge, and so forth) are not readily apparent to observers, and the actors themselves may have differing perceptions of the 'same' event. Also, the event may be described in multiple ways. The labeling of an incident and the ascription of responsibility for it is not enacted by a distant, neutral observer or judge, but by interactants variously positioned and aligned in social contexts. We have no recourse but to consider actors' accounts because the meaning and significance of events is a consequence of such discursive, communication practices. For example:

To 'He did it' ('He hit her') it can be pleaded:
1. 'Accidentally' (she got in the way when he was hammering a nail).
2. 'Inadvertently' (in the course of hammering a nail, not looking at what he was doing).
3. 'By mistake for someone else' (he thought she was May who had hit him).
4. 'In self defense' (she was about to hit him with a hammer).

5. 'Under great provocation' (she had just thrown the ink over him).
6. 'But he was forced to by a bully' (Jones said he would thrash him).
7. 'But he is mad, poor man.' (Hart, 1955: 162–3)

Each of these seven pleas accounts for the 'same' event, and if believable, implicates differing social, moral, and legal consequences. If one avows that one hit another 'accidentally,' 'inadvertently,' or 'by mistake,' one is denying responsibility, at least in part, for the event because of lack of intent. Now actors may be reproached for not being more careful in watching what they were doing, but that is of a different order of seriousness than intentionally hitting another. If one claims 'in self defense' or 'under great provocation,' one is not denying responsibility or intentionality, but justifying the act – as perhaps unfortunate but appropriate given the circumstances. Hitting another – even to death – can be justified under certain circumstances as in time of war. If one is 'forced to do it,' this is a kind of transference of responsibility to another agent, the one who forced me. This account evokes thorny ethical and legal problems, such as in the case of the soldiers' defense for killing civilians as taking orders from commanders (Backman, 1977). Finally, if 'mad or insane', actors may not be held responsible, but their autonomy may be taken away just because they are no longer accountable for action. The point here is that in constructing an account an actor can draw on a variety of contextual and background conditions which can alter the understanding and evaluation of the incident in question. In a sense, the events in our lives are never final and complete because at any point our actions are open to further reinterpretation – our personal histories can be revised.

The Consequences of Accounts
The previous section's heading, 'Re-presentation of Action,' captures the Janus-faced work of accounts. In a straightforward sense, accounts involve the use of language to *represent* the action in question. Accounts can draw on various cultural assumptions about action to verbally (re)construct the event. At the same time, accounts involve a *presentation* of, not only the action, but also the accounter's self and relationship to the recipient. Accounts can serve impression management, face saving, and relational alignment purposes. How these representational and presentational functions of accounts are interactionally achieved through talk will be a major focus of this work.

Recipients of accounts commonly attend to both the representational and presentational functions. Recipients are often less interested with the account's veracity and more concerned with maintaining the ongoing interaction and relationship. Even when accounts are questioned or challenged, the resolution of the breach looks more like negotiation or seeking alignment than it is rendering a judgment.

This social reconstruction of meanings thesis needs some qualification: '[F]ew excuses get us out of it *completely*: the average excuse, in a poor situation, gets us only out of the fire into the frying pan – but still, of course, any frying pan in a fire' (Austin, 1961: 177; emphasis in original). Austin's wry observation suggests the interactive nature of accounts processes. For accounts to transform, or even modify others' evaluations, others need to accept, or at least not overtly reject, the proffered accounts.

Social Accountability as Language Game

The word 'accountable' in ordinary language originates from the metaphor of 'keeping an account' of one's conduct:[3] '[T]he doing of an untoward act can be *charged* to one, or *registered* for further notice, or "placed as an entry on one's *record*." Outside of institutional contexts, of course, there are no formal records, but only reputations' (Feinberg, 1970: 124; emphasis in original). The individual's reputation, or 'face,' may be restored, maintained, or even enhanced by face-work accounts (Goffman, 1967a).

This view of 'the individual' offering accounts needs to recognize how the language game of social accountability constitutes the individual (Shotter, 1985, 1987). That is, the individual as cultural member acquires the local knowledge of social accountability practices – the group's vocabulary of motives, rules of practical action, standards of evaluation. Our sense of having individual options (strategies, tactics) needs to be seen as implementing the cultural resources provided by the language game of social accountability.

Social accountability as a language game involves a 'vocabulary of motives' (Mills, 1940), or in other words, a set of conceptually interrelated terms which comprise the moves within the language game (Wittgenstein, 1953). For instance: 'assessment,' 'failure,' 'offense,' 'blame,' 'ability,' 'responsibility,' 'obligation,' 'knowledge,' 'constraints,' and so on represent part of our lexicon of social accountability. These terms are interrelated into an implicit action theory, or what I call a folk logic, of what counts as appropriate or right conduct. The relations among these terms are conceptual (Coulter, 1983) and comprise a 'logical grammar' of human action

(Wittgenstein, 1953). For example, the notion of 'constraints' implicates a limitation on an actor's 'abilities,' or the notion of 'blame' entails a belief about 'responsibility.' This vocabulary, and the interrelations among its terms, constitutes the ways we think about, structure, and finally evaluate, our own and others' actions. This folk logic of practical action involves a web of common sense understandings about social and moral orders.

By way of speculation, imagine a world that does not have accounts as a move in the language game of social accountability; what would be the consequences? Persons seemingly would have no verbal way to explain themselves or respond to accusations. One's claims to good character conceivably would be much more easily tarnished if one could not tell one's side. As a consequence, persons would likely feel more obligated to adhere to social norms and feel constrained from deviating, since transgressions could not be ameliorated verbally. It would be even harder for persons to decline invitations or offers, since as Heritage (1988) observes, persons at times accept invitations for that which they do not want when they cannot come up with a 'good excuse' to get out of it.

Also, society needs a communicative form for forgiveness and relieving guilt and shame, such as apologies, accounts, and explanations, lest the burden of failure become unbearable (Duncan, 1962). In systems theory terms, social relations would lack a repair mechanism for the individual to restore equilibrium following a disruption. So this thought experiment of a world without accounts throws into bold relief the interactional work accounts do for us, particularly how they lubricate social relations by discursive means.

Accountability serves regulative functions for the social group by constraining the individual's range of actions. But if the individual can generate a plausible account in anticipation of being censored, this 'defense in hand' may allow him/her to deviate from norms which would have been less likely without such prepared accounts. So, while calls for accountability may constrain the individual, accounts may enable the individual to circumvent such constraints.

Limits to Accountability

While there are multiple dimensions of accountability and ways to account, the domain of human affairs for which actors can be held accountable is restricted in certain ways:

> One can be held accountable only for those activities and outcomes over which one exercises control. . . . Having a realm of inevitability is important because it limits . . . responsibility to manageable proportions. It defines areas over which one has no control and, therefore, cannot be

held accountable. Moral codes that survive for any length of time are likely
to include some ways of limiting responsibility. (Wuthnow, 1987: 77)

The realm of the inevitable is generally associated with bodily
functioning and its limitations. For example, being tired and unable
to stay awake or concentrate are commonly drawn upon as excusing
conditions, say, for not completing a project by a deadline. But the
realm of the inevitable is not always unambiguous. Is the contracting
of diseases, such as cancer, inevitable? For example, medical patients
at times confess to feelings of guilt for contracting such diseases, or
not trying hard enough to recover. What counts as inevitable
(namely, that for which persons cannot be held accountable), while
having a biological cause, is simultaneously a social construction
(Harré, 1991).

Preview

Much of the previous research focuses on distinguishing the various
types and functions of accounts. The focus of this monograph is on
how accounts talk is interactionally accomplished in context. That is,
what makes accounts sequentially relevant, and what do persons
make relevant about the problematic and context in the course of
accounting? What makes certain talk heard as successful or unsuccessful accounting?

In the following chapter a reading of the accounts literature is
presented. My reading is divided into two main sections, the first an
attempt to sketch out the principle issues and answers that have been
put forward about accounts. The second section critiques certain
trends in the literature, particularly the view of accounts as an
abstracted speech act performing a range of social functions. Such
findings are due in part to the artificiality of non-naturalistic methods
of studying accounts. Researchers relying on memory or imaginative
reconstructions of accounts, or subjects evaluating a hypothetical
situation promote an idealized image of accounts.

My own perspective on accounts is set out in chapter 3. A
conversation analytic perspective and methodology is combined with
some theoretical leads from social constructionism into a synthetic
perspective I call 'conversation analytic constructionism.' Conversation analysis is the most successful of the new naturalistic,
observational methodologies in providing analytic tools to describe
the workings of communicative interaction. Accounts episodes are
interactively described, that is, how accounts are sequentially
organized, how accounts become relevant as a response, and what
accounts make relevant about the event or surrounding context.

In addition to the conversation analytic attention to interactional sequencing and relevance of accounts, I address the issue of how actors construct accounts. Here I draw from a social construction of realities perspective. What counts as a good or acceptable account depends on our socio-cultural assumptions, norms, and ideologies of right, practical, or permissible conduct – the group's folk logic of action. The classical notion of taken-for-granted understandings is not sufficient because there are often competing and contradictory rules and assumptions, and even when there is consensus, these apply to different people in different ways. Attention must be given, not only to socio-cultural norms, but also to how the actor uses them in practice to apply to this situated context. Social constructionism also offers some interesting leads on the uses and logic of affect in doing social accountability, an idea developed further in chapters 5 and 6.

Chapter 4 provides a statement of methodology and methods for doing this accounts analysis. The main rifts in the social sciences today are over disputes in methods and methodology. My formulation of conversation analytic constructionism needs to be seen as an alternative to mainstream empiricism. This chapter addresses some central issues in methodology and lays out steps for doing this kind of research.

The remaining six chapters comprise the second part of the work. Chapters 5 through 9 are empirical studies of accounts and accountability in different contexts of social accountability.

In chapter 5, a couple therapy session is examined as a site for telling problems and the giving of accounts. Such relationship troubles are told to the therapist in front of an overhearing relational partner. Telling problems involves descriptions of past events or relational patterns; such talk is not a neutral description but is used in the service of implicating blame and responsibility of one's partner. Affect display is developed as a device to frame how to take what is being said – as emphatic, exasperated, angry, and so on. Also, the competing accounts and assessments of the couple's folk logics of relationships are interactionally negotiated with the therapist's specialized logic.

Social accountability episodes are often emotionally charged. In chapter 6 I pursue further how emotion is used and displayed in ordinary conversations in pursuit of social accountability. Affect is treated as part of a discursive practice and having certain social organizational features and implications, rather than as an internal motivational state. Emotions can be nonverbally or paralingually displayed, verbally avowed by the speaker, or ascribed of others. Such affect displays, avowals, or ascriptions can be powerful statements of criticism or defense in social accountability, so such features need to be included in the accounts analysis.

Chapter 7 examines the talk between a Zen teacher and students in a North American Zen monastery. This study takes social account-ability more broadly than the previous chapters and focuses more on answers students offer about their Zen understanding and the interactional challenges and assessments from the teacher. Students are called upon to give an answer to a Zen question or *koan*, but given Zen beliefs about language, discursive, rational, logical answers are not valued. So the student faces a communication problem of how to answer the question in language, but avoid the proscriptions against intellectual, rationalistic talk. Strictly speaking, this chapter is not about accounts in the specific sense developed in the prior chapters, but about the accountability of understanding.

Chapter 8 examines accounts in a welfare application interview. This institutionalized setting provides bureaucratic rules and pro-cedures which structure the course of such interviews. In everyday practice, such institutional rules and procedures may fail to cover the range of contingencies which can arise. In the case examined, the applicant offers narratives to justify her need for assistance, while the caseworker insists that she follow institutional procedures. However, the case is complicated by previous court decisions and conflicting statements from other branches of the welfare agency. Both appli-cant and caseworker partake in recurring and repeated social accountability practices of complaints, justifications and defenses. No clear resolution of the problematic is evident in this transcript, but we do get to see how accounts work to justify a course of proposed action, and how recurring complaint–accounts sequences intensify the interaction.

Chapter 9 looks at social accountability talk in broadcast news interviews. The questions put forward by news interviewers at times can be heard as critical assessments or challenges to the policy, position, or actions of the interviewee. The interviewee's answers can be heard to justify, explain, or account for the conduct in question. A unique feature of this context is that these criticisms and accounts may be observed by a mass television/radio audience. While interviewees may rehearse their answers, in the news interview itself the prepared answer must be inserted as at least minimally relevant to prior questions. As is well recognized, politicians are notoriously skillful at avoiding accountings to difficult questions, but inter-viewees cannot blatantly step around criticisms because the inter-viewer can make relevant such dodges in follow-up questions. In this chapter, the various techniques for raising criticism through question and accounts through answers are examined as interactional ac-complishments.

Chapter 10 provides me with a final moment to look back at the prior social accountability studies and address the issue of context. Context cannot be viewed by a 'container' metaphor or taken unproblematically as a variable to be added to the explanatory equation. Instead, context is conceived as both shaping the accounting practices as well as shaped by these practices.

Conclusion

Accounts are a recurring phenomenon in everyday life. 'Recurring' because all too often our performance falls short of the desired or the expected which leads to some failings on our part. So some way is needed to ameliorate such failings and assuage criticism. Accounts can serve these functions as a response to these problematic situations. Accounts enter as a move in the language game of social accountability. How such episodes of accountability get resolved can be consequential for a person's claims to face, good character, and relationships with others.

Notes

1. The capacity to be accountable for actions differentiates humans from other animals. As the eighteenth-century philosopher Thomas Reid observed: '[Brute-animals] have appetites and passions, but they want that which makes them moral agents, accountable for their conduct, and objects of moral approbation or of blame' (Reid, 1977 [1788]: 69).
2. This passage from Genesis is used as an epigram in McLaughlin, Cody, and O'Hair (1983).
3. My thanks to John Adams for engaging me on this issue of accounts as metaphor.

2

A Reading of the Accounts Literature

> Talk, we hold, is the fundamental material of human relations. . . . Our concern here is with one feature of talk: its ability to shore up the timbers of fractured sociation, its ability to throw bridges between the promised and the performed, its ability to repair the broken and restore the estranged. This feature of talk involves the giving and receiving of what we shall call *accounts*. (Scott and Lyman, 1968: 46; emphasis in original)

In coining the term, 'accounts,' Scott and Lyman (1968) draw attention to a central social repair function of speech and open up an area for analytic investigation. Since this classic work much has been written on accounts and related forms of social accountability discourse. This chapter attempts to provide a reading of the accounts literature to sort out some basic issues and positions: What counts as an account? What functions do accounts serve? What are the processes of accounting? What strategies are used in offering accounts? What perspectives have been taken in doing research on accounts? After this cataloging of distinctions, I turn to a critical assessment of the literature in the Discussion section. This sets the stage for my own perspective developed in the following chapter and further empirical studies of accounts and accountability in chapters 5–9.

The Emergence of Accounts as an Object of Study

Why the recent cross-disciplinary interest in accounts and social accountability? This interest stems from a larger groundswell of research into human symbolic systems and meaning-making structures and practices as reflected in the key terms: language, communication, speech acts, discourse, texts, rhetoric, and the like. The *linguistic turn* in fields such as philosophy, sociology, anthropology, and social psychology moves the study of language-in-use from the periphery to a more central disciplinary concern. At the same time, disciplines which have traditionally studied language-in-use, such as linguistics, rhetoric, and speech communication, became increasingly concerned with the functions of language in a variety of diverse social contexts which expanded research horizons beyond the linguistic intuitions of academics (Levinson, 1983) or the public speaking of trained orators (Adams, 1985). Language studies broadened their scope from formal-structural models to pragmatic, functional, or discourse perspectives. How speakers use language in social situations and what functions these speech actions perform become of primary analytic interest.

Language-in-use, or speech, comprises a primary way in which people engage in social life; indeed, it is only through talk that persons can participate in many social activities and relationships. Speech cannot be regarded as simply an epiphenomenon of more basic constructs like 'attitude', 'social role,' or 'cognitive schema' (Cicourel, 1972; Potter and Wetherell, 1987). As a consequence, accounts as a particular type of speech practice came to be seen, not as mere rationalizations for 'more real' underlying meanings, but as phenomena worthy of study in their own right – as a 'language game' for the social repair of problematic events (Wittgenstein, 1953). The 'things we can do with words,' such as account for troubles, can be consequential for practical and moral action (Austin, 1962).

The Vocabulary of Social Accountability

In perusing through the social and human science literatures, the reader finds a number of terms and concepts which are similar to the notion of accounts, for example, explanations, excuses, justifications, apologies, disclaimers, verbal defenses, motive-talk, aligning actions, and so on. Some of these related concepts dovetail and overlap with accounts. The notion of social accountability will be taken as an umbrella term to cover these various actions, discourses, and speech practices. To sort out this profusion of terms used to capture aspects of social accountability processes, this chapter will survey some of the main ways of accounting for accounts.

Accounts as a Phenomenon

To begin consider the basic question, What counts as accounts? The term 'accounts' is used rather loosely in the research literature, so there arises the problem of multiple meanings of the term. Accounts finds currency in both a conceptual and non-conceptual sense. The non-conceptual use commonly occurs in social scientific texts in much the same sense as its use in everyday parlance – to mean 'a description.' 'a reason for' or 'an explanation.'

Scott and Lyman (1968, 1970) are the first to provide a systematic treatment of accounts as a concept. As seen in the epigram, they define accounts as an individual's talk designed to mend a social breach resulting from a problematic situation. Problematic situations may be discrediting to the actor (for example, failure) or offensive to others (for example, insults). The emergence of a problematic situation reflects the condition that persons can be held accountable for their conduct and called upon by others to account for themselves. Verbal accounts serve as explanations for apparently 'untoward' or 'unusual' actions; accounts attempt to prevent, or repair, these problematic situations and restore social equilibrium between participants. The development of this concept bears a close affinity to Goffman's investigations into face-saving practices (1967a) and remedial actions (1971).

A second use of the term refers to the 'descriptions,' 'ordinary explanations' or 'self-reports' about everyday activities (Antaki, 1988) or personal relationships (Harvey et al., 1990). This sense of accounts includes a broader range of discourse than Scott and Lyman's notion (1968). Accounts are not circumscribed as responses to a problematic situation, but include references to unproblematic or routine situations. This conception focuses on how persons portray their ordinary actions, practices, and relationships to others; how persons render these accountable through language. Accounts of everyday, mundane activities merit social scientific attention because such talk embodies persons' sense-making procedures.

A third sense of accounts has been developed as part of attribution theory (Weiner et al., 1987; Synder and Higgins, 1988). A broadened view of attribution theory involves not only descriptions of what happened or who caused it, but also moral accounts and self-presentational accounts (Tedeschi and Reiss, 1981). In addition, this conception may include the mental representations of events. That is, accounts can be both verbal reports or explanations (consistent with the above uses) as well as the private cognitions of other persons, acts, or events (Antaki, 1987).

A fourth use of the term accounts can be found in ethnomethodology (Garfinkel, 1967; Watson and Sharrock, 1991) and conversation analysis (Sacks, 1989 [1964]). On this view, accounts involve the various ways persons present their activities so as to render them sensible, normal, understandable, proper, and the like. Persons continually account for their actions such that others can make sense of what they are doing 'for all practical purposes' (Garfinkel, 1967). On this view, accounts do not depart from the ordinary focus of interaction into efforts to mend the problematic with justifications or excuses as with Scott and Lyman (1968). Instead accounts need to be seen as an ongoing, sense-making feature of the interaction. For example, an officeworker seated at a desk shuffling papers, jotting notes, making telephone calls, and the like may be seen to account for his/her activities to co-workers as engaged in what we may gloss as routine work.

When a person's actions (verbal or nonverbal) are not accountable by normal typifications or commonsense understandings, then this may create an unusual or problematic juncture such that the person may be questioned by others and need to account in Scott and Lyman's (1968) sense for those actions. For example, Sacks (1989 [1964]: 250–1) recounts how as an adolescent he used to go for walks at night in his neighborhood. Growing up in an 'exclusive' suburb where few people walked at night the police would sometimes stop and question him about what he was doing. So, walking at night in an exclusive suburb apparently is not a routinely accountable activity, and thereby demanded an account.

Accounts are not continually called for from others just because persons' actions – such as walking – are usually understood in routine taken-for-granted ways – *they account for themselves.* It is only when this sense of the routineness or the taken-for-granted fails to explain another's actions that we call another to account. So the Garfinkel and Sacks sense of accounts as ongoing, sense-making procedures is ultimately consistent with the more circumscribed Scott and Lyman sense of accounts as excuses and justifications (Heritage, 1988).

While there are clearly overlaps among these different uses of accounts, the primary interest here will be on the tradition arising from Scott and Lyman (1968) – talk used to transform pejorative ascriptions and resolve problematic events.

Ways of Accounting
In this section I review different types of accounts and related social accountability phenomena. Accounts are distinguished into two main kinds, *excuses* and *justifications* (Scott and Lyman, 1968). Drawing on Austin's (1961) classic formulation, excuses serve to account by admitting the negative significance of the event, but denying all or some of the actor's responsibility for it. To say, 'I was held up by heavy traffic on the way over,' can be heard to offer an excuse since it implicitly acknowledges that arriving late may be offensive, but the actor's responsibility is minimized by being portrayed as due to circumstances beyond control. Justifications, on the other hand, involve claims in which the actor implicitly accepts responsibility, but denies the offensive character of the event in question. To account by saying, 'I needed to finish that project before I left the office,' attempts to justify arriving late due to an appeal to the higher consideration of completing work.

The underlying notion of responsibility is central to understanding and evaluating human action. Indeed, responsibility is commonly synonymous with being accountable. As Goffman observes, '[T]he question of responsibility must be raised . . . for without knowing how those involved in an act attribute responsibility for it, we cannot in the last analysis know what it is that has occurred' (1971: 99). So accounts designed to excuse will address the conditions of offensive action which can alleviate or modify the actor's responsibility, while accounts designed to justify will accept responsibility and address the characterization of the incident in question.

Persons can account for conduct in diverse ways. The 'accordion-effect' comes into play: one may say a lot or a little, be concise or verbose in accounting. Accounts can be seen to range along a continuum which has on the far end an *actional* perspective of carefully thought out and calculated *reasons* for action, and on the other end, *movements* arising from *causal* conditions such as physical reflexes (Burke, 1969; Toulmin, 1970). Consider how reasons and causes can be used in forming accounts.

In perhaps the canonical case, an account may be heard as a kind of *reason* for action, an explanation for 'why' or 'how' an action was committed (Draper, 1988). Reasons are often marked by 'because statements,' as in 'I did X because of Y' (Antaki, 1990). A familiar form of reason-giving involves stating one's *intentions* to explain one's conduct (Anscombe, 1960). Intentions can specify the actor's ends and express a means-to-ends relation in accounting, such as, 'I was sarcastic in order to get her to leave.' Intentions can be used to portray the actor's relationship to the action as in the more common type of instance, 'I didn't mean to make him cry by what I said.' Another's action taken in isolation may require the actor's intention to be made understandable in a larger context, what Harré (1977) calls an 'action-act recategorization,' for instance, 'I took your ball, but I was going to return it when I was finished playing.' The specification of the actor's intentions works to indicate the point or the direction of the action and thereby account by making it intelligible as part of a larger act sequence.

Persons also can account for their behavior in terms of bodily movements based on *causes*. Behaviors, such as blushing, tripping, illness, sleepiness, and the like, can be used as an object in an account to excuse some behavior. The account can be constructed to say, 'I didn't mean to spill coffee on you, but I tripped on the rug,' or 'I won't be able to come to work today because I'm not feeling well.' Bodily movements are an interesting kind of behavior for the study of accounts because they imply that what the person did or did not do was beyond control – that there was no choice in the matter. It does not make sense to ask for a reason for movements because movements are not within a person's power, they are based on the causal mechanisms of the body or external environment. Toulmin points out that it is inappropriate to ask for another's reason for blushing – blushing is something one cannot prevent (1970: 10). In such a situation one may have reasons for *not* blushing, but one cannot help it. There is, however, a common usage of asking, 'Why are you blushing?' But such a query is not asking for one's reason, in the sense of being a warrant for action, but of what background circumstances blushing signifies. Causal accounts suggest that one had no choice or control over the matter.

How an action or event is *described* is crucial for understanding what happened and who is culpable. Actors commonly identify incidents by favored descriptive terms. Backman (1977, 1985) calls this rhetorical transformation of redescribing or offering a different label for the act in question 'conventionalizations,' for instance, 'I'm just teasing' to modify a seemingly insulting remark, or 'I'm not giving you an ultimatum, I just want to reschedule.' Atkinson and Drew (1979: 139–40) observe that witnesses in court cases frequently justify their part in events by descriptions of the scene, for example, 'We were under gunfire at the time.' Descriptions of scenes, events relationships, and so on can be crucial for recounting what happened, establishing the facts, and ultimately who is responsible.

Narratives also can function as an account by verbally reconstructing a temporal sequence of particular events and the actor's part in them so as to justify actions, for example, in therapy (Labov and Fanshel, 1977) or to explain failed relationships (Gergen and Gergen, 1983; Weber et al., 1987). Narratives as a discourse genre work as accounts when tellers re-present past events in such a way to defend their conduct. Narratives allow the teller to offer explanations at greater length.

Not only can narratives work as accounts, but also accounts can be seen as part of a larger, ongoing narrative – telling a life story (Sarbin, 1986; Fisher, 1987). Accounting not only ties into an individual's narrative, but such narrations are themselves connected with other narratives. As MacIntyre remarks, '[N]arrative selfhood is correlative. I am not only accountable, I am one who can ask others for an account . . . I am part of their story and they are part of mine . . . [T]his asking for and giving of accounts itself plays an important part in constituting narratives' (1984: 218, cited in Addelson, 1990: 142–3).

Another discourse form commonly associated with accounts is *apologies*. Apologies are utterances which acknowledge the actor's culpability for the event along with an expression of remorse. Goffman takes apologies as a kind of ritualistic performance of 'splitting the self in two': a blameworthy part which is cast into the past and a reformed part which is ready to abide by the rules (1971: 113–14). In contrast to excuses, apologies in their canonical sense admit responsibility for the misdeed. However, apologies often co-occur with excuses, as in the form: '[apology]-but-[excuse].' 'I'm sorry I didn't get the paper in on time, but I had two exams last week' (Owen, 1983: 96). On a *prima facie* level, it seems odd that apologies and excuses cohere together since apologies concede fault while excuses deny at least some responsibility. The fact that these two acts do frequently co-occur suggests that persons are less concerned with the logic of speech acts or the propositional content of the message, but more with the expressive character of speech as regards mending relational alignments.

Motives A parallel development in rhetoric and in philosophy to the work on accounts is the notion of 'motives' (Peters, 1958; Burke, 1969). Persons describe or explain their own, or another's, actions by citing the actor's motives. Avowing motives or ascribing them of another are common communication practices particularly when actions are questioned, for instance, 'We weren't plotting anything, we were just talking before the meeting' or 'She's saying that as a way to show off to you.' The notion of motive has currency in everyday parlance as well as the social sciences. Detectives may search for the suspect's motive for the crime. Court cases provide good examples of reconstructing motives for crimes. It may be a fact that Jones was killed, but what motives led to this will constitute how the event is labeled – as murder, as manslaughter, or as accident. In such cases much of the courtroom exchanges involve portraying the accused's conduct by innocent or guilty motives.

Motives are 'shorthand terms for [defining] situations' and thereby providing a way to see actions in a desirable way, as having a particular point or purpose (Burke, 1936: 29). 'Motive is not in this regard a thing in the world but a way of conceiving social action' (Blum and McHugh, 1971: 101). In this literature, motives do not refer to a person's internal states – to 'the subjective springs of action.' Rather, motives are the avowed or imputed words which 'stand for anticipated situational consequences of questioned conduct' (Mills, 1940: 913). Motives need to be distinguished from the psychologist's notion of motivation which posits inner states as *causes* of behavior (Peters, 1958). In other words, a distinction needs to be drawn between 'motive-talk' and motivation (Hewitt, 1984). Motive-talk works as a social object to present actions as understandable once the actor's motive is recognized. The picture can become more complicated: the recipient may doubt the actor's avowed motive, or the issues of hidden motives, multiple motives, or unconscious motives may be raised. All of these point to how the notion of motive works as a way to see or identify or typify the actions in question. So motive-talk can function as accounts to defend the actor's conduct from others' approbation.

Motives are given as a reason for behavior when there is a departure from conventional expectations, or the ends of one's actions are not clear (Peters, 1958). Not all actions require motives, for instance, the giving of birthday presents or getting married. These activities are done for reasons, but to ask for someone's motives implies that something is fishy, that is, there are certain conditions or intentions which are devious or out of the ordinary. One may indeed have motives for commonplace activities; giving birthday presents to influence the boss, or marrying someone for their money. But to presume that every action is done with a motive is to blur the useful distinction in ordinary language between reasons and motives.

The terms in ordinary language for describing motives are not precise and devoid of ambiguities. As Burke (1969) suggests, speech cannot be rid of this open texture, so analysts should examine 'the resources of ambiguity' present in the actor's avowed motives which makes possible the transformation of meanings.

The kinds of motives actors give for their actions themselves need to be explained. The motives that make action intelligible in one place or time do not readily translate to other cultures or historical epochs. For instance, contemporary Western, middle-class ideologies explain economic success or failure in terms of individual effort; by way of contrast, some traditional cultures account for failures by fatalistic explanations or appeals to codes of honor (Brown, 1987; Buttny, 1987b). Such historical and cultural differences in ways of explaining or justifying action is captured by the notion of 'vocabularies of motives,' that is, a group's taken-for-granted moral and practical reasons for actions (Burke, 1936; Mills, 1940). A vocabulary of motives works to provide the cultural resources for understanding or evaluating actions.

These notions of motives and accounts clearly overlap and in some respects are functionally equivalent. As seen above, one can cite motives as a way to account for actions. Generally, though, motives have not found much currency in recent research, probably because of the potential confusion with the concept of motivation. The notion of accounts captures more clearly the lingual or interactive aspects of social repair. The pioneering work on motives has provided the most important conceptual precursor for accounts research.

Approaches to Accounts

Functions

One of the driving interests in the research on accounts stems from the larger issue of the social construction of realities (Berger and Luckman, 1966). How is it possible that the social meanings of action and ascriptions of responsibility can be transformed through accounts? There is a *changeable* and *negotiable* character to the significance of events. Seemingly problematic events can be retrospectively reconfigured through interactants' ascriptions and redefinitions. Accounts, then, can be viewed as the use of language to *interactionally construct preferred meanings for problematic events*.

This reconstruction-of-social-meanings thesis leads to a view of accounts as not merely a *representation* of action, but as a *presentation* of the actor's preferred interpretation (Burke, 1969). The performance of an account serves a *formative function*; language is used rhetorically to shape how others see us and our actions (Duck and Pond, 1990). This formative conception of speech reflects a functional view of accounts. A primary focus of research is how accounts *function* in social interaction – to change or mitigate the problematic event. The very idea of speech used to account for conduct is a functional concept.[1] Functional in that the emphasis is on what speech *does* in interaction, to justify, excuse, mitigate, explain, and the like. In the course of offering accounts, one is simultaneously attempting to preserve face and maintain social relationships.

Face saving   This *face-saving function* is probably the most cited explanation for accounts. The self, and how it is seen by others, is the basic organizing principle of social interaction (Goffman, 1967a). To achieve the status of full-fledged members of society, one must avow claims to a right or good character, in terms of socially-approved statuses, competencies, goals, and the like. When one's actions are not consistent with one's claims to good character, this may be discrediting because it is expressive of social or moral failings. This inconsistency between the claimed and the performed creates a social disequilibrium which moves the individual to attempt to correct the incident through accounts and thereby prevent threats to face. Social equilibrium can be restored when the recipient accepts the proffered face work.

The problematic events which arise in everyday life are at times less about substantive or material matters (an accident, such as damaging another's property; or committing a crime), than about ritualistic concerns (declining an invitation; criticizing one's spouse in front of others). Goffman develops this analogy of the *ritualistic* or *ceremonial* features of interaction by conceiving of the self as a kind of 'sacred object' which must be attended to with appropriate concern. Social interaction becomes seen as structured by rules protective of one's own 'face' or the face of others (Goffman, 1967c; Brown and Levinson, 1978). Accounts, or ways of saving face, are needed when this ceremonial order of face-to-face interaction becomes disrupted. While this distinction between the substantive and ritualistic features of interaction breaks down (Morris, 1985; Schegloff, 1988), the conception does draw our attention to the expressive features of action – what conduct reflects about moral character and interpersonal alignments (also see Shotter, 1985).

For Synder et al. (1983), face gets developed by the construct of self-image. So 'excuses are explanations or actions that serve to lessen the negative implications of an actor's performance, thereby maintaining a positive image for oneself and others' (Synder et al., 1983: 45). Persons strive to preserve their self-image in the face of threats by attending to both an *external audience* (consistent with impression management) and an *internal audience* (which reflects the individual's values). The individual attends to the 'revolving images' of both the external and internal audiences.

Social relationships   Accounts, in addition to protecting one's own face, serve *relational functions*. When our actions are offensive to others, accounts can lubricate social interaction so as to restore 'relational alignment' (Stokes and Hewitt, 1976; Morris, 1991) and 'achieve joint conduct' (Shotter, 1984). Our actions express both our 'demeanor' about ourselves and our 'deference' towards others (Goffman, 1967b). An offender may need to take a deferent posture in relation to the offended party. The very act of offering an account to the offended party may itself be seen as a sign of deference. However, an offender may present an account which expresses that the corrective process is not being taken seriously, as when a high school student sarcastically accounts for an absence to the teacher. Such a demeanor and lack of appropriate deference may intensify the breach rather than mitigate it because of the expressive implications in the manner of doing the account. In offering an account, one is simultaneously projecting a construction of the person to whom it is offered (Shotter, 1989). The point here is that the ways persons account to others explicitly sends a message about the event in question as well as implicitly sending a message about their relationship (Watzlawick et al., 1967).

This relational dimension to the corrective process is witnessed also by persons who accept accounts publicly which privately they do not believe. This common form of 'blinking' is due to the desire to maintain a relationship rather than adjudicate minor offenses. What is really at stake is often not so much the event itself, but the actor's claims to good character and amicable relations with others.

Social control   A third kind of function accounts perform is social control. The necessity of giving accounts for deviation from social norms or rules serves a social control function in regulating behavior. Being held accountable or answerable to others works as a constraint on one's actions. This social control function involves more than simply matching conduct to social rules and invoking accountability for deviance. Instead, social control is seen as an emergent feature of interaction which arises from how persons orient to and actively respond to the regulative function of the rules. For instance, Much and Shweder (1978) examined how situations of accountability arise in a kindergarten setting. While teachers invoke rules for social control purposes, such 'rules are continually *tested, employed, clarified, and negotiated*' by kindergarteners and teachers (Much and Shweder, 1978: 20; emphasis added). The accusations made and the accounts offered reveal how rules are used and responded to in accountability practices.

On the one hand, the individual may be seen as constrained from deviating from group norms or rules because of the social control function of accountability. But on the other hand, how rules apply to the individual with what weight and what authority, are matters which can be interactionally negotiated, especially through accounts (Sabini and Silver, 1982). So individuals can be seen to follow, circumvent, or even modify the rules to coordinate actions. In short, the social control function of accountability reflects the dialectic of human action between societal constraints and individual autonomy (Pearce and Cronen, 1980).

Accounts Processes
A second main issue in accounts research has been a depiction of the process of accounts-giving. This issue of process is captured by the related labels: 'corrective process' (Goffman, 1967a), 'remedial interchange' (Goffman, 1971), 'accounts episodes' (Morris, 1985), 'accounts phases' (Schönbach, 1990), 'accounts sequences' (Buttny, 1987a), or 'situations of accountability' (Much and Shweder, 1978). There are three questions which comprise this issue of process: What are the *components* (that is, the parts, elements, or stages) of the process? How are these components *interrelated* or *connected*? What are the *variations* from the canonical format?

The accounts process may be seen to have four basic components or parts. The process begins with the occurrence of (1) a *problematic event* for which the actor may be (2) *held accountable* through interlocutor's *finding fault, criticism*, or *questioning*. This in turn leads the actor to offer (3) an *account* which then needs to be (4) *evaluated* by the recipient as acceptable or not.

Initiation of accounts processes   In ordinary or routine circumstances, accounts are not needed just because one's actions are self-explanatory or accountable in obvious ways given interactants' shared, background typifications and taken-for-granted knowledge (Schutz, 1964). When persons are seen to diverge from expectations or act in unusual ways, they may be questioned or criticized by others for such conduct. What an actor can be reproached or held accountable for reflects the commonsense understanding of local normative standards. Such circumstances have been variously labeled: a 'problematic situation' (Scott and Lyman, 1968), 'virtual offense' (Goffman, 1971), 'failure event' (Schönbach, 1980), 'predicament' (Schlenker, 1980), 'disjuncture' (Lutfiyya and Miller, 1986), 'incident,' 'breach,' and the like. These range in degree of seriousness from minor (forgetting an acquaintance's name) to major (stealing money from an acquaintance). The point here is that the event becomes recognized by interactants as no longer routine and ordinary, but instead, problematic or unusual.

This recognition of the problematic marks a necessary but not sufficient condition for the beginning of the accounts process. For instance, Smith's recognition of Jones' presumed misconduct does not necessitate that Smith will raise the issue with Jones. The incident may be minor or Smith may be more concerned with amicable relations with Jones than adjudicating the misconduct.

Problematic events may be offensive to others and/or discrediting of the actor. Actions which are offensive may lead others to accuse the offender for such breaches. Following the initial offense, the offended party may 'blame' (Pomerantz, 1978), 'challenge' (Goffman, 1967a), 'rebuke' (Sanders, 1991) or 'find fault' (Morris, 1988) with the offender. Or, less overtly, the offender may be indirectly questioned (Rosenblum, 1987), the issue may be hinted at, or the offended party may propose an account for the offender (McLaughlin et al., 1983) as a 'priming move' (Owen, 1983). The point here is that the act of criticism or probing makes necessary the practice of accounting. The blame-accounts exchange is a central form of practical and moral action. As already seen, actors want to maintain their claims to good character and will attempt to remedy the problematic. Accounting for actions is a form of 'remedial work' (Goffman, 1971).

While it is common for accounts to be prompted by the inter-locutor's blame or question, this is not invariably the case. For instance, Smith may not even notice the problematic character of Jones' actions, but Jones may volunteer an account in anticipation. Further, the failure event may not be offensive to another, but discrediting to the actor. Such discrediting failure events preclude a reproach from others – it would cease to have a function. The point here is that discrediting failure events may lead to accounts without a prior reproach. A reproach is not a necessary condition for accounts (Buttny, 1985, 1987a).

Resolution of the accounts process   For the problematic event to be ameliorated, the accounts offered need to be evaluated as acceptable by the recipient. 'Evaluation' is a constituent feature, not only of accounts episodes, but of practically all forms of social interaction. Persons continually monitor their own and others' actions according to situational standards of propriety. But in accounts episodes, evaluation is conceived more specifically as the recipient's assess-ment or judgment about the account's acceptability. As Goffman (1971) observes, the person offering accounts needs some sign of their sufficiency from the recipient, lest the accounter feel obliged to continue to offer more accounts. So evaluation includes not only a cognitive dimension, but also a communicative act which conveys the recipient's assessment. Evaluation describes the final part of the canonical accounts sequence: problematic event–blame–accounts–evaluation.

To be credible, accounts need to cohere with the recipient's 'background expectancies,' that 'taken-for-granted knowledge' which reflects the acceptable beliefs and standards of the group (Scott and Lyman, 1968). When the account fails to offer a sufficient explanation for the problematic event, the account may be con-sidered unacceptable and deemed 'illegitimate.' Accounts need to be 'normalized' within the background expectancies of the group, otherwise they may be deemed 'unreasonable.' For example, John Hinckley's account for shooting President Reagan as wanting to attract the actress Jodi Foster is considered unreasonable and even a criterion for insanity. The social circle to whom the account is offered may have different standards of evaluation. Being too high to attend class may be understandable to a student's peers, but usually not to the teacher or parents.

A recipient may dispute the adequacy of an account or, more indirectly, display hesitation, or make an ironic comment. Such negative evaluations may lead the actor to 'recycle' the accounts sequence by offering further explanation or different accounts

(Morris, 1985). If the actor's accounts are unsuccessful in mending the breach, then the interaction may escalate into a confrontation episode (Newell and Stuttman, 1988).

The evaluation of accounts is affected by how credible the speaker is perceived to be by others. Goffman's (1971) observation that accounts may be accepted publicly even when they are not fully believed privately, led Blumstein and colleagues (1974) to distinguish the 'honorability' (private assessment) of an account from 'honoring behavior' (public actions). The public honoring of accounts is affected, not only by its honorability, but also by situational constraints, most notably *status or power differences*. Subordinates are more likely to honor accounts from those of higher power or status positions (Blumstein et al., 1974; Semin and Manstead, 1983: 99, 110–11). In addition, subordinates offer more accounts to those of higher status when seeking desired ends. In a study of employment interviews, Ragan (1983: 165) found that applicants (subordinates) offered many more accounts (twenty to three) than those offered by interviewers.

This notion of evaluation may be misleading if a 'judicial analogy' is taken too literally for ordinary situations of accountability. Goffman (1971: 116) suggests that invoking some sort of balance principle of distributive justice (the greater the harm, the greater the compensation) will be limited in explanatory scope because much of the remedial process is 'ritualistic' rather than 'substantive.' In everyday circumstances, accounts are often readily accepted, especially for minor offenses, even when the content of the accounts is not fully believed. Offender and offended alike frequently want to bring the remedial process to a rapid and mutually agreeable close. Interactants are primarily concerned with finding ways to achieve 'mutual alignment of conduct so that some kind of joint action can proceed' rather than the secondary consideration of adhering to social norms (Stokes and Hewitt, 1976).

Even for more serious incidents which involve substantive matters, the evaluation of accounts may be seen as a kind of negotiation by the use of regulative rules (Morris and Hopper, 1980; Geist and Chandler, 1984). The emphasis here is not on the content of the particular rules, but on how communicators achieve consensus about rules. The application of the general rule to a specific situated context is often not definitive for participants (Buttny, 1986). The rules do not apply in the same ways and with the same consequences for different categories of persons. Consequently, to achieve consensus may involve verbal negotiation designed to show one's relation to the rules, future intentions, and alignments with others.

Strategies
A third main issue in the literature involves the accounting strategies persons employ in responding to problematic events. The notion of strategies involves the questions of: Why did the actor *select* this account from the *range* of other possible responses? and, What do the actions taken *express* about the actor, the actor's view of events, and the actor's view of relations with others?

Accounts are taken as a form of 'impression management' strategies (Goffman, 1959; Schlenker, 1980; Tedeschi and Reiss, 1981; Semin and Manstead, 1983). Impression management is rooted in the idea that the individual is motivated to protect or defend against threats to social identity which arise from predicaments. The more severe the predicament, the more accounts will be offered. A routine, script-like account may suffice for minor offenses, but for major ones much more explanation will be required. Compare the accounts required for accidentally washing your turtle down the sink to accidentally drowning your baby in the bathtub (Scott and Lyman, 1968).

Accounts are selected which are believed to maximize the ratio of rewards to costs for the person, that is, to minimize the negative implications arising from the predicament (Schlenker, 1980). For instance, accounting strategies may be used such as: presenting an act as meaningless, or as a joke, not to be taken seriously, or as due to extenuating circumstances, like drunkenness. Offenders may adopt a deference strategy in which they overstate the seriousness of the offense with the hope that the recipient in turn will cooperatively minimize the magnitude of the fault. Accounting strategies may not only be about an action or event, but about the individual *qua* person; one may offer accounts which redefine the self – a renunciation of a past self (for example, being a drug addict) which is no longer true of the person today (Goffman, 1967a, 1971).

One may try out various accounts for a failure event on different audiences to see which is the most effective. This trying out of accounts may be mentally rehearsed beforehand in anticipation (Tompkins and Cheeney, 1983). This mental rehearsal allows the actor a chance to intrapersonally test the adequacy of the accounts (Harré and Secord, 1973). But persons cannot offer just any accounts. To be convincing, accounts need to be congruent with the 'reality constraints' of the situation – the severity of the predicament, the audience's knowledge and beliefs about the situation (Semin and Manstead, 1983). What is 'true' about an event may need to be negotiated by consensual agreement between the actors and others.

The selection of accounting strategies depends on the nature of negative ascription from others. Synder et al. (1983) offer a strategies model of excuses. Excuses are oriented to three main components of the problematic event: first, the link which implies responsibility between the person and the negative performance. Excuses of innocence and denials typically occur here. If the first component is unsuccessful, then the individual may adopt an excusing strategy to attempt to reframe or alter the impact of the event. If all else fails, a last strategy is to attempt to lessen responsibility by conceding that one did the act, but citing various qualifying circumstances.

Weiner et al. (1987) examined how excuses are presented so as to avoid anticipated anger from others. They found that 'good excuses' – those that lessen personal responsibility – portrayed the event as due to 'external, uncontrollable, and unintended causes.' These results are interpreted from a naive theory of emotions framework: people use an implicit theory of emotions in which they predict how the causes of an event will affect others' emotional response. The causality for the event is then presented to others according to this good excuses model.

Cody, McLaughlin, and colleagues offer a model of accounts strategies which attempts to predict the type of accounts strategy and evaluation of this account based on the antecedent reproach type and situation variables (McLaughlin, Cody and O'Hair, 1983; McLaughlin, Cody and Rosenstein, 1983; Cody and McLaughlin, 1985, 1988, 1990). Accounts are conceived of as possessing varying degrees of 'mitigating' or 'aggravating' effects on the face of the communicators. Accounts types are modeled along a continuum from the most mitigating to the most aggravating: 'concessions,' 'excuses,' 'justifications,' and 'refusals.' In selecting an accounts strategy to manage a failure event, concessions and excuses are more mitigating than justifications and refusals because 'they threaten the speaker's but not the hearer's face' (McLaughlin, Cody and O'Hair, 1983: 211).

Their model claims that accounts sequences are a function of congruent levels of mitigation and aggravation between reproach and account, and between account and evaluation. The type of accounts strategy selected to manage failure events is based on a 'general principle of reciprocity of affect.' that is, 'congruent levels of mitigation and aggravation.' The evidence for the matching response is stronger for aggravating reproaches and accounts, than for the mitigating end of the continuum. This reciprocity principle works for interpersonal settings, but does not hold for formal situations, such as traffic court. In traffic court, concessions were found to lead to the most aggravating evaluation (Cody and McLaughlin, 1988).

Discussion

To this point the accounts literature has been portrayed by a rhetoric of consensus – in terms of generally accepted answers to standard social scientific issues: definitions, functions, processes, evaluation, and strategies of accounts. But now I want to take a more critical view of some of these writings. The literature on accounts may be seen as a microcosm of the current pluralism and disparate perspectives throughout the social and human sciences (Shweder and Fiske, 1986; Dervin et al., 1989). Presenting a review of the accounts literature based on a trope of progress or cumulative knowledge is at best suspect, and at worst misleading. This chapter is entitled 'a reading' rather than a review to call into question the idea of linear progress and unity in the accounts literature. Instead of a unified theory or dominant paradigm, the reader finds everything from interpretative descriptions (accounts as paying ceremonial homage to the face of another as a sacred object) to discourse analysis (close readings of accounts found in conversational transcripts) to mainstream empiricism (credibility studies of accounts) and to critical studies (why some accounts seem to count more than others).

The largest rift is between the empiricist paradigm and what might be broadly called interpretativism. Consider the litany of contrasts for what counts as good research: explanation–understanding, prediction–thick description, control of conditions–naturalistic observation, variables–social practices, experience far–experience near concepts, extensive sample–intensive analysis. Generally empiricism identifies with the terms on the left-hand side of the polar contrasts while interpretativism aligns with the right-hand side. While some cross-fertilization has occurred, on the whole, each paradigm has developed its own epistemological standards and exemplars of good research. Theoretical and methodological commitments influence how the researcher approaches the phenomenon being studied: what to look for, the appropriate analogies to work with, what kinds of questions to ask, what counts as good evidence, and even how to write up the study (Gergen, 1982; Bochner, 1985).[2]

A Critical Reading of Some Accounts Research

At the conclusion of their review of the accounts literature, Semin and Manstead (1983: 122) call for more research (a) in *naturalistic contexts* which (b) examines the *relations between the offense and the account*. Semin and Manstead's assessment remains largely accurate today. I attempt to develop their critique here, and in the next chapter, present a position which satisfies these criticisms.

Regarding (a), a limitation of much of the accounts research is that it does not examine accounts in naturally occurring settings (this criticism is not specific to this literature, of course).[3] In much of the empiricist or neopositivist research, accounts phenomena are formulated, not from naturalistic observation, but from the researcher's memory or by imaginative intuitions. Accounts are studied from respondents' written reconstructions of a past social accountability event, or respondents' evaluation of a vignette or hypothetical situation. Relying on the researcher's intuitions, or respondents' reconstructions and hypothetical evaluations results in broad glosses of the phenomena and must raise doubts about ecological validity. Also, these methodological procedures result in a conception of a person offering *the* account, as though accounts are invariably achieved as a *single speech act*. Such a paradigmatic image of accounts as a single speech act abstracts accounts out of their sequential context, independent of antecedents and other co-occurring acts, in order to operationalize as a variable.

Accounts have received the most scholarly attention for how they *function* in various problematic situations. Accounts have been shown to serve three main functions: to preserve interactants' face, to maintain social relationships, and for social control. Consider the variety of functions which accounts are claimed to perform: to 'change,' 'transform,' 'redefine,' 'make intelligible,' 'reframe,' 'legitimate,' 'warrant,' 'reconfigure,' 'qualify,' or 'modify' the significance of the event in order to 'save face,' 'manage impressions,' to 'align' or 'coordinate' actions so as to 'achieve consensus' and 'mitigate' (or 'aggravate') social relations and thereby 'maintain' (or 'restore') social solidarity and equilibrium. How many more ways can we find to specify the functions of accounts?

This functional conception has been valuable for focusing on what accounts *do as an act*, instead of simply examining the account's propositional content, or inquiring whether the account accurately represents 'what really happened,' or treating accounts as rationalizations for more 'real' underlying reasons. However, by framing the question as how accounts function, we are naturally led to examine the impact accounts have on an audience in repairing the problematic event or saving face, and overlook the shape of accounts as communicative phenomena. The empiricist tack of operationalizing accounts as a variable to be associated with other variables tends to shut off further investigation into what accounts look like as talk embedded in an interactional episode (Potter and Wetherell, 1987: 79–81). This approach sacrifices the complexity or naturalistic richness of accounts phenomena.

The issue of the credibility of accounts and their effectiveness in influencing others' evaluations leads some researchers to compare different types of accounts, for instance, to ask what kind of accounts are most effective, excuses or justifications? This is the wrong question to ask, in my view, because it abstracts the account out of interactional context and assumes a general use of the account-type as an individual speech act. Credibility studies typically have respondents evaluate hypothetical vignettes to compare the relative efficacy of different types of accounts. The problem with this approach is that it is based on a faulty judicial model of evaluation. Such research protocols cast the recipient as an audience, a detached observer of events merely evaluating, rather than situated in the interactional context as a co-participant (Shotter, 1981). For some everyday offenses, the recipient of an account is *not* primarily concerned with the account's truth or falsity or its credibility as these studies assume, but rather with the performative aspects of the act as remedial (Goffman, 1971; Antaki, 1987). Communicators in such circumstances are frequently more concerned with maintaining their own and others' face, and relationship, rather than in judging the veracity of the account. This image of the audience for interpersonal accounts directs attention to processes which are often of secondary importance.

Another problem with non-naturalistic research is that accounts are conceived of solely as verbal texts or as speech acts with little attention paid to their nonverbal dimensions. When accounts are examined in naturalistic contexts, their nonverbal aspects (for example, eye contact and the paralingual features of intonation, volume, and pacing) become crucial in how to interpret interactants' positioning, understandings, and assessments. An utterance may not be heard as critical without attending to its paralingual dimensions, such as intonational emphasis or increased volume. For instance, the verbal utterance, 'What other time?', can be conventionally heard as a question or request for information. But when the placement of the utterance in sequential context of a conversation is considered, a somewhat different understanding emerges. Consider M's utterance (arrow 1) in the following transcript (see Appendix for transcription conventions):

```
1     (Canceling plans to go to Boston)
M:    ((with rising intonation)) I'm not gonna take– be able to take
      ↑ you to Bos:ton Fran:
F:    > I understand we'll–< ↓ we'll go another ti:me.=
→  M:  = > Wh↑at other time? <
      (1.5)
F:    > In the sp↑ring I'm gonna have my car up here <
      (1.2)
F:    I'll bring it up after ah:
```

[

→²→ *M*:   Something will come up hhhhh
→³→ *F*:   Oh <u>come on don't</u> be pissed.

Notice that M immediately latches a response (arrow 1) onto F's agreeing to postpone, and this is produced with a rapid pace, emphatic vocal quality, and rising intonation. Such paralingual cues help us to hear M's utterance, not simply as a request for information, but as displaying affect such as disappointment or frustration with the postponement. M's subsequent assessment is more explicitly marked with a noticeable outbreath hearable as negative affect (arrow 2), and recognized as such by F (arrow 3).

The call for studying the nonverbal aspects of communication is nothing new, of course, but it has been neglected in this literature probably because our primary image is accounts as verbal explanations. When transcripts of naturally occurring accounts are examined, there is no individual act which does all the corrective work (Atkinson and Drew, 1979: 139–40). The point here is that analysis must move beyond the conception of accounts as a single speech act or variable which is effective (or not) in changing social meanings, and also consider how accounts are interactionally organized and constructed as discursive practices.

Regarding Semin and Manstead's second criticism (point (b) above) much of accounts research glosses how accounts work as a response; typically it is assumed that one is *merely reacting* to an accusation, rather than *actively construing* and formulating the problematic to use in producing an account. This latter notion of the interactional construction of events will be central to my approach developed in chapter 3, but first I want to show the problems with the standard structural-functional model.

Social systems, in order to maintain equilibrium, need some mechanism for members to repair or correct disruptive occurrences. This equilibrium or balance imagery provides the generative mechanism for the role of accounts within the structural-functional model. When a state of disequilibrium arises within a social system, persons need to draw on repair mechanisms – in the form of accountability and accounts – in order to restore equilibrium. If accounts as repair mechanisms do not function adequately to restore equilibrium, then the routine operation of the social system may be disrupted, and in extreme cases, may lead to system disintegration (for example, marital break-ups, severing social relations).

The root metaphor of social relations between interactants being in a state of equilibrium or disequilibrium can be traced to balance theory (the paradigm in social psychology in the 1960s when accounts research crystallized), and to general systems theory adopted across the social sciences. Even the commonsense representation of justice portrayed by balanced scales seems to be an influence on thinking about accounts. But these metaphors seem of limited utility since the imagery of balance and equilibrium invokes a hydrologic paradigm of communication as a product of 'forces' (Geertz, 1983). While a balance metaphor underscores that accounts function to repair social breaches, it overlooks *how* this repair function gets accomplished through the interactional work of participants. This equilibrium model does not take us far enough, at least for the concerns of social communication theory, because it offers a gloss on accounts as interactive phenomena by focusing on resulting balanced states.

A more recent approach explains the relation between the initial reproach resulting from an offense, and the account as based on a principle of 'congruence' or 'reciprocity' (McLaughlin, Cody and O'Hair, 1983; McLaughlin, Cody and Rosenstein, 1983; Cody and McLaughlin, 1985, 1988, 1990). For interpersonal accounts, an aggravating reproach from an interlocutor will likely elicit a reciprocal aggravating account in response (a justification or denial), while a mitigating reproach will likely lead to a congruent mitigating account (a concession or excuse). But this modeling of account-giving as a matching or reciprocity to the level of mitigation or aggravation from the antecedent reproach seems too reactive and reductive of an explanation. Persons do not simply offer accounts to reciprocate to a prior reproach. If this were the case, then interpersonal communicators would invariably select mitigating reproach strategies since they could predict a mitigating account in response.

While reciprocity is a basic norm in social relations, in my view, this explanatory model over-extends its bounds. Instead of a monistic principle of human action, such as reciprocity, analytic attention needs to be given to the *multiple* moral and practical beliefs, norms, and ideologies of the culture which are implicit in persons' accountability practices. Given that accounts are everyday explanations, instead of looking for a more abstract principle to somehow subsume all these different explanations, begin by looking at the lay explanations themselves as cultural inscriptions or speech practices reflecting implicit, moral/practical reasoning – the group's folk logic of everyday action.

At the end of the day, my reading of the accounts literature leads in the direction initially marked by Goffman, Scott and Lyman, and more recently developed by the methodological breakthroughs of conversation analysis and the conceptual leads from social constructionism (see chapter 3). The research on the types, functions, and processes can be extended through more rigorous analytical tools to do the naturalistic, descriptive work of locating accounts in context and how interactants' alignments and positionings are displayed through such discursive practices.

Notes

1. The notion of 'function' should not be equated with the functionalist perspective.
2. To borrow from C.P. Snow, we may say there are 'two cultures' of social scientific research (Gergen, 1982).
3. For instance, Antaki (1990: 271) cites a recent review of attribution theory in which only one unpublished study used naturalistic conversational transcripts as data.

3

A Conversation Analytic Constructionist Perspective on Accounts

Accounts are most extraordinary. And the use of accounts and the use of requests for accounts are very highly regulated phenomena. (Sacks, 1989 [1964]: 219)

This chapter examines naturally occurring instances of accounts in order to describe their workings – how accounts are structured and constructed through talk. Of the naturalistic approaches attempting to provide analytic tools and vocabularies to describe of social interaction, ethnomethodology and conversation analysis (Garfinkel, 1967; Sacks et al., 1974) rank as the most successful. To anticipate, I develop a version of conversation analysis to address the issues of how accounts become relevant as a response and what accounts make relevant, how accounts sequences interactionally unfold, how accounts are reflexive, and how such talk displays context. Also, I attempt to extend conversation analytic concerns into the domain of the emotions, and the folk logic of accounts. These latter two issues recently have been advanced by social constructionism (see for example, Gergen, 1982; Shotter, 1985; Harré, 1986). These social constructionist leads could be further extended by drawing on conversation analytic methods. A synthesis of these two perspectives is presented, hence the chapter's title, 'A Conversation Analytic Constructionist Perspective on Accounts.'

A Conversation Analytic Approach to Accounts

Conversational Order
Conversation analysis[1] starts from the premise that conversation unfolds sequentially through participants taking turns at talk (Sacks et al., 1974). In the course of turn-taking, persons participate in a number of conversational practices: beginning and ending the encounter, telling stories, requesting, questioning, answering, praising, blaming, accounting, and all the various speech activities engaged in through talk.

The analyst attempts to describe the *structure*, or *sequential organization*, of these conversational practices, and what *functions* they perform in context. Instead of the traditional tact of 'looking through' language to something presumed to be more basic – attitudes, goals, or cognitive structures – the project is to describe how conversation practices are accomplished in and through language use. The interest is not in language per se, but in the social action and interaction achieved by language – as it has come to be called, 'talk-in-interaction' (Schegloff, 1991). How is the conversation significant or consequential for the participants as shown in their talk? How do they use conversational resources to display, understand, and respond to one another's utterances?

Conversational exchanges are central to the conversation analytic methodology since the initial part of the exchange *opens up* and *calls for certain relevant responses* from the recipient. Only through such conversational exchanges can many of the activities of social life become accomplished. For instance, a speaker's request 'calls for' a range of relevant response-types from the addressee, such as: 'comply,' 'deny,' 'partial or conditional compliance,' 'ask questions about the request' and so on. Of course, a person's response may not be relevant to the request, but such responses will be heard as 'avoiding the issue,' 'changing the topic,' or simply, 'not hearing the request.' So, the relevance of a response to a prior communicative act (request) suggests a minimal sense of conversational order – a 'sequential contiguity' (Sacks, 1987 [1973]). That is, persons monitor their interlocutor's next turn at talk as *responsive* or *relevant* to their prior turn. This does not guarantee that one will receive a relevant response, but the *absence of a relevant response is noticeable*. Such absences provide the grounds for the initiator to pursue a relevant response, for example, by restating or rewording the request, doing so in a louder voice, inferring reasons for the absence, or issuing a challenge.

This sense of sequential contiguity of conversational exchanges allows us (as conversationalists or as analysts) to look 'forwards' as well as 'backwards' from a particular communicative act. *Forwards* in the sense just discussed – a request looks forward or projects a response such as complying. *Backwards* in the sense that a response can reveal how the recipient takes or understands the prior utterance. For example, a question may indicate that a prior answer was unexpected (arrow):

1   (FO1aCOOK.2)
M: .hhh When do you have your last te:st.
    (0.8)
D: I don't have one this week
    (0.4)
→ M: You don't have one this wee:k?=
D: =No:: I've just um (1.0) I've gotta write a repo:rt

Notice how M's utterance (arrow) both informs us about her understanding (or lack of understanding) of D's prior answer as well as projecting a next response from D. The point here for accounts analysis is that an utterance can be used both *retrospectively* and *prospectively*. Retrospectively an utterance can display the person's understanding or assessment of the prior turn, and prospectively an utterance can project certain relevant next turns. Given this sequential nature of conversation, the analyst needs to consider (a) what a given utterance projects or makes relevant as an interlocutor's response, and (b) what the response reflects about the recipient's understanding and evaluation of the prior utterance. These two points comprise a central core of the conversation analytic approach.

Accounts Sequences
The case was made in chapter 2 that the Scott and Lyman (1968) sense of accounts (that is, talk designed to mitigate a problematic) is ultimately consistent with the broader Garfinkel (1967) notion (Heritage, 1988). The more circumscribed Scott and Lyman sense will be used as a starting point for accounts analyses.

The above notion of sequential contiguity applies to our interest in accounts in the following way. Some utterances can be identified as certain kinds of actions *by virtue of their sequential positioning*. This commonly occurs with accounts. An interlocutor's accusation, criticism, or complaint projects a range of responses from the addressee. The next speaker's talk in the slot following the criticism will be monitored as responsive or not to that initial act of criticism. To put this another way, a criticism creates a 'sequential environment' to hear subsequent talk as replying to that criticism.

In the following transcript, A's response to B works as an account by addressing the prior criticism through challenging the comparison between 'last night' and B's projected situation.

> **2**
> *A*: I was wondering if you're going to that Japanese movie at the State?
> *B*: Should I say that I'm going to go and then not show up
> → *A*: Well that's not exactly comparable to last night

Notice there is nothing inherent in the form or content of A's utterance (arrow) alone such that it can be heard as an accounting action. B's prior criticism or ironic complaint creates a sequential context for interpreting A's talk as accounting. In another sequential context, this utterance could perform different actions,[2] such as issuing a complaint or downgrading a compliment.

Talk can be heard as doing an account, not solely due to its positioning after a criticism, of course, but also because that talk attempts to retrospectively transform the pejorative or odd sense of an event. As seen in transcript 2, B minimizes the problematic character of 'last night,' or in transcript 1, D explains the unusual state-of-affairs of 'no test' during finals week. In response to criticism, seldom is there a simple 'agree–disagree' or 'acceptance–rejection'; instead respondents discursively account for their positioning. Accounts need to be seen as both *prospectively made relevant* by the antecedent criticism and *retrospectively making relevant* contextual materials to cohere in one's telling.

A conversation analytic perspective offers both a *structural* view of accounts as responses occurring in the slot following a criticism, and a *discursive-practice* view of how accounts work to transform unwanted problematic meanings. At first glance, this discussion may seem like a rehash of the accounts literature on process (chapter 2). Each raises the issues of (a) the discourse units or parts, and (b) how these get connected, such that one follows coherently from the other. Conversation analysis extends our understanding of process.

Conversation analysis provides the most insight into (b). Accounts commonly follow criticisms, of course, but what is the basis for this regularity? Accounts become a way – a practice – to address the truth or falsity of the criticism (Sacks, 1975: 62). Bilmes (1988a) extends this structural explanation for criticism–accounts exchanges. Consider the attributions made of others: if the recipient of the attribution does not deny, correct, or qualify the attribution in some way, then this absence of a response may be heard as agreement with the prior attribution (Bilmes, 1988a: 167–9). This may be formulated by the ordering principle: assume others agree with the attributions made of them unless they contradict it.[3] A response becomes relevant following an accusation, blame or complaint to show one's positioning or alignment to that critical attribution – what may be called a *self-defense rule*. This rule interactionally provides for a slot after the blame for the accused to respond to critics. This self-defense rule may be formulated as: upon receiving a blame, make a response (denial, account, remedy, and so on) lest no response be heard by others as an admission to the blame. This self-defense rule is an application of Bilmes' (1988a) broader 'ordering principle' for the attributions made of others; that is, if the recipient of the attribution does not deny or change it, then it can be assumed that the recipient agrees for all practical purposes. So this self-defense rule explicates what I call the folk logic underlying accounting practices. In the following section, this criticism–account exchange gets elaborated by the notion of 'adjacency pairs.'

Adjacency-Pair Organization

Some conversational exchanges seem so familiar as to be conventional, for example, question–answer, request–comply/deny, greeting–greeting, invitation–accept/reject, offer–accept/reject, assessment–agree/disagree, accusation–denial, and so on. These exchange formats have been identified as adjacency pairs: two contiguous utterances from different speakers which are heard as connected, such that the first part of the pair makes the occurrence of a second-pair part expected or relevant (Schegloff and Sacks, 1973: 295–7). But not all adjacent utterances work as adjacency pairs. These adjacent (or contiguous) utterances are heard as a connected pair in that the initial utterance 'sequentially implicates' a certain limited range of responses. Implicates in the sense that certain responses are expected or 'conditionally relevant.' The notion of adjacency pairs presents a simple but powerful organization in conversational sequencing.

The sequential ordering of the first-pair parts and second-pair parts of adjacency pairs is not an invariant relation. Persons can be idiosyncratic enough to do practically anything at times in response to a first-pair part. While these exchanges like question–answer or greeting–greeting are common enough, the adjacency-pair structure is not based merely on an observed regularity. The ordering of adjacency pairs needs to be understood as 'rule-governed' or as a 'normative organization' (Heritage, 1984, 1988). Normative in the sense that *deviations* from the projected second-pair are *relevantly absent*, and thereby, something for which one can be held *accountable*. The significance of these two points is that it allows the analyst not only to identify a conversational structure, for example, adjacency pairs, but also to show how deviations from it are marked by the participants. It also allows us to see accounts as a more general phenomenon than it is customarily conceived of as a reply to a reproach.

The relevant absence of a response   One way to demonstrate this normative organization is by considering the consequences of a lack of response, or silence, to a first-pair part of an adjacency pair. For instance, one could simply remain silent in response to a question. But if no response is offered following a question, then this lack of response is *noticeably* and *relevantly absent*. The noticeable absence of a response following an act such as a question provides evidence for the above-mentioned notion of conditional relevance.

Silence following a first-pair part is not only noticeable, it also provides the grounds for *drawing inferences* about the person who does not respond. Such inferences based on silence are highly context sensitive. For instance, the lack of response to an accusation may involve a range of candidate inferences such as: 'admission of guilt,' 'attempted avoidance,' 'display of being above having to answer,' or simply 'failure to hear or understand the speaker.' In courtroom settings, defendants who remain silent following accusations commonly are heard as conceding guilt (Atkinson and Drew, 1979: 113). Given that conversation unfolds on a turn-by-turn basis, one way of demonstrating that a response is noticeably absent is for the initiator to repeat the first-pair part when a response is not forthcoming.

> **3**
> S: It makes a big difference?
>   (0.8)
> →¹ S: (   ) you're saying what?
>   (3.0)
> →² S: Makes a big difference in <u>what</u>?
>   (1.6)
> W: Well first things first . . .

Evidence for conditional relevance is displayed by the fact that the questioner prompts (arrow 1) and then repeats the question (arrow 2) in pursuit of an account.

A person may elect not to repeat the question when a response is not immediately forthcoming. Instead, the questioner may elect to wait for an answer (see arrows).

> **4**
> *Teacher*:   Why do you practi::ce?
> →   (14.8)
> Student: I practice
>   (9.9)
> *Student*:   I know it I can't say it
> *Teacher*:   How do you practice
> →   (16.6)
> *Student*:   I practice be:ing (0.9) I practice being here

Clearly silences following a question, or other first-pair parts, can have various reflexive meanings for participants, such as the difficulty of answering as in transcript 4. So the fact that participants repeat the question or wait for an answer shows that responses can be noticeably absent.

Accounts as alternate second-pair parts   A second way to demonstrate the normative organization of adjacency pairs is seen by the fact that persons may account for their not responding to the first-pair part in the way projected. Accounts serve as explanations for the absence of the projected second-pair part. For instance, when a request is not (fully) granted, the respondent may account for lack of compliance.

    5 (MU/E/113)
    Child: I want a' apple .hh two p.hh apples each
            (1.6)
→ *Mother*: Half an apple each= I don't think we've got so many apples

    6 (Optician's office: adjust frames)
    Client: What about the big boss, or doesn't he do it?
→ *Assistant*: He's with a patient right now

Accounts function in other kinds of adjacency pairs, such as explanations for declining invitations:

    7
    A: Would you like to come over for dinner Saturday night?
    B: I can't, I have other plans hon'

    8 (FO1aHARD.1, 53–6)
    M: ↓ S:o do you wanna go to wu::h (0.8) George's >with us<
          tomorrow afternoo:n
              [   ]
    D: No: Mother I ca:n't (.) I've got– u:h I'm meeting a gir:l
        at two: and we've got to um (1.0) pt (.) study

Also, accounts are used as a way to decline offers (see transcript 9) or resist advice (see transcript 10).

    9
    A: I'll make some coffee for us.
    B: We'll all be real nervous.

    10 (FO1aLLAN.5, 117–24)
    M: Why 'ont you go over there with him.
        (0.9)
→ *D*: We:ll it depends on if I'm invited–
→   Mother on business (0.4) you don't always
    M: .hh Well I mean you could go by and see Patty Sue.
        (.)
→ *D*: *I don't know Patty Sue* ((breathy))

Accounts work within the normative organization of adjacency pairs as providing a second-order response to resist a projected action from a first-pair part. Such sequences are structured by an adjacency-pairs rule: given an interlocutor's first-pair part, respond with either the projected second-pair part, or give an account for why it is not forthcoming. Failure to provide one of these responses counts as a violation of the adjacency-pairs rule (Bilmes, 1988b: 44). Violating this basic rule of social exchange may have consequences for face or politeness.

In addition to these claims about sequential organization, notice that in the practice of accounting persons draw on resources which cite 'constraints' or 'inability' rather than, say, an 'unwillingness' (Turner, 1976; Drew, 1984; Heritage, 1988). This inability to do the proposed action implies a 'no fault' quality to the response. These resources for accounting are similar to those found by attribution theorists for 'good excuses': conditions 'external, uncontrollable, and unintentional' (Weiner et al., 1987: 323). Notice that conversation analysis not only lists these resources, but goes beyond the level of social psychological strategies to describe their use and sequential organization in talk.

Preference Organization
In the discussion of adjacency-pair organization it was seen that the first-pair part and second-pair part are connected by the notion of conditional relevance. An initial utterance makes relevant and projects certain types of response. But there are a *range* of responses which can be made relevant to a first-pair part. For instance, as a response to a request, a complying, denial, question, or statement of pre-condition all can be relevant. The conditional relevance rule cannot inform us about what kind of response will follow a request; it only directs attention to a range of relevant responses. However, these responses are *not structurally equivalent* – there are *differences* in how these second-pair parts are *sequentially organized*. These differences in sequencing of the response are captured by the conversation analytic notion of 'preference organization.' Accounts figure into this as a communicator's way to do a dispreferred response.

Preference for agreement   The notion of preference organization derives from the observation that there seems to be both a 'preference for agreement' and a 'preference for contiguity' in conversation (Sacks, 1987 [1973]). Agreements with the proposed initial action tend to occur in contiguous relation to the initial utterance and with little delay (see transcript 11). Disagreements, on the other hand, commonly are produced in a 'weakened fashion,' are pushed back into the response and are surrounded by various components to display reluctance, such as: pauses, filled pauses ('ah'), qualifiers, particles ('well'), and accounts to explain the disagreement (Pomerantz, 1984). For example, compare accepting

versus declining an invitation. Accepting is produced with a preferred sequential organization (transcript 11), while declining ex-
hibits a dispreferred organization (transcript 12).

11   (SBL:10:12)
A: Why don't you come up and see me sometimes.
                                         [   ]
B: I would like to.

12   (SBL:10:14)
A: Uh if you'd care to come over and visit a little while this morning I'll
     give you a cup of coffee.
B: hehh Well that's awfully sweet of you, I don't think I can make it this
     morning .hh uhm I'm running an ad in the paper and-and uh I have
     to stay near the phone.

B's response in transcript 12 displays many of the features of
dispreference: the rejection gets delayed by the use of 'hehh,' 'Well'
and an appreciation. The rejection itself is qualified or softened plus
an account is given after as explanation. Drawing on a distinction
from linguistics, preferred responses are conversationally 'un-
marked,' while dispreferred responses are marked by features such
as pauses, prefaces (for example, 'uh,' 'well') qualifiers, token
agreements, hesitations, appreciations, apologies, and accounts
(Levinson, 1983: 332–7).

The concept of preference should not be confused with one's
personal preference, but rather refers to certain structural features of
the talk. For instance, one may personally prefer not to accept an
invitation to a party, but this will not prevent one's rejection from
being dispreferred as a conversational structure (Potter and Wetherell, 1987). These reluctance components or delay features indicate to
participants that disagreement is forthcoming. These discourse units
may be said to be 'other attentive' in that they allow the one making
the first part, say, an offer, the opportunity to revise the projected
action (Drew, 1984; Heritage, 1988). A recipient may begin to
decline an offer which leads the initiator immediately to reform the
offer in a more acceptable way even before an account is offered.

13
A: Listen I got a nice letter from Frank=you want me to read it ↑ to
     ya?
     (0.8)
B: Well ah: (   )
               [   ]
A: I'll send it=I'll send it to ya:

In the following adjacency pairs, the action in the left of the bracket represents the preferred response to the first part, while that on the right is the dispreferred response: (1) request – [comply/deny], (2) offer – [accept/decline], (3) invite – [accept/decline], (4) assessment – [agree/disagree], (5) question – [expected answer/unexpected answer]. In these adjacency pairs, the preferred second part may be broadly said to be in agreement or aligned with the 'projected' response of the first part. Dispreferred responses, in contrast, are comprised by accounts along with other elements – the above-mentioned reluctance components or delay features.

These conversation analytic findings about accounts as a way of doing dispreference expand our understanding beyond the received view of accounts as 'replies to reproaches.' Within the adjacency-pairs organization, persons account as a way to explain certain classes of responses, such as not doing the proposed action, such as an invitation, offer, or request.

There are some notable exceptions to this pattern of preference for agreement. For instance, the preferred response to self-deprecations (Pomerantz, 1984) and to accusations (Atkinson and Drew, 1979) is *disagreement* rather than agreement. This preference for disagreement in response to accusations may be seen as an exception to the general pattern of preference for agreement. This exception may be explained by supposing that conversation is guided by a sociability norm such that participants agree to mutually uphold each other's claims, evaluations, offers, invitations and so on. Generally, agreement is affiliative, so agreeing would be organizationally preferred since it meets the sociability requirements. But accusations breach this sociability norm by critically evaluating another's deeds. Once an interlocutor violates the sociability norm through the accusation, the respondent then may reciprocate through disagreeing with the accusation.

Constructing the Events to Account For

Accounts can be used as a resource to examine what respondents make relevant (implicitly or explicitly) about the problematic in question or the surrounding context. Much of the traditional accounts research glosses how accounts work as a response – typically it is assumed that one is merely reacting to the prior blame, rather than actively construing and formulating the problematic to use in producing an account. As blames prospectively make accounts relevant, so accounts can also be seen retrospectively to frame the respondent's version of events. As regards the latter retrospective framing of events, what does a person make relevant through accounts about the criticism, problematic event, or other features of the background context?

So, then, the relevance of accounts will be approached from two sides. On the one hand, the prior blame creates the conditional relevance for an account as a response, but on the other, how persons actively make relevant aspects of the prior problematic event to use in the production of their account must be examined. Accounts may be seen as produced as a function of (a) the conditional relevancies arising from the antecedent blame, and (b) what respondents can make relevant to cohere in their accounts. Item (a) addresses the *structure* or *sequential organization* of accounts talk, while (b) reveals accounts as *discursive practice*. Both (a) and (b) are central to a conversation analytic perspective on accounts.

The reflexivity of accounts Accounts need to be seen as a person's response to a problematic event. In one sense this point seems hardly noteworthy, but in another it is crucial in that accounts pick out and make visible the person's positioning and alignment in relation to others in the context of the problematic event. The nature of the problematic event and persons' stance toward it are often displayed in and through accounts. Often the problematic event is not known or mutually understood until it is addressed during the accounts episode. Accounts, then, will be used as a frame to reveal the person's stance toward the others and the problematic event.

Disagreeing with others may be softened or weakened by particles, such as 'well,' qualifiers, and delaying disagreement. These ways of accomplishing disagreement, or denial of blame, are simultaneously reflexive of the actor's positioning vis-à-vis the event – as displaying reluctance, uncertainty, politeness, and the like. In contrast, strong disagreements reflect the actor's immediate or direct positioning toward the blame. These various methods of accounting allow the actor not only to justify disagreeing with a blame, but also to display it as 'strong' or 'weak,' as 'certain' or 'uncertain,' and so on. How one sequentially organizes responses to blames accounts for, not only the problematic in question, but also the actor's alignment toward it and toward the interlocutor. The kinds and ordering of conversational resources persons use reflexively indicate how they want their utterances to be heard – as reluctant, very polite, abrupt, and so on.

Accounts in Context
Accounting practices reflect the context in which they occur. An exemplary study of accounting practices in context comes from

Atkinson and Drew's (1979) work on 'defenses' (justifications and excuses) in a judicial setting. The turn-taking system of the court-room is different from ordinary conversation: speaking turns are pre-allocated such that the counsel asks questions and the witness provides answers. The standard adjacency-pair format, accusation–denial/concession, is much more elaborated in this setting. For instance, to avoid a 'flat denial' of an accusation, the counsel engages in the conversational tasks of asking questions to get the witness to agree to certain 'facts' and 'descriptions of events.' The counsel uses this interactional construction of facts and events to draw an inference of guilt. To deny an accusation, the witness needs to address the facts from which the accusation was constructed. If the denial cannot be heard to address these facts or events, then this absence will be noticeable and implicate that the witness failed to answer the accusation.

Defenses from the witness occur in two types of sequences, *prior to* and *post* noticing of failure by counsel. In these defenses the witness attempts to avoid self-blame, while also avoiding disagreeing with the information in the prior question. Avoidance of self-blame can be accomplished by mitigating the implicated blame or withholding agreement with the prior question, but rarely is there outright disagreement with the prior question. An interesting finding in cross-examination discourse is that excuses and justifications occur following questions which do not directly accuse the witness. This reflects the witness's recognition that counsel's questions are leading to blame, and the witness's desire to mitigate such blame. So the adjacency-pair format with the excuse or justification as a second-pair part will be inadequate for such cases.

When accusations are made by counsel, accounts often co-occur with a 'rebuttal' of the presupposition contained in the prior question. Accounts provide reasons for the implicated failure, in these data, for not taking a given action. Accounts are often formed as 'constraints' on witnesses by citing factors which exhibit the impossibility of taking an action with the proviso 'if circumstances would have allowed.' These constraints are formulated to appear as strong as possible (also see Pomerantz (1986) on 'extreme case formulations'). In addition to constraints, witnesses cite other actions they were engaged in. So the account for not doing X is presented by the importance or the priority of doing Y.

The importance of context comprises a central theme in the forthcoming social accountability studies of therapy, news inter-views, and Zen teacher–student interviews. The structure and practice of accounts will reflect and be reflected by the communi-cation context.

Accounts as Social Constructions

Thus far I have approached accounts from a conversation analytic perspective, addressing issues of: interactional sequencing, how accounts become relevant and what accounts make relevant, reflexivity, and context. While conversation analysis provides the richest vocabulary and analytic tools for capturing social interaction, I do have a few sticking points. The conversation analytic concern with empirical observation is at once a strength, but some versions lead to what seems to be 'positivistic-like' epistemological claims (Atkinson, 1988). For instance, the view that the analyst reports conversational facts as captured on the transcript thereby avoiding interpretation and constructions. To my mind, in doing social research constructions are unavoidable because the selection of terms with which to identify, observe and describe phenomena are already theoretical commitments. We cannot describe human action and interaction in a theory-neutral way (Hanson, 1960; Brown, 1977). The choice of a descriptive vocabulary contains theoretical assumptions and root metaphors. It is at this point that I want to introduce social constructionism to conversation analysis to emphasize that there are no theory-neutral descriptions of social interaction. The notion of social construction should not be taken as ironic or as a minimization (as in 'It's only a social construction, it's not real') of accounts analysis.[4] Instead constructionism should be seen in contrast to a naive realism in which the researcher observes and then unproblematically describes social facts. Social constructionism draws attention to how our theoretical terms and analytic vocabulary, plus 'writing the social text,' becomes a constitutive feature of our observations and descriptions (Gergen, 1982; Shotter, 1989; Brown, 1992; Edwards and Potter, 1992).

In addition to these epistemological matters, I want to raise some empirical questions about accounts which conversation analysis has yet to address. Conversation analysis has said little about *affect*. Conveying one's emotions, whether in nonverbal displays or verbally, can be a powerful technique for persons in doing social accountability. Social constructionism offers some leads into the discursive uses of affect in accounting.

The Discourse of Affect in Accountability Practices   As argued in chapter 2, accounts are often conceived of as verbal texts or speech acts with little attention paid to their affective or nonverbal dimensions. But when accounts are examined in naturalistic contexts, nonverbal and paralingual components (for example, intonation, volume, pacing, silences, eye contact) become crucial to understanding persons' actions. As Bateson (1972) shows by his 'report–command' distinction, nonverbal and vocal components work as 'frames' to signal how to take what is being said – as ironic, intensified, angry, and the like (also see Goffman, 1974). For instance, in accusing another, the actor's increase in volume reinforces what is said verbally to intensify the actor's position and display anger. These seeming minutiae of pausing or intonational emphasis are the very stuff which interlocutors use to produce and understand each other's meanings.

Actors can use *multiple* levels of expression to convey their assessments and alignments with others. These nonverbal or vocal components are especially significant in the *display of affect*. Nonverbal components can be employed to convey messages which would be too threatening to say verbally, such as implied meanings involving challenge, deference, dominance, and the like. The nonverbal channels, particularly vocal intonation, can allow actors to express critical assessments and negative affect, but simultaneously be able to verbally deny intent, if called to account: 'Speakers need a form of communication which is *deniable*. It is advantageous for them to express hostility, challenge the competence of others, or express friendliness and affection in a way that can be denied if they are explicitly held to account for it' (Labov and Fanshel, 1977: 46).

In addition to displays of affect, persons can talk about their emotions as a way to account or call another to account. An actor can verbally *avow* an emotional state (a first-person statement), such as anger to convey criticism, or depression to excuse the role performance. Also, an actor can *ascribe* an emotion to an interlocutor (a second-person statement), such as a bad mood or an unjustified emotion like jealousy in order to hold them accountable. Such ascriptions can be taken as criticism or complaints and lead recipients to offer accounts to justify their own emotion.

If satisfactory accounts cannot be found to justify an emotion, this may lead the actor to reconsider the basis for the emotion. The use of affect in doing accountability implies social relations and an appraisal of events (Averill, 1980, 1991). The demand to justify one's emotions shows that the discourse of affect involves more than an 'inner' feeling, but must appeal to cultural norms or some other negotiated standards of intelligibility. Certain appraisals may not hold up when formulated and aired before others – they may be taken as unwarranted, as excessive fears or as jealousy.

The uses of affect in social accountability practices implicate the actor's appraisal of conduct: '[E]motion can be viewed as a cultural and interpersonal process of naming, justifying, and persuading by people in relationship to each other' (Lutz, 1987: 5). So, a discourse of affect combined with its implied appraisal can be seen to presuppose a cultural logic of 'right' action. This latter construction of a cultural logic of 'right' action, or simply a folk logic, is what I want to attend to in the following section.

Accounts as Constructions from a Folk Logic

Social accountability practices reflect ordinary persons' moral or practical reasoning for action. Such moral and practical reasoning invokes a cultural system of beliefs, values and ideologies implicit in the discourse to warrant the account's claim. This cultural system provides members with a logic for action, that is, for what is right, moral, or at least, acceptable. What counts as 'right,' 'smart,' or at least 'passable' conduct depends on the group's (culture's) system of beliefs, values, and ideologies – a folk logic.

Typically this folk logic is not articulated in a propositional form, but rather is implicit. To offer an account for one's actions presupposes an array of action concepts which are largely taken-for-granted or tacit in the commonsense understanding of human action. Analysis may be enriched by making such presuppositions explicit and verbally analyzing the commonsense assumptions of moral or practical human action. The project here will be to examine, not only the propositional content of what is claimed in the actor's blame or account, but also how a folk logic is implied or presumed. This notion of folk logic broadly resembles the classical concepts of 'taken-for-granted beliefs' (Schutz, 1964) and 'vocabulary of motives' (Mills, 1940; Burke, 1969). But folk logic differs from these classical conceptions in that it draws attention to how persons implement and negotiate the propriety of action *for the particular event* through accountability practices. How do such taken-for-granted assumptions, moral orders, and ideologies *apply* in *this* particular situation? Given that there can be competing or contradictory beliefs, how do persons invoke such background understandings in support of their accounts? That is, folk logic is not simply a set of implicit rules and shared beliefs, but includes the *practice of using* these rules and beliefs through blames and accounts.[5]

The notion of practice is central to understanding folk logic (Shotter, 1985). Practice captures the sense of how a culture's general moral beliefs, values, and ideologies can be *implemented* (put to use) *by an actor in a particular situated context*. Accountability practices typically involve more than the simple application of general rules to a particular case. In many cases there are competing folk logics that could apply in a situation. Whether working from 'the top down' (rules to cases) or 'the bottom up' (defining the situation in accordance with rules) (Sigman, 1987), accountability practices involve discursive negotiation for the labeling and propriety of events.

The folk logic invoked through a blame or account does not fully constrain or determine what actors will do. It is not uncommon for different persons to offer competing accounts based on different folk logics for the 'same' event. In the following transcript competing folk logics are evident; the tenant draws on a prior agreement of a 'twenty-four hour notice' before showing the house. Making relevant this agreement, and implicitly its breach, serves as a mild rebuke of the realtor as well as an attempt to coordinate future actions. But the realtor's account invokes a folk logic of 'the timeliness of doing business' which implicates exceptions to the twenty-four hour notice.

14   (Realtor–tenant telephone conversafion)
Realtor: But today they'll just look around on the outside and if they like– what they see then they'll make an appointment for the inside
Tenant: Okay did you– you had mentioned <u>before</u> that you told the brokers you want twenty-four hour notice=
Realtor: =Yea:h but ya know that hh I– I have the same problem I had this ah person come in the other day and ah (0.7) they're (1.4) they're really earnest buy(hh)ers they– they have cash on the barrelhead they don't finance or anything they just come in with cash and it's ah hard to turn them down, but I had to turn them down because I– I <u>did</u> ah ya know it was in the morning and I showed her (.) about an hour after I had ah (.) ah first contacted=
                 [   ]
Tenant: Yeah
Realtor: =her and I showed her the– the properties so
Tenant: Yeah *yeah*

Consider how the folk logics invoked through blames and accounts are used, evaluated, and interactionally negotiated. Given that there can be competing folk logics to account for the same event, how does one folk logic rather than another get applied in this situated context. Accounts provide a valuable site for examining a person's understanding of how general cultural rules apply to a specific situated context (for example, 'twenty-four hour notice' versus 'the timeliness for doing business'). Of course, a person's accounts may be challenged or disputed, but this can only be negotiated through further appeals invoking folk logics.

The accounts used in institutional or specialized contexts may employ different logics for understanding and evaluating actions. What counts as an acceptable account will vary depending on whether it is told to one's friend, one's boss, or one's therapist. The logic of action may differ as a function of context. The folk logic of everyday contexts must be distinguished from the 'logic' of institutional or specialized contexts (for example, courtrooms, employment interviews, therapy sessions).

Conclusion

In chapter 2 I discussed Semin and Manstead's (1983) criticisms of the accounts literature and in this chapter put forward conversation analysis and social constructionism as ways to satisfy these criticisms. Conversation analysis provides innovations to resolve both of their complaints: (a) it offers methodological tools and practices for a radically naturalistic and empirical form of research, and (b) focuses on the connection or sequential linkage between the criticism and the account by the concept of conditional relevance. Relevance is the key to this methodology because it focuses analytic attention on how an act, such as a criticism, opens up the call for a response, such as an account, as well as how the accounting response displays an understanding or assessment of the prior act.

The relevance of accounts can be approached, so to speak, from two directions. On the one hand, the prior blame creates the conditional relevance for an account as a response, but on the other, persons actively make relevant aspects of the prior problematic event to use in the production of their account. This latter point of what actors make relevant in the course of accounting reflects the social construction of realities thesis. Actors may be seen as not so much responding to the propositional content of an interlocutor's reproach, but as constructing a version of events in the course of accounting. That is, selecting what about the problematic to account for and implicating the actor's positioning in this. So, accounts may be seen as produced as a function of the conditional relevancies arising from the antecedent blame, and what respondents can make relevant to cohere in their accounts. These two features make conversation analysis a powerful methodology for the study of human interaction: conversation is orderly and attended to by participants as orderly, and is mutually accomplished by participants on a moment-by moment basis.

The perspective one uses influences how one will 'see' the phenomenon. The social constructionist perspective draws attention to the actor's active construction of events through accounting. Such constructions are possible because of the cultural group's assumptions, vocabularies, and ideologies of right or practical action which are applied to a situated context through the actor's use of folk logic.

This folk logic may be achieved, not only through verbal accounts, but also by nonverbal affect displays. Given the sometime emotionally charged character of accountability episodes, it is crucial to see the multiple levels of meaning that may be drawn on.

Notes

1. My presentation of conversation analysis is designed to lead to the main concern of accounts. For a general introduction or review of conversation analysis, see: Atkinson and Drew, 1979: ch. 2; Levinson, 1983: ch. 6; Heritage, 1984: ch. 8; Zimmerman, 1988; Beach, 1990; Nofsinger, 1991: chs 3–5.
2. Sacks (1975: 62) observes that the utterance, 'everyone has to lie,' can be used in making a complaint or excuse, and we might add any number of different actions depending on its sequential placement.
3. Humor provides an interesting exception because critical attributions of others can be made under the guise of humor. Drew (1987) shows how persons often respond to teases with accounts designed to correct the teasing attribution.
4. My thanks to Rod Watson. See Watson (1992) for a critique of social constructionism.
5. Jayyusi formulates a similar notion of everyday logic; 'This is not a logical necessity, but one that is a possibility built into the informal logic of conversational resources and interactional methods available to interactants, resources that include the logic of the concepts involved and our commonsense knowledge of the social world' (Jayyusi, 1984: 107–8).

4

Accounts Analysis: Methods and Methodological Issues

The question naturally arises of how this synthesis of conversation analysis and social constructionism gets implemented in doing research. There have been misunderstandings in some quarters about these new qualitative methods – from there being 'no method,' to being 'subjective,' 'relativistic,' and even 'nihilistic' (Bostrom and Donohew, 1992). These difficulties are due, not only to the growing pains of new ways of doing research, but also due to a seeming unwillingness from some empiricists to allow qualitative methods. I present my response to this debate in the first section below, followed by a discussion of methods for doing conversation analytic constructionism.

Methodological disputes

The largest rift in accounts research, and indeed throughout the social sciences, stems from differences in methodology and methods. Over the past thirty years or so the social sciences have witnessed a philosophical reaction against the 'received view' of positivism and mainstream empiricism, and have constructed new paradigms and ways of doing research (Bernstein, 1976, 1985; Pearce and Cronen, 1980; Geertz, 1983). Methodological commitments and practices influence and constitute how the researcher orients to the phenomenon, the kinds of questions that should be asked, and the criteria for what counts as good research. Here I want to address empiricist criticisms of conversation analytic constructionism and offer my replies – if you will, to account for my accounts analysis.

Some empiricist critics do not see activities like conversation analysis or social constructionism as social scientific methodologies (Cappella, 1990). Or, these investigations are relegated as pre-scientific procedures for discovery of hypotheses – the 'logic of discovery' rather than the 'logic of justification' (Kaplan, 1964). Qualitative approaches get criticized as not empirical, but merely as subjective readings of texts. In my view, this criticism confuses 'empiric*al*' with 'empiric*ist*.' To the extent that empirical means forming and justifying claims based on observations, a methodology like conversation analysis is not only empirical, but by that criterion, appears more empirical than empiricism. Conversation analysis is a radically empirical approach to studying talk-in-interaction. Conversation analytic methods require much more painstaking time and effort in doing naturalistic observations and formulating careful descriptions of the talk than is called for by, say, standard empiricist coding schemes (Beach, 1990) or operational definitions of variables (Cicourel, 1964). Empiricists' practices distance the researcher from the phenomena and avoid naturalistic observations of the particulars of social interaction. For instance, standard empiricist coding schemes may achieve inter-coder reliability, but at the cost of abstracting the unit of behavior out from the interaction sequences in which it occurs. This casts doubts on the comparability of these behavioral units.

Qualitative methods such as conversation analysis have not yet formulated methods in a textbook fashion comparable to quantitative social science. This reflects both the newness of the approach and the difficulty in working with conversational materials. But this present lack of a textbook does not imply that there are no methods. Methods represent a logic of argument for presenting evidence, rather than a foolproof guarantee of knowledge (Jackson, 1986; Jacobs, 1990). So attention needs to be given to how qualitative methods use data in support of claims or to falsify competing claims.

A related criticism is that conversation analysis is merely interpretative, and not replicable because of the possibility of alternative interpretations of the same text. Alternative interpretations of the same transcript are possible, but this does not mean that the methodology is subjective. First of all, a conversation analyst does not simply give an interpretation or reading of a text, but instead examines a participant's conversational actions and how an interlocutor's responses display uptake, understandings, and assessments of the prior turn. The analyst is not attempting to read the mental state of the speaker; all of the features of the talk-in-interaction are publicly available in participants' verbal and nonverbal actions and moves. Conversation analytic claims are replicable in that other readers can examine and criticize the analysis since the data – the transcripts – are included in the manuscript. Conversation analysis, probably more than any other method, makes its data available for first-hand inspection by the scholarly community.

The analyst of tapes and transcripts is engaged in what might be called a hermeneutic process of observing the conversational materials, proffering an analysis, going back to the materials to check that analysis, making adjustments and refinements, observing again, adding to or modifying the analysis (Taylor, 1978). Such research practices involve 'a tacking back and forth' between observation and analysis.[1] At the end of the day there is no certainty that your claims are right. There is no bedrock sense-datum, no foundations as supposed by empiricism, to certify knowledge claims.

Alternative interpretations of the same transcript are possible because different researchers bring different perspectives or different concerns to the materials. It is not so much that researchers disagree as that they adopt a different theoretical language or descriptive vocabulary. As discussed in chapter 3, the problems with naive realism lead me to social constructionism. The intractable problems of foundationalism and the theory-laden nature of observations do not imply a rampant relativism (Bernstein, 1985). Researchers can present findings in an open manner to fellow researchers for their reviews and criticisms – to carry on the scholarly conversation (Rorty, 1979). For instance, an operating principle of conversation analysis is to get down to specific cases. This alone is no guarantee of consensus, but most of the time this hermeneutic process and scholarly conversation seems to work pragmatically. The criteria for evaluation are not unfamiliar: insightfulness, clarity, precision, usefulness, generality.

In addition to criticisms about matters of validity there are also empiricist criticisms about the generalizability of conversation analytic claims. It must be granted that generalizability may not be initially justified due to a limited sample. The focus on the particular precludes amassing a sufficiently large sample to warrant generalization. On the other side of the coin, proceeding on a case-by-case basis allows for a more intensive analysis of the dynamics of social interaction. It seems inadequate to make broad generalizations about social interaction which pale when faced with the richness or complexities of the particular case (Scheff, 1990). One solution to this problem is through the gradual accumulation of different studies of the phenomenon to warrant generalizability. Indeed, many conversation analytic studies do use a sufficiently large sample size to support generalizations.

Conversation analysis strives to be a 'structural science,' rather than a 'parametric science' like mainstream empiricist research (Harré, 1977; also see Coulter 1983). Parametric sciences want to specify the interrelationships among discrete variables (causal, correlational) into explanatory or predictive propositions. In contrast, conversation analysis works as a structural science in that its program is to describe the structures of interaction, that is, sequential organization or social order. For instance, notions developed in chapter 3, such as turn-taking, adjacency pairs, or preference organization, describe the interactional structures which participants use in doing accounts. The research project involves describing how these various conversational practices are interactionally structured and how they function for interactants. So, conversation analysis may not satisfy the demands of traditional empiricism, but instead has developed methodological procedures to support knowledge claims about talk-in-interaction, and thereby has opened up a new area for inquiry, an area previously considered too random or chaotic for social scientific study. Now we know that talk is finely structured and part of an interaction order.

Methods

This methods section is a reconstruction of the procedures I have used in doing studies of accounts and social accountability (chapters 5–9). The procedures below are listed as numbered steps for matters of presentation. But these steps should not be taken as discrete, linear steps, or be employed in a mechanical-like fashion; in practice they work in a more reflexive, circular fashion. These procedures should be thought of as ways to handle data so as to discover and support claims. Some of these points have been examined already (and some key points at greater length in chapter 3), but I reiterate them here due to the value of presenting them in a list-format and also to show 'the method in the madness.'

Step 1: Transcribe and Observe Naturalistic Accounts Phenomena

The advent of tape-recording technologies (both videotape and audiotape) allows for the repeated observation and detailed description of talk-in-interaction in ways which were not previously possible (Hopper et al., 1986). Instead of the researcher relying on memory, imaginative reconstruction of events, or coding schemes, analysts can now study tape recordings of naturalistic discourse (Heritage, 1984). Tape recordings offer the advantage of repeated observation and writing up transcripts to inscribe salient verbal and nonverbal units (Psathas and Anderson, 1990). This provides the researcher with an observational base with which to ground descriptions and construct claims.

Repeatedly observing the tape recordings reveals features of interaction which commonly are 'seen but unnoticed' during the actual conversation, or could not be accurately remembered at a fine-grained level. Recordings can capture fleeting moments of interaction which, if attended to at all, could only be glossed by traditional methods. The analogy of the tape recorder to the microscope in biology is fitting due to this revelation of the particulars of social interaction (Scheff, 1990).

Transcription can be a painstaking and lengthy process. It has been estimated that transcribing takes ten times as long as the real-time conversation (Potter and Wetherell, 1987). Despite this labor-intensive commitment, transcribing is an invaluable discovery procedure for revealing 'what is going on' in the talk. The practice of repeated hearings and/or viewings allows the researcher, not only to write up the transcripts, but to observe closely. Transcription is observation (Zimmerman, 1988). There are a variety of transcription conventions available, although the Gail Jefferson conventions have become canonical for conversation analysis and related approaches. A modified format is used in the present work (see Appendix).

Decisions need to be made on how detailed to transcribe the recordings. The level of specificity depends on the research question. Accounts phenomena can be usefully analyzed at varying degrees of specificity. For instance, in chapters 5 and 6, I am interested in how affect enters the performance of accountability and accounts. Affect can be displayed in multiple ways: through vocal cues (for example, intonation contour; volume shifts) and nonverbal displays (for example, eye contact; body positioning). To capture such phenomena as paralingual and bodily moves requires rather fine-grained transcription conventions. On the other hand, my study of a welfare interview focused primarily on the recurrence of the actors' verbal justifications and explanations, so transcribing the dialogue seems sufficient for these purposes. The questions the researcher wants to raise dictate the level of transcription.

Step 2: Sample Size
The time-consuming procedures of repeated observation, writing up transcripts, and close analysis mean that often the researcher must initially sacrifice a large sample size for the 'close look' at a few cases. Working on a case-at-a-time basis provides the researcher with an opportunity to do a more 'intensive' analysis of the phenomenon, than is possible by standard 'extensive' methods (Labov and Fanshel, 1977; Becker, 1988). Before instances can be counted or coded, the researcher must have a sense of what the phenomenon looks like – how it is organized (Beach, 1990). The payoff from these intensive labors comes in the non-intuitive descriptions of talk-in-interaction which cannot be captured by traditional methods.[2]

Research strategies typically either focus on a *single case* (such as, a therapy session), or collect a *corpus of cases*. The single case analysis allows for a more in-depth examination and can provide a good test for the adequacy of concepts and models. The second tack is to gather a number of instances of the phenomena. The acts being performed and the interactional patterns which they comprise can be located and described (see steps 3–4). Claims to generalizability of the pattern can then be supported by standard inductive principles.

Step 3: Analysis – From Utterances to Actions

Having drawn up a transcript, identify what the interactants are up to. The words are inscribed on paper, but what are these utterances being used to do – what actions are being performed and what moves are being made? To paraphrase Austin (1962), describe what interactants are doing with words.

As analysts we begin with our own cultural knowledge, or intuition, of what is going on in the talk. But this intuition must be based on some publicly available data in the transcript. Instead of relying solely on conventional understandings of the utterances, examine what the talk is being *used to do in context*, how it *functions* for members. For instance, consider the interactional work of the utterance, 'I don't know' (arrow).

> **1**
> *S*: Why did you tell me it was a good thing I told you now (.) I'm happy you told me?
> *W*: I don't 'cause eh <u>be</u>cause Sam it's just (.)
> →   *I don't know*
>   (4.1)
> *W*: .hh
>   (12.1)
> *W*: I just don't like to <u>think</u>what would happen.

W uses 'I don't know' (arrow) in a way somewhat different from its conventional use of reporting one's cognitive state. 'I don't know' works in a more complex fashion here in performing moves: to self-interrupt, to preclude her continuing with her account, to display affect such as frustration. The general point is that an utterance can be used to perform a variety of interactional moves; attention must be given to its use in its particular, situated context, that is, its 'indexicality' (Garfinkel, 1967).

A second technique to identify what is going on in the talk is to look to how interlocutors understand or interpret each other's utterances. Instead of a conversation analyst being understood by the analogue of a reader of a text, the analyst can look to how interactants interpret one another as displayed in responses to other's prior turn. The analyst cannot see into the interactants' minds, of course, but interactants' uptake and responses to prior moves are empirically available. This uptake and responses can be used as a way to identify the interactant's recognition, understanding, and assessment of the prior actions. Such displays reveal how the respondent takes the prior act. For instance in transcript 1, W's initial answer displays recognition of S's request for an account for what she said previously. The same conversational resources (for example, verbal utterances, pauses, volume, intonation) which interlocutors use to convey and respond to each other's messages can also be observed by the analyst (Schegloff and Sacks, 1973).

In some cases, an utterance may be metacommunicatively identified as a particular kind of act by a participant. As seen below, John labels Mary's prior avowal, 'I'm depressed' (arrow 1), as an 'excuse' (arrow 2).

       2   (Coulter, 1990: 185)
       Mary: – (as if I'm sick) (   )
 ¹⟶   I'm de<u>press</u>ed
       John: (I mean) uh-uh I don't feel like a custodian
                  (1.5) ya know
       Mary: Yee:eah?
       John: But I'm not gonna see someone come up with a
 ²⟶   weak excuse like I'm depressed I'm gonna sleep away

But interlocutors' labeling each other's utterances as an action cannot be relied upon for analysis because it occurs relatively infrequently.

The above-mentioned technique of using the interlocutor's response to a prior for action identification works well when such understandings are interactionally displayed, but such uptakes and understandings are not always unambiguously available. In some cases the analyst may not know how to label an utterance as an action: the talk may be unclear or vague to the interactants themselves, interactants may not exhibit an understanding, or our cultural knowledge may not suffice in the context. Further, talk can serve multiple interactional moves, so the analyst must attend to the possibility of more than one action being performed through an utterance. Despite anomalies, these conversation analytic procedures provide the best available, context-sensitive methods for the discovery and support of what persons are doing with words.

Step 4: Analysis – From Actions to Interactional Sequences
The next step is to examine the *connectedness* among the participants' actions to uncover the *sequential ordering* of accounting. In other words, describe the *patterns* or 'language game' of social accountability. Having located an instance of accounting, look to what gives rise to that account, and in turn, what does that account

give rise to. Accounts can be used as a site to examine the *antecedents* and *consequents* of accounts. More importantly, examine what *connects* these parts together as a coherent discursive practice of accounting.

As regards the antecedents of accounts, recall the previous treatment of the adjacency pair, blame-accounts. The actions of blaming and of accounting may be seen as *connected* by the analytical notion of conditional relevance. That is, on the condition of A's blame of B, some accounting action becomes relevant or expected from B. The connectedness or relation between these actions of blaming and accounting is not simply one of causality or correlation, but of practical necessity. 'Practical necessity' captures the 'demand' element in situations of accountability, the import of making a move in the language game: of responding to the blame because without an account, A's blame will be heard as unchallenged by B and taken as accurate. Talk-in-interaction unfolds on the contingencies of such a move-by-move basis.

As regards the consequents of accounts, what responses do accounts make relevant from the recipient? Accounts project some response of evaluation or assessment from the recipient to indicate the acceptability of the account. Thus, the three-part accounts sequence: 'blames–accounts–evaluation.' But the connection between the account and the evaluation does not appear as strong as the connection of conditional relevance between the blame and the account. In the slot following an account frequently there is no explicit evaluation from the recipient. Such a lack of response, say by moving to another topic, can be heard as tacit agreement, for all practical purposes, with the account. This seems to reflect a rule that disagreement with a prior needs to be displayed, while agreement can be tacitly assumed. An account is a kind of disagreement with the prior blame, so it needs to be performed, otherwise others will presume the accused agrees with the blame.

Accounts may be found in other kinds of sequences than following blames, as part of other kinds of language game. Persons may account to explain the problematic emerging from their own failures, what might be called a 'problem-telling accounts sequence.' This kind of accounting arises in a different sequential environment than the more familiar blames-accounts sequence. Following the telling of problems, instead of blaming, responses such as questioning or probing from the recipient become relevant. So a somewhat different accounting sequence can be identified: (a) problem-telling, (b) questioning/probing, (c) accounting.[3]

Accounts also operate in a third kind of language game – as a dispreferred response in some adjacency pairs (see chapter 3). For example, in response to an invitation, one may do declining the invitation by offering accounts of constraints, along with related dispreferred moves, which portray the actor as prevented from accepting the invitation. Accounts do similar kinds of work as dispreferred responses to offers and requests. In these sequential environments accounts do not work as responses to blames or questions, but rather preclude their occurrence. Of course, if these accounts as dispreferred responses prove unsatisfactory, then blames or a problematic could emerge.

These methods of locating accounts and their antecedents and consequents allows us to see that accounts occur as responses in at least three different kinds of sequences: 'blames-accounts,' 'telling problems,' and 'as dispreferred responses.' The methodological importance of uncovering patterns or accounts sequences is that these reveal the organization or structure of accounts-talk-in-interaction.

Having identified a pattern, consider the *exceptions* to this pattern, what Heritage (1984) calls 'deviant case analysis.' What are the interactional consequences of deviations from the pattern? Persons may resist doing the expected or normative response. For instance, a person may remain silent in response to a blame or question about problems. Not giving an account in defense may result in the accusor inferring guilt, or some related critical ascription, for this noticeable absence. Another example: persons who fail to give an account for declining an invitation may be heard as inconsiderate of the inviter's expression of good will. As a friend once remarked to me while doing an afterburn from such an incident, 'He didn't even bother to make up an excuse.' The point of looking to how members respond to deviations by these various sanctions is that these patterns are 'normatively organized' (Heritage, 1988). That is, these patterns are not mere regularities, but are interactionally oriented to as the right or appropriate ways of acting. So actors are accountable, not only for their actions, but also for their accounting for their actions.

Step 5: Analysis – What Accounts Make Relevant
In step 4, attention is given to how accounts are 'made relevant'; here the focus is on what persons make relevant through accounts about the prior blame, problematic event, or background context. In other words, as blames project accounts, so accounts can be seen retrospectively to frame the problematic event at issue. The *nature*, *magnitude*, and *consequences* of the problematic event are themselves *interactional constructions* which are made relevant by the actor in the course of the accounts talk. Interactants may disagree over, say, the magnitude of the problematic, but this itself can be

addressed in the accounts talk. It is commonly assumed that the account simply responds to the prior blame without considering that this account is an active construction of events drawing on contextual resources.

Persons often account by making relevant some conditions, events, or states-of-affairs which interlocutors either *do not know about* or *do not fully appreciate*. For instance, notice how F's accounts in transcript 3 make relevant features of the problematic state-of-affairs to lessen her responsibility:

3
> *M*:   But wait >I mean< are we leaving this up in the air?
> *F*:   NO I'M GONNA TRY – I'M GOING TO WRITE TO HER AGAIN, I'M GOING TO
> TELL HER like Marge please there's my phone number please call
> me, tell me by the– whatever the fifth coming before the fifth
> (1.9)
> *F*:   (   ) you know (.) SHE NEVER WROTE ME LAST YEAR SO you know
> (3.6)
> *F*:   I'll– Mike I'll see what I can do ↑ ya know

In response to M's complaint of 'leaving this up in the air' F responds with an emphatic denial and reassertion of her solution to the problematic by writing to Marge. By this making relevant of Marge's lack of response plus her citing what happened 'last year,' F is able to construct implicitly the problematic as something beyond her control, and therefore, that for which she is not fully responsible, but she is nonetheless 'trying.'

Step 6: Analysis – Accounting as Interactional Achievement
Examine accounts talk as an 'interactional achievement' or 'joint accomplishment' among interactants. Accounts do not spring full blown from the mind of the speaker; how they are ordered and produced is contingent in part on the recipient. Accounts talk admits of an 'accordian effect' in the sense that a speaker may say a lot or a little dependent on the receptivity of interlocutors. How a sequence unfolds needs to be seen as a co-enactment between participants.[4]

Consider how the following accounts sequence gets interactionally achieved.

4
> *S*:   Makes a big difference in <u>what</u>?
> (1.6)
> → *W*:   Well first things first
> (2.6)

```
   W: .hh About this other thing about uhm if you have to work on
      Saturday night?
   S:  (                          )
          [                   ]
2→ W:          No no I want to talk about this first
   S: Okay
      (3.2)
3→ W: I'm not going to be happy no.
4→ S: >I'm not saying you should be happy<
      [                                ]
5→ W: I   u   n   d   e   r   s   t   a   n   d I understand okay?
      (1.1)
6→ W: I understand and I kno:w (1.3) there's nothing you can do about
      it . . .
```

In response to S's question, W marks a shift to a prior consideration which must be addressed 'first' (arrow 1). As W begins to account, S attempts to come in, but W reasserts (arrow 2) the importance of this prior consideration by overlapping S with emphatic intonation so as not to allow a shift. So how the account gets told – in what order – is monitored and interactionally negotiated between participants.

As W returns to her account (arrow 3), S quickly inserts a display of recognition for the problematic condition (arrow 4). W immediately moves to hold the floor by again overlapping with S and repeating 'I understand' (arrow 5) as acknowledgement tokens and transition to continue with her account. The point here is to show that accountings are contingent on the moment-by-moment moves, actions, and displays of interlocutors.

Step 7: Method of Expansion – Making the Implicit
Explicit
To understand why certain discourses work to account, while other discourses do not, draw on the cultural beliefs and assumptions about human action – the folk logic of action. Given that folk logic is implicated in a criticism, account or evaluation, methods are needed to make the implicit explicit. Formulating folk logic may be approached through using a method of expansion: interpreting what is said in terms of background contextual knowledge, tacking back and forth between the part and the whole, and reading the part in terms of the whole, and the whole in terms of the part (Much and Shweder, 1978; Shotter, 1985: 172). Such methods begin with the actor's assertions, and then attempt to uncover what is implicated by them. A folk logic is not a formal deductive logic, but rather involves the cultural system of interrelated beliefs, values, and ideologies which can be drawn on by members to warrant action. In some cases

describing the folk logic may be uninformative simply because it is readily evident as commonsense knowledge to cultural members (also to researchers and readers). Cases in which different actors invoke conflicting folk logics for the 'same' action usually proves to be more interesting for this kind of analysis. Not uncommonly conflicting rules and norms get applied to the same event, so how actors account for the event – which folk logic is brought to bear – can be consequential. This is especially the case in institutional settings (for example, welfare interviews, therapy), where specialized logics of action become relevant. These institutional logics may conflict with the folk logics of clients. So these methods of revealing or uncovering folk logics and institutional logics, and how these are interactionally applied by members to the situated context, becomes important for accounts analysis.

Conclusion

These methods represent a list of procedures for putting to practice conversation analysis and social constructionism to particular cases. Such procedures direct analytic attention to the talk itself as a primary datum of social accountability and accounting. These methods can be useful for both discovery and support of claims about conversation. But no methods are foolproof; there is no guarantee that using them will reveal something interesting. In the end, this goal of uncovering something interesting is the payoff from employing these new methods.

The current fragmenting of social scientific methodologies has been at once a strength and a weakness for the investigations of accounts and social accountability. A weakness because the diverging starting points and disciplinary assumptions, particularly between mainstream empiricism and the new paradigms, means that there is little cross-fertilization among approaches. But, overall, this diversity of approaches opens up new ways to conceive of and study social life. Until recently conversation was thought too idiosyncratic to be studied scientifically. Methods such as conversation analysis provide the best available analytic tools to describe the workings of accounts as talk-in-interaction.

Notes

1. I borrow this felicitous phrase from Vern Cronen.
2. As Pomerantz comments, '[T]he value of Ethnomethodological and Conversation Analytic studies is that we are able to identify features of interactants' interpretive work that otherwise are undefined, hazy, and undifferentiated' (1990: 234).

3. The following case may be identified as D telling problems, M questioning or probing about these problems, and D further accounting for the problems.

(FO1aHARD.1)

D: .hhh We:ll– I tell you what– You think about it and you call me back and tell me if you're gonna visit Ja:n cause if you're no:t I wanna go to Jazzercise in the morning (.) Cause I'll be wastin a time. .hhhh But– (0.7) I feel like I should go visit Ja:n because I feel like that's what God wants me to do.
   (0.9)

M: pt .hh we:ll do you mean you're not gonna go if I don't go:?
   (0.2)

D: .hhh I don't know. uh– I– (.) uh no: I don't think I wi:ll. Cause I don't know how to– .hhh I feel real haw– uh awful about this but I don't know how to handle– (0.2) I don't know how to handle it

4. While practically all social scientific approaches to human communication give lip service to the transactional character of communication, conversation analysis is one of the few methods which is able to follow this in its methods.

5

Blame–Accounts Sequences in Couple Therapy: Accountability for Relational Problems

> [P]articipants in therapy and in conversation normally do not argue the propositions directly, but argue whether or not the events being talked about are instances of these general propositions. . . . There are many propositions that a person might endorse but that would be difficult for him to assert explicitly: for example, 'I am better than you.' One of the specific characteristics of therapy is that both patient and therapist are presumably working towards making certain propositions explicit. (Labov and Fanshel, 1977: 53)

A setting which offers a rich body of material for the analysis of accounts is a therapy session. Therapeutic interviews may be viewed as a particular kind of conversation,[1] or language game, designed for intensive talk about problems. Couple therapy, in particular, provides an interesting context for accounts analysis since participants present their telling of problems as well as account for their partner's problems. The project here is to examine telling problems, blame and accounting in a therapeutic context. A couple therapy interview is used to consider: (1) how persons make relevant aspects of the problematic event to cohere with their preferred account, and (2) how nonverbal and paralingual dimensions of blames and accounts are used to frame or display persons' meanings and affect. (3) Analytic attention is given to the common sense, folk logic of the clients as well as the therapeutic logic of the therapist to describe how the interaction is conjointly accomplished and relational meanings are negotiated.

Couple Therapy as a Site for Problem Talk and Accounts

The discourse of relational problems often takes the form of the teller describing him/herself as reacting to the unjustifiable actions of his or her spouse – 'You (actively) did something to (passive) me and I (having no choice) had to respond as I did' (Lannamann, 1989). In telling problems, participants also may be implicating blame and allocating responsibility to their relational partner. These interactional tasks of telling problems, blaming, and accounting get accomplished through *descriptions* of one's own and one's spouse's actions and dispositions. An interesting feature of descriptions is that the interactional point may be *implicated* rather than explicitly said.[2] So in the following analysis, attention is given to how problems are told through descriptions in order to see how blame is implicated.

Couple therapy is often characterized by recurring instances of blame or criticism made by relational partners of one another. Repeated blaming in therapy contexts usually indicates the importance or salience of an underlying proposition over which partners disagree. Repetition of criticisms is heard as a 'challenge' which may have face-threatening implications particularly if the complaint employs the same word choice (Labov and Fanshel, 1977: 95). Recurring blames may give rise to accounts as a way to defend against the change implied by the blame. Repeated 'blame–blame' or 'blame–defense' sequences may have the character of patterns, for example, 'I nag because you withdraw,' and 'I withdraw because you nag' (Watzlawick et al., 1967). These patterns are not desired, but interactants may feel enmeshed within the pattern and unable to change (Cronen et al., 1979).

The therapist as participant possesses a specialized knowledge of interpersonal relationships and therapeutic intervention strategies. The couple, on the other hand, bring a commonsense knowledge and folk logic of relationships and ways to solve their problematic features to the session. Given the therapist's specialized knowledge, there is a tendency for the researcher to view therapy from the perspective of the therapist's framework. But the present project takes couple therapy as conversation, so it must be considered how therapist and clients alike co-create and mutually accomplish the interaction. The following analysis will not privilege either the point of view of the therapist or the clients; rather this analysis will examine both as contributing to how blame–accounts sequences are interactionally negotiated and achieved.

The therapist in the following study has independently written a paper describing his perceptions and the intervention strategies he uses in the session analyzed here (Sluzki, 1990). This unique source of information will be drawn upon at relevant points to help us understand what the therapist is doing. The present paper is not a mere duplication because it is a more intensive analysis focusing on blame-accounts sequences, while the Sluzki paper (1990) gives an overview of the entire session from a therapeutic intervention perspective.[3] This therapist works from a systems theory perspective (Sluzki, 1978, 1983). A principle from systems theory which pertains to accounts analysis is the view that 'the way a sequence of events is punctuated and reality is organized results from (arbitrary) agreements by the participants' so 'a change in punctuation . . . may radically alter interactional rules and family myths' (Sluzki, 1978: 392). For instance, the therapist attempts to repunctuate a blames-accounts pattern to change the couples' interactional rules.

Accounts in therapy have not been previously examined, and yet accounts seem to be an important way that clients tell their side and defend themselves against blames. In particular, this analysis will focus on the following research questions:

1. How participants make relevant aspects of the prior problematic event to cohere with the folk logic of their accounts.
2. How participants use the nonverbal dimensions of interaction to display their positionings, alignments and affect in blame-accounts sequences.
3. How clients and therapist interactionally negotiate and construct the import and significance of events.

Blame–Accounts Sequences in Couple Therapy

A videotape of a couple therapy consultation is used here.[4] The participants are a therapist, Sluzki, and an unmarried couple, Jenny and Larry. The following episode is selected for analysis because it contains instances of telling problems, blames, and accounts as well as a therapeutic assessment of these.

1   (Episode)
    Sluzki: What kinds of problems were there.
           (1.2)
    Jenny: Uhm hh (0.4) again back to th– >you know what I said
           originally I think ya know< just this:: inabil:ity to:
           communicate feeling like we were .hh (1.0) living in: in: you
           know sep<u>arate</u> (0.9) <u>houses</u> and that we weren't <u>real</u> ↓ ly: (0.6)
           <u>working</u> as a ↓ couple we ↑ <u>weren't</u> like a couple, I mean we
           really didn't have .hh (0.9) a re<u>lation</u>ship >so to speak< I
           mean uhm I felt that if if things happened to Larry he couldn't
           talk to me about them
           if (   )   .hhhh
           [   ]
    Sluzki: He didn't talk to you about it?=
    Jenny: =<u>No</u> he(.hh)'s >he's< <u>very</u> introverted and and very ah:
           <u>private</u>, very private person=
    Sluzki: =Um hum
    Jenny: And he: (doesn't)
           [-   ]
    Sluzki: When things happen to you what?

Jenny: >When things happen to me I mean< now: with therapy it's
it's it's more (0.6) ah it's easier for me now t' to talk about
things I ↑ wa:nt to talk about things (0.6) I mean my feelings
are more on the surface and I have a need to=

Larry: =I think it's not ther:apy I think I think it's just her personality
.hh=

Jenny: =But therapy certainly brought a lot of that out=

Larry: =Could be

Jenny: I mean I feel more comfortable about talking about my
˙feelings (.) an:d expressing them=

Larry: =We're different in that way, she has a problem she likes
to talk (0.5) about it or reiterate on it (0.4) a num:ber of times
a large number of times (.) in my view
                                    [   ]
Sluzki: >Yes that's a problem<

Larry: An:d and I (0.4) so (1.1) on that issue (0.7)
she's probably, if there is (0.4) an objective way to look at
it, I think she's probably (.) over does the talking
about problems and I (0.6) tend to under (0.6) talk those
                              [   ]
Sluzki: (   ) (0.9) Uh hm

Larry: Hhh and I think the balance between us is (0.5) is ah: about
right hhhhh
              [   ]
Sluzki: Um huh
          (1.2)

Jenny: *Well: I don't know*
          (0.6)

Sluzki: Yeah:

Jenny: I'm not so sure that I – I (.) overdo it though
          (0.4)

Jenny: >Because I talk to< other people: (.) ya know about problems
and they seem to have .hhh similar reactions >you know when
they have a problem< they they seem to (0.7) talk to me:
about it just the way >I talk to them about it so< I mean if I'm
comparing myself to other people that I know I don't feel like
I'm: .hhh overly:: reactive or: anything like that
          (0.5)

Jenny: I mean that again is very subjective=

Sluzki: =Absolutely
              [   ]
Jenny: Ya know

Sluzki: Yeah
          (0.7)

Jenny: So:: (0.8) the way he views: (0.6) uhm my: (0.6) over-reaction
or the way somebody else would look at it they might think

	that I'm even under-reacting to certain problems so it's again ↑ very subjective.
Sluzki:	Um hmm
	(0.5)
Sluzki:	Ah:: in addition to that this is an old discussion.
Jenny:	*Uh huh*
	(0.8)
Sluzki:	Yeah?=
Jenny:	=An old one?
Larry:	Yes=
Jenny:	=Yeah yeah: (.) definitely an old one

                                    [   ]

Larry:	You know ob-obviously you=

                                                [   ]

Jenny:	Uh hum
Larry:	=don't believe that you overdo problems otherwise you=

                                              [   ]

Jenny:	Um huh
Larry:	=wouldn't do: it (.) I mean you think you handle=

        [   ]   [   ]

Jenny:	Uh hum right
Larry:	=problems correctly and I think I do but what I'm saying is: (.) you obviously don't think you do it incorrectly otherwise you would *change* it, and I don't think (.) I do it incorrectly otherwise I would change it but I think wha–what the=

          [   ]

Sluzki:	Yeah:
Larry:	=prob– what's happening is ah (1.2)– is that (.) uhm: we both have a different idea on what's the correct way to handle (0.5) problems that ↑ come up
	(1.4)
Sluzki:	*Yeah*
Larry:	That's all.
Sluzki:	Uhm (2.3) .hh one way or another (.) you are involved in a:: in a: very particular ritual . . .

Telling Problems

The analysis begins with the telling of problems and blaming which creates the relevance for accounts. Clients in an initial therapy interview face the conversational task of saying why they are there and this typically involves what may be glossed as telling problems. Problems are a commonsense category which clients convey through claims, descriptions, and narratives of their circumstances, their partner, and their interpersonal relationship. Problems are told, not for their descriptive adequacy alone, but to make an interactional point – to complain, ascribe blame, or allocate responsibility.

In this episode, how is Jenny's talk heard as telling problems? The therapist's initial question requesting information about problems creates a slot or the conditional relevance to hear the answer as about problems. Jenny initially formulates the problems by the ascription, 'just this:: inabil:ity to: communicate,' and then proceeds to describe this problematic by a series of contrasts between their present relationship and how it should be. Her ascriptions here are heard as telling problems because they implicate a 'deficiency' in their relationship given the folk logic that intimate couples should have 'good communication.' In other words, the relational identity of intimate couples may be seen as a 'membership category' for which various 'category-bound activities,' such as good communication, are expected (Sacks, 1972). 'If an incumbent category . . . does not enact category-bound obligations . . . then these matters may be claimed as noticeably absent and as *specifically accountable*' (Watson, 1978: 106–7; emphasis added). Quite simply, this deficiency is inconsistent with an intimate relationship, so it is displayed as problematic, and thereby creates the relevance for an account.

An organizational feature of this telling of problems is that it references a previous telling:

2
Sluzki: What kinds of problems were there.
            (1.2)
Jenny: Uhm hh (0.4)
→₁   again back to th– >you know what I said originally
→₂   I think ya know< just this:: inabil:ity to: communicate

Jenny formulates the problem by referring to 'what [she] said originally' (arrow 1). By drawing on what she has said previously, she allows us to understand the emphasis she puts on 'this::' (arrow 2), in that it is used as an indexical marker of the problem as already told. The intonational emphasis achieved through the elongation on, 'this:: inabil:ity to: communicate' (arrow 2), displays her exasperated affect with the problem.

The participation framework of couple therapy typically involves the telling of problems directed to the therapist and monitored by the relational partner. In transcript fragment 2, the therapist's query is directed to Jenny. Her answer is delayed by a between-turn gap, the particle 'Uhm,' and the audible outbreath. Such delay components display the difficulty of telling problems. Jenny turns her gaze from the therapist to briefly look to Larry and then casts her eyes down as she begins to tell the problem. In transcript fragment 3 (below)

Jenny's eye gaze is transcribed along with her problem telling from
fragment 2.

3

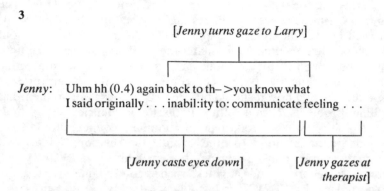

[*Jenny turns gaze to Larry*]

Jenny: Uhm hh (0.4) again back to th–>you know what
I said originally . . . inabil:ity to: communicate feeling . . .

[*Jenny casts eyes down*]   [*Jenny gazes at
                                            therapist*]

Larry synchronizes his gaze with Jenny's: he looks at her and then
casts his head down as she does. Jenny's looking to Larry may be an
appeasement or cooperative gesture, but her gaze aversion and
casting eyes down displays the difficulty in retelling the problem.
Larry's nonverbal synchrony here also seems to display coopera-
tiveness with Jenny, and the difficulty or even embarrassment with
telling the problem.

Allocating blame   Problems are told in therapy not merely for their
descriptive adequacy, but for their interactional point. Jenny's telling
can be heard, not only to tell problems, but also to allocate blame and
responsibility to her Larry. Such implicit blame becomes displayed
when she turns from *relational descriptions* to *descriptions of Larry*:

4
	Jenny:	Uhm I felt that if if things happened to
→¹		Larry he couldn't talk to me about them
		if ( ) .hhhh
		[ ]
→²	*Sluzki*:	He didn't talk to you about it?=
	Jenny:	=No he(.hh)'s >he's< very introverted and and
		very ah: private, very private person=

Her use here of 'he couldn't talk to me' (arrow 1) draws upon a
similar folk logic of deficiency as she used in the description of their
relationship, 'inability to communicate.' The important difference is
that ascribing a deficiency to Larry implies that he is responsible for
their relational problems. So Jenny may be seen as moving from
telling problems about their relationship to telling problems about
Larry and thereby allocating blame to him.

The therapist's query (arrow 2) (that is, a partial repetition or mirroring of Jenny's description) appears to display recognition of her shift. Jenny, then, explains Larry's inability to communicate by the personality ascriptions 'introverted' and 'private.' These descriptions are marked by her intonational emphasis on 'very' and 'private.' She gives an immediate reply by latching an emphatic 'No' on to the end of the therapist's question. Her audible inhalation and repetition in the production of 'he's' displays her exasperation. Critical emphasis is marked through the use of 'very' to intensify the personality ascriptions 'introverted' and 'private,' as well as through the use of repetition in 'very ah: private, very private person.' These paralingual features of Jenny's answer are instructive here for the way this utterance is heard, for these same words said with a different intonation and pacing could be heard as, say, sympathetic, rather than as critical. These paralingual features also are used for an affect display of exasperation or frustration.

Therapeutic Responses to Blame
In two-party conversation the occurrence of a blame by the first party makes conditionally relevant a response from the second party, such as a denial, admission, account, or counter-blame. But this adjacency-pair format does not work so neatly in three-party conversations such as couple therapy. The 'participation framework' (Goffman, 1981) of couple therapy affects the interactional sequencing. In the above episode Jenny's criticisms of Larry are *told to the therapist* so that the latter's questions or comments become expected (Sluzki, 1978: 373). Of course, Larry could respond to these criticisms, but in so doing he may appear to be interrupting or precluding the therapist's intervention. So following a criticism in couple therapy there appears to be competing conditional relevancies between the therapist's interventions and the relational partner's response.

In the present episode the therapist responds to Jenny's criticism of Larry in different ways: compare arrows 1 and 2.

5

Jenny:	I felt that if if things happened to Larry	
	he couldn't talk to me about them	
	if ( ) .hhhh	
	[ ]	
⟶ *Sluzki*:	He didn't talk to you about it?=	
Jenny:	=No he(.hh)'s >he's< very introverted and and	
	very ah: private, very private person=	
Sluzki:	=Um hum	

> *Jenny:*   And he: (doesn't)
> 　　　　　　[　　　　　　]
> → *Sluzki:*   When things happen to you what?
> *Jenny:*   >When things happen to me I mean< now: with therapy it's
> 　　　　　it's it's more (0.6) ah it's <u>easier</u> for me now t' to talk about
> 　　　　　things I ↑ wa:nt to talk about things (0.6) I mean my feelings
> 　　　　　are more on the surface and I have a need to=

At arrow 1, the therapist mirrors Jenny's description of Larry just at
the point where she moves from telling problems to allocating blame.
Notice though that Sluzki substitutes 'didn't' for Jenny's use of
'couldn't' (arrow 1). The therapist's substitution of terms here is due
to the logic of the use of 'couldn't' versus 'didn't'; the former implies
ascriptions about abilities and competencies, while 'didn't' implies
what happened in a particular case. Therapeutically the focus on
actions rather than on capabilities allows more for the possibility of
change. However, Jenny does not appear to pick up on this
distinction because she answers the therapist's question by explaining
Larry's personality traits which imply abilities rather than specific
actions.

A potential problem which therapists want to avoid in couple
therapy is the appearance of forming a coalition with one of the
clients (Sluzki, 1975). The therapist wants to remain 'equidistant'
from both clients (Sluzki, 1990). In the present sequence, the
therapist does not allow Jenny to continue with her criticism of Larry
because this is the third occasion where she describes his deficiency at
communication. Instead the therapist asks her how she handles such
circumstances (arrow 2). This kind of query has been called a
'difference question' in that it is designed to have clients describe
their differences as a first step to seeing their complementarity.[5]

Larry's Matching Criticism and Account

As mentioned above, a potential communication problem for clients
in couple therapy is how to respond to a criticism which is told to the
therapist. In the present episode the therapist's intervention had
shifted the focus from Larry's deficiency at communication to Jenny's
description of her own behaviour which makes a response to her
criticism more difficult for Larry. But Larry responds to Jenny's
self-description by denying that therapy is the reason, and instead
ascribing it to her 'personality.' His disagreement displays recognition of Jenny's prior criticism of him. In formulating the reason for
her talkativeness by, 'it's just her personality .hh,' he is openly
disagreeing and minimizing her prior assessment of the importance of
therapy. He also appears to use this personality ascription as a way to

match her personality ascription of him. Personality ascriptions seem to be more critical than action ascriptions.

Larry's critical description of Jenny's behavior is contrary to her own self-description (compare fragment 6 and fragment 5).

6

Larry:	=We're different in that way, she has a problem she likes
→	to talk (0.5) about it or reiterate on it (0.4) a <u>num:ber</u> of
→	times a <u>large</u> number of times (.) in my view
	[ ]
Sluzki:	>Yes that's a problem<

Larry's formulation of Jenny's behavior (arrows) is produced, not only by lexical choice, but also by *repetition* (of 'number of times') and by the *intonational emphasis* (on 'number' and 'large'). He also gives emphasis to 'talk' by moving his head forward while saying it and pausing afterwards. His display of affect intensifies his response to Jenny's repeated negative descriptions of him. The therapist's overlapping '>Yes that's a problem<' at once shows agreement with Larry and also works to encourage him to continue in telling his side. Again the therapist uses the strategy of maintaining equidistance between the couple. Jenny has made many more criticisms of Larry than he of her (in this episode and also earlier in the interview), and also she presents him as the one who needs therapy, so the therapist needs to display support to Larry to accomplish an equidistant alignment.

Making relevant the problematic to account for   A blame makes an account conditionally relevant, but a blame does not determine the content or character of the account. In producing an account, one makes relevant certain aspects of the problematic event which are designed to cohere with one's preferred reading of events.

In the present episode Larry offers an account which responds to Jenny's prior criticism of him and of their relationship:

7

Larry:	An:d and <u>I</u> (0.4) <u>so</u> (1.1) on <u>that</u> issue (0.7) she's
	probably, if there is (0.4) an objective way to look at
	it, I think she's probably (.) <u>over does</u> the talking
	about problems and I (0.6) tend to under (0.6) talk those
	[ ]
Sluzki:	( ) (0.9) Uh hm
→ *Larry*:	Hhh and I think the balance between us
→	is (0.5) is ah: about right hhhhh
	[ ]
Sluzki:	Um huh

First of all, given the participation framework of couple therapy it is not until this point that Larry is able to respond to Jenny's prior criticism some nine turns earlier. He makes relevant her prior criticism by his formulation, 'I (0.6) tend to under (0.6) talk those.' Notice how his self-description here is in marked contrast to Jenny's previous critical description of him (transcript 5).

Secondly, his self-description (transcript 7) can be produced without explicitly disagreeing with Jenny's prior assessment. In fact, it can be heard as a partial concession to her criticism. But his formulation minimizes its blameworthiness by deletion and substitution of descriptive terms.

Thirdly, Larry begins the account by reiterating his criticism of Jenny talking too much about problems. He ascribes blame both to her and to himself, but in ways which *complement* or *balance* each other. He attempts to transform her characterization of their problematic relationship by offering an account of their relationship based on a folk logic of 'balance.' His formulation of their relationship minimizes their relational problems. This minimization is heightened by his muffled laughter in presenting his balance solution of her problem (see transcript 7, arrows).

Larry's balance account here does not fit neatly into any of the extant accounts taxonomies. It is not an excuse because there is no denial of responsibility, nor is it a justification because fault is conceded. The difficulty in categorizing it arises from the fact that most accounts are defenses for the individual's problematic actions, while Larry's account is a minimization of their problematic relationship.

Jenny's counter-account   Larry's account is told to the therapist, however Sluzki offers no evaluation or alignment with the account. Instead the therapist uses the minimal response 'Um huh' (transcript 8) as acknowledgment token.

8

Larry:	Hhh and I think the balance between us is (0.5) is ah: about right hhhhh
	[ ]
Sluzki:	Um huh
	(1.2)
→ *Jenny*:	*Well: I don't know*
	(0.6)
Sluzki:	Yeah:
Jenny:	I'm not so sure that I – I (.) overdo it though

The between-turn gap after therapist's 'Um huh' allows Jenny to respond with an account of her own. She begins to account with a qualified disagreement with Larry's criticism (arrow). The elongation of 'Well:' to initiate the account displays her qualifier to the prior claims (Owen, 1981). The tempo and volume of Jenny's softly spoken, hesitant disagreement is in *marked expressive contrast* with Larry's muffled laughter produced in offering his account (transcript 7, arrows). So her disagreement is displayed paralingually as well as verbally.

Jenny's account makes relevant the prior criticism (transcript 7). She indicates that she is responding to Larry's criticism by: 'I'm not so sure that I – I (.) overdo it though' (transcript 8). Notice that she does not explicitly respond to what appears to be the main point of Larry's account – that the 'balance' between them is right – though, by implication, she can be heard as disagreeing with this. She uses the similar verb, 'overdo,' that he used in formulating her actions, 'she probably over-does the talking about problems . . .' (transcript 7), to make relevant the problematic to address in her account.

Jenny's account then presents a rebuttal of Larry's prior criticism by giving reasons to support her disagreement.

9

Jenny: *Well: I don't know*
          (0.6)
Sluzki: Yeah:
Jenny: I'm no so sure that I – I (.) overdo it though
          (0.4)
Jenny: >Because I talk to< other people: (.) ya know about
          problems and they seem to have .hhh similar reactions >you
          know when they have a problem< they they seem to (0.7) <u>talk</u>
          to me: about it just the way >I talk to them about it so< I
          mean if I'm comparing myself to other people that I know I
          don't feel like I'm .hhh overly:: reactive or: anything like that
          (0.5)
Jenny: I mean that again is very subjective=
Sluzki   =Absolutely
            [   ]
Jenny: Ya know
Sluzki: Yeah
          (0.7)
Jenny: So:: (0.8) the way <u>he views</u>: (0.6) uhm my: (0.6) over-reaction
          or the way somebody else would look at it they might think
          that I'm even under-reacting to certain problems so it's again
          ↑ very subjective.

Jenny's account compares her talking about problems to other people's talk about problems as reasons or evidence to justify her position. The folk logic invoked here, 'being like other people,' is used to normalize her actions. She then formulates the upshot of her account as how much to talk about problems is 'very subjective.' This subjectivity assessment is used to explicitly deny the previous criticism that she overdoes the talking. In sum, this account attempts to transform the event from problematic to something subjective, and thereby, not unjustified.

Evaluation

Upon an account's completion a response to the account is relevant or becomes expected from one's interlocutor. As already mentioned, the participation framework of couple therapy involves the client telling problems or giving accounts directed to the therapist in front of their relational partner. Clients expect that the therapist will assess these problems or accounts (Sluzki, 1978). In the present episode two very different kinds of responses to Jenny's account are seen, one from the therapist and the other from Larry.

Therapist's reframing response   Following Jenny's account Sluzki responds, not to the account, but to the couple's blame–accounts sequence by labeling it 'an old discussion.'

> **10**
> *Jenny*:   . . . so it's again ↑ very subjective.
> *Sluzki*:   Um hmm
>   (0.5)
> *Sluzki*:   Ah:: in addition to that this is an old discussion.
> *Jenny*:   *Uh huh*
>   (0.8)
> → *Sluzki*:   Yeah?=
> *Jenny*:   =An old one?
> *Larry*:   Yes=
> *Jenny*:   = Yeah yeah: (.) <u>definitely</u> an old one

By formulating the couple's blame-accounts sequence as 'an old discussion,' the therapist breaks frame with the content of the couple's accusations and defenses, and instead makes relevant the character of the discussion itself – as a recurring pattern. From a systemic perspective, the therapist views the couple's interactional pattern as a conjoint attribute, rather than from a commonsense, individualistic perspective of blame and accounts (Sluzki, 1990). So the therapist refuses to evaluate Jenny's or Larry's accounts, but instead assesses both of their blame-accounts as 'old' – as part of a mutually produced pattern. Also, by commenting on the couple's discussion itself the therapist is able to remain neutral and avoid taking sides.

This formulation, 'an old discussion,' displays the therapist's implication for the couple *not* to continue in this pattern of blame-accounts. The therapist proposes a reframing of the couple's interactional pattern – a change from their individual *folk logic* to a *therapeutic, systemic logic*. The therapist needs to know whether the couple agrees with his assessment, as seen by his prompt (arrow).

This sequence appears to be similar to a therapeutic strategy identified by Davis (1986) in which the therapist reformulates the client's telling of problems in psychotherapeutic terms that can be managed by therapy. The therapist then seeks consent from the client to pursue solutions for this reformulation of the problems.

What is at issue in both Davis' (1986) materials and mine is how is the interaction to be labeled or identified – by a folk logic or by a therapeutic logic? This is crucial because how action and interaction are defined has implications for future action. If Jenny's ascription of Larry as deficient communicator holds, then the implication is for him to change; if Larry's balance account is accepted then little change is needed; and if the therapist's reframing (namely, 'an old discussion') is accepted, then minimally the couple will stop this old pattern. In short, which account or assessment will hold is consequential for what should be done next.

An account or an assessment may be seen as the actor's interpretation of events which has implications for future action. An interpretation may be seen as a *proposal* which needs to be agreed to or accepted by one's interlocutors in order to hold. Larry only minimally accepts Jenny's criticism of him by his balance account, and she rejects the criticism of her by her comparison-to-others account. Even the therapist, in the membership category 'expert of interpersonal relations,' needs to have his assessment aligned with interactionally for it to hold.

Jenny begins to align with Sluzki's proposal by agreeing verbally while shaking her head, and by intensifying the therapist's formulation with the modifier 'definitely an old one' (transcript 10). Larry also appears to agree with the therapist, but instead returns to the topic of Jenny's account.

Evaluation sequence In the following transcript Larry turns to evaluate Jenny's prior account. He accomplishes this return to topic (or continuing with the 'old discussion') by formulating the gist of her account 'you don't believe that you overdo problems.' This formulation is prefaced by the assessment, 'obviously,' produced with emphatic intonational contour which works to minimize the significance of her account.

11

Jenny:	=Yeah yeah: (.) <u>definitely</u> an old one
	[ ]
Larry:	You know ob-<u>obviously</u> you=
	[ ]
→ *Jenny:*	Uh hum
Larry:	=don't believe that you overdo problems otherwise you=
	[ ]
→ *Jenny:*	Um huh
Larry:	=wouldn't do: it (.) I mean you think you handle=
	[ ] [ ]
→ *Jenny:*	Uh hum right
Larry:	=problems correctly and I think I do but what I'm saying is:
	(.) you obviously don't think you do it incorrectly otherwise
	you would <u>change</u> it, and I don't think (.) I do it incorrectly
	otherwise <u>I would</u> change it but I think wha–what the=
	[ ]
Sluzki:	Yeah:
Larry:	prob– what's happening is ah (1.2) is that (.) uhm: we both
	have a different idea on what's the correct way to handle (0.5)
	problems that ↑ come up
	(1.4)
Sluzki:	*Yeah*
Larry:	That's all.
Sluzki:	Uhm (2.3) .hh one way or another (.) you are involved in a:: in
	a: very particular ritual . . .

The sequential positioning of Larry's evaluation here appears to be taken as ill-timed as seen by Jenny's responses. Jenny's marked use of the minimal responses, 'Uh huh,' displays her recognition of the ill-timed positioning of Larry's evaluation (arrows 1, 2, 3). Typically 'Uh huh's' are used as continuers and are positioned at 'the boundaries of turn-constructional units' (Schegloff, 1981; Goodwin, 1986). In the present case, the initial use of 'Uh huh' (arrow 1) is positioned well before Larry completes a turn-constructional unit, or move. This use of 'Uh huh' (arrow 1) seems to display recognition of being interrupted and the evaluative character of '<u>obviously</u>.' In addition to its marked positioning, 'Uh huh' is produced rapidly and with little intonational contour. Instead of signaling to continue it seems designed to *challenge* Larry's right to the floor and to returning to the 'old discussion.'

Jenny's eye contact in this evaluation sequence also displays her negative assessment of Larry's returning to the 'old discussion.' She looks at Larry as he overlaps her, but then averts her gaze and looks down as he finishes the formulation of her account (transcript fragment 12).

12

Larry: you don't believe that you overdo problems otherwise you
    [ ]   ↑ [ ]
Jenny: Uh hum   ↑ Uh hum
            [Jenny breaks gaze with
             Larry and looks down]

Jenny casts her eyes down while Larry continues. This gaze aversion seems to signal a *distancing* from Larry's evaluation and return to the 'old discussion.'

During the course of Larry's evaluation, Jenny brings her gaze up and looks briefly at the therapist as though to display her misalignment with Larry's evaluation. After she casts her eyes down again, the therapist utters the minimal response, 'Yeah:' produced with a flat intonational contour, to Larry. So Jenny and Sluzki appear to coordinate their reception to Larry's evaluation.

13

Larry: incorrectly otherwise I would change it but I think wha–what
                     [ ]
Sluzki: |_____| Yeah:
            |
        [Jenny gazes at Sluzki and
         then casts her eyes down]

Larry appears to recognize the lack of responsiveness and distancing from the therapist and Jenny as seen by his minimization of his own evaluation 'That's all' (transcript 11).

In sum, the marked placement of minimal responses and eye gaze aversion are used here by Jenny as a kind of mitigated challenge to Larry's misalignment with the therapist's reframing. Not only is an account open to evaluation, but so is the evaluation itself subject to evaluation.

Discussion

Examining a couple therapy session raises the question of how blame-accounts sequences get shaped by the therapeutic context. The issue of *context* needs to be addressed. The accounts offered in a couple therapy session are likely to differ in certain systematic respects from other contexts, such as when the couple is just by themselves. The notion of context is often taken as a 'container' for interaction, and different patterns of interaction are explained by appealing to different contexts. However, context may be approached in a more fruitful way by claiming that the extent to which context matters, should be manifested or displayed in the talk itself (Heritage, 1984).

The following is a provisional description of how blames and accounts are used in couple therapy. As already seen, much of the talk in couple therapy is organized by a participation framework of the therapist asking questions and the clients giving answers. Through answering questions, clients tell problems, make criticisms and offer accounts. Most of the clients' talk is directed to the therapist, but it is monitored and can be responded to by their relational partner. Clients express complaints about their relational partner to the therapist in the partner's presence. Criticizing another to a third party in his/her presence has been likened to 'gossiping in the presence of.'[6] Clients often refer to their partner by a third-person pronoun ('he' or 'she').[7] Such third-person reference seems distinctive of therapy and other kinds of mediation sessions, for example, courtroom discourse.

The membership category of the therapist affects the blame-accounts interaction. The therapist is, in effect, a virtual stranger to the clients so they must provide more background description and elaboration of problematic events than if the couple were just by themselves. Clients need to be more explicit and do more verbal work to describe and explain themselves in presenting their preferred meanings. Clients' discourse also reflects their perception of the 'therapist as expert.' For instance, clients frequently defer to the therapist's questions, interruptions and evaluations, and at times attempt to align with the therapist 'against' their partner. The therapist appears to exert considerable control over turn taking, for example, by directing questions, by cutting short criticisms and by drawing out underlying assumptions which results in a decrease in overlaps and marked silences.

Accounts in therapy may be part of a recurring blame–defense pattern. Such recurring accounts have not been previously examined. These accounts function to resist the change implied by the prior blame. Clients use accounts to 'tell their side.' The therapist, on the other hand, wants to get the couple to break such recurring patterns by reframing their punctuation of events.

By way of summary, the project here has been to do an analysis of blame-accounts sequences in couple therapy. By examining naturally occurring discourse, the nonverbal components of accounts can be included in the analysis. While the call for considering the nonverbals of communication is nothing new, it is especially important for accounts analysis because the nonverbal levels display how inter-actants frame their messages and display affect. For instance, we saw how Jenny used emphatic intonational contour, rapid pacing, and repetition to display exasperation while doing criticism; or how she averted eye contact and produced 'Uh huh' rapidly and with little intonational contour to display disagreement and distancing from Larry's evaluation of her account; or how Larry synchronized his eye behavior with hers to display the difficulty or embarrassment in the problem's telling; or how he used a muffled laughter to display minimization during his balance account. The most expressive nonverbal features in these materials seem to be eye contact and the paralingual dimensions of intonation, pacing, and pausing. The framing capacity achieved through these nonverbal aspects suggests that blames and accounts are multidimensional activities which display meanings at different levels, rather than their traditional conception as simply explanatory verbal texts or speech acts.

Secondly, we saw that problems are told to the therapist by descriptions of one's partner to implicate blame of him or her. How does one select and *make relevant* through talk some aspects of the prior problematic event in one's account? The multiple relevancies inherent in problematic events are why the notion of a response is crucial in describing accounts. Accounts are not determined by the antecedent criticism; accounts need not respond to the previous speaker's main point. What is made relevant from the prior problematic is designed to cohere with one's folk logic in the attempt to transform meanings. For instance, Larry responds to Jenny's deficiency crticism by *minimizing* its significance through a deletion and substitution of terms. This minimization of the problematic is then used in his account with the folk logic that they balance each other out. She, in turn, makes relevant his criticism of her over-talking about problems by paraphrasing his words in her denial. She attempts to rebut the criticism in her account by the folk logic of comparison to others. The therapist makes relevant the recurrence of the couple's discussion rather than the content of their criticisms and accounts to get them to see the recurrence of this pattern. In a sense, the prior problematic event is continually open to revision depending on the folk logic one can make relevant in the course of one's account and its evaluation.

Notes

1. The exemplary work in viewing therapy as conversation is Labov and Fanshel (1977), but also see: Pittenger et al. (1960), Turner (1976), Wodak (1981), Davis (1986), Peyrot (1987), Scheff (1990), and Gale (1991). Therapists and psychologists have examined the cognitive and social bases of everyday problems, but little attention has been given to the interactive dimensions of how communicators tell problems, account for their actions, and narrate their lives.

2. As Atkinson and Drew (1979: 107) point out:

    [D]escriptive work which speakers do is reported as 'telling a story', . . . 'blaming', 'justifying', . . . and so on – and may be reported as such even though no prefatory or declaratory, 'here's a story . . .', 'well, I blame . . .', etc., was used. This is to emphasise that describing is not merely an appendage to other interactional work; rather it is often through constructing descriptions that certain interactional tasks may be accomplished.

3. There are a series of works analyzing different aspects of the same therapeutic interview: Gill et al. (1954), Pittenger et al. (1960), Turner (1976), and Mellinger (1987).

4. My deepest thanks to Sara Cobb and Carlos Sluzki for making the videotape of the therapy session available to me. For a complete transcript of this session, see Sluzki (1990).

5. My thanks to Jack Lannamann for pointing this out to me.

6. I owe this analogy to Sheila McNamee.

7. Shotter (1984: ch. 9) uses this distinction in an interesting critique of attribution theory and as a reason to prefer a social accountability perspective.

6
Discursive Affect in Situations of Social Accountability

Emotion words form part of the vocabulary of appraisal and criticism, and a number of them belong to the more specific language of moral criticism.

Emotion concepts . . . are not purely psychological: they presuppose concepts of social relationships and institutions, and concepts belonging to systems of judgment, moral, aesthetic, and legal. In using emotion words we are able, therefore, to relate behavior to the complex background in which it is enacted, and so to make human actions intelligible.

These passages from the linguistic philosopher Bedford (1962: 119, 126) broaden the view of the emotions from internal states to their discursive aspects in invoking social accountability. As shown in the previous chapter, persons assess and defend conduct on multiple levels. The uses of affect in social interaction comprise an important, if neglected, dimension of social accountability. Emotions, such as anger, and feelings of exasperation or tension, seem to be common reactions during social accountability episodes. For example, an accusation may be intensified by the accusor's show of anger, displayed through emphatic intonational contour in uttering the accusation. Or, actors may verbally avow feelings, such as depression, as a way to explain their unusual behaviors. The point here is that the uses of affect can be consequential in the performance of social accountability practices. Yet, with few exceptions, the literature on accounts and social accountability overlooks the domain of the emotions and focuses largely on strategies of verbal accounting.

The focus of this chapter will be on the *discourse of emotion* in doing social accountability, rather than on the traditional approach to emotion as a physiological or psychological occurrence. In my research on accounts in therapy (chapter 5), I was struck by how participants used affect displays in forming complaints and giving accounts. Here I want to extend this investigation beyond the therapeutic setting to everyday talk. As I began to examine tape recordings and transcripts of accounts episodes, I noticed that the emotions worked in ways beyond the previously described nonverbal and paralingual affect displays. Persons constructed criticisms and accounts *by verbally avowing emotion* (for example, 'I'm mad') or *by ascribing it to others* ('You look upset'). The concerns here will focus on how affect works interactionally as a procedure for doing social accountability – evaluating, prompting an explanation, accounting, and the like. The uses of affect can make accountability relevant to the situated context and project a certain range of responses from interlocutors. The avowal of an emotion such as anger, for instance, is a way to frame events as out of the ordinary and problematic, and thereby to implicate another's responsibility for provoking the speaker's emotional reaction. So how affect is conveyed or displayed in the practices of social accountability will be the focus of this chapter.

Perspectives on the Social Accountability of Affect

The idea of looking at the role of affect in accounting also comes from my readings in different literatures on the emotions and their relevance for accounts. So before beginning the accounts analysis of discursive affect, some of the main leads from these literatures will be highlighted.

Embarrassment and Accounts

A line of research on the emotions which has examined social accountability and accounts is the work on embarrassment (for a review see Cupach and Metts, 1990). Embarrassment is conceived of as an unwanted emotional eruption occurring when an actor's self-presentation is discredited through the actor's deeds, some situational contingency, or the actions of others (Semin and Manstead, 1982). Embarrassment constitutes a problematic condition for the actor due to the incompatibility between the expressive features of the situation and the actor's claims to good character which can be a threat to face (Goffman, 1967c). By way of contrast, young children do not become embarrassed by being naked in front of others or publicly talking aloud to themselves because they have not yet been enculturated into societal practices and its system of rules. Once one acquires these competencies, one is held accountable for their proper expressive functioning, or embarrassment is a price one pays for their neglect. The possibility of embarrassment throws into bold relief the demands for expressive performances compatible with the actor's statuses. For instance, the physician who engages an unrobed patient in a mutual gaze during a medical examination may inadvertently provoke embarrassment in the patient (Heath, 1988). In brief, embarrassment may be seen as a culturally acquired response to failed performances in which the actor is aware of being seen.

Usually embarrassment is a relatively short-term, emotional

response. Interaction returns to normalcy when the emotion subsides and composure is regained. Persons may offer accounts as coping strategies to manage these embarrassing incidents. But not only does the actor suddenly experience a loss of poise or discomfort, but this very disruption makes face-saving practices more difficult.

Social embarrassment offers an interesting site for the examination of accountability and accounts. While our concern here is not with embarrassment per se, but with the accountability of affect, the embarrassment literature raises some issues for further development: first, embarrassment presumes the actor's appraisal or evaluation of actions, events or character. Indeed, such critical or negative appraisal of circumstances is a necessary condition for embarrassment to arise in the first place. Secondly, embarrassment can reflect circumstances which create the necessity for accounts to explain or mitigate the discrediting social meanings.

Other emotions and feelings also can be relevant in social accountability episodes, such as anger, sadness, exasperation, tension, and the like.[1] Generally these comprise what might be called the 'negative' emotions in that they reflect some problematic or blameworthy social conditions. The focus in this chapter will not be on a single emotion, such as embarrassment, but on the discursive character of various negative emotions which work as part of social accountability practices.

A Social Constructionist View of Emotion

The evaluative nature of affect discourse is one of the principle insights of social constructionism (Averill, 1980, 1991; Gergen, 1985; Harré, 1986; Lutz, 1987, 1990; White, 1991). The connection of affect to social accountability comes in that a person's avowal, ascription, or display of negative affect implies the person's negative or critical evaluation, appraisal, or assessment: '[E]motion-concepts function in accounts that explain action that is in some way considered untoward or problematic within a situation' (Coulter, 1986: 126). The expressions of affect, such as anger, sadness, or exasperation, work interactionally to demonstrate to others (and to oneself) that circumstances are out of the ordinary or problematic. For instance, to avow anger implies some appraisal of an incident which justifies one's emotional reaction. Affect display works interactionally to demonstrate or intensify a person's critical assessment of the event. The uses of negative affect may be seen as a person's procedure for presenting an event as problematic – for showing the seriousness of the event – to mark it as out of the ordinary and as a way to intensify it.

The discourse of emotion needs to satisfy certain cultural and situational conditions to be considered 'reasonable' or justified in the eyes of interactants. A person may be said to be *excessively* or *unjustifiably* angry, jealous, or depressed. If circumstances do not warrant a particular emotion or feeling, then others may question or reproach the actor for such displays of affect. One may be held accountable for: (a) the 'extent' of one's emotion (feeling insanely jealous or not jealous enough), (b) the 'direction' of emotion (one may feel depressed when one should feel happy), or (c) the 'duration' of emotion (grieving too long or too little) (Hochschild, 1979: 564). For example, becoming angry over a tease may lead interlocutors to accuse the actor of being overly sensitive. Of course, the actor may offer accounts of background conditions which make the reaction understandable, but it is only through such further appeals to contextual information that render the emotion appropriate. Persons often make efforts to justify their emotions, and if they cannot do so, this may even lead them to *alter their feelings* in accordance with what can be justified. This demand to justify one's emotions when called to account shows affect is discursive in that it involves more than an 'inner' feeling, but must appeal to cultural norms or some other standards of intelligibility.

Folk logic of affect   The uses of affect in social accountability practices implicate the actor's appraisal of conduct. What counts as a justified or reasonable show of affect may be seen to be based on a folk logic of emotion, that is, the cultural group's commonsense understandings, shared norms, and moral codes for appropriate affective responses, demeanor, and self-presentation.[2] The folk logic of emotion is implicated in those accounts which invoke the 'passions'; persons may portray their behavior as passive, as merely reacting to others' deeds, or as being overcome by feelings which constrain other actions. Whether or not such claims are an accurate representation of psychological processes is beside the point; what matters here is the discursive use of affect.

Typically folk logic is not articulated in a propositional form, but rather is implicit. To offer an account for one's actions presupposes an array of commonsense assumptions of moral/practical human actions and passions. The folk logic inherent in such affect discourse becomes most apparent in those cases in which an actor's affect is challenged or questioned by others. As already seen, actors may be reproached for their anger or disappointment if contextual conditions do not warrant such displays. This suggests the further point that emotion as a form of assessment must be justifiable, otherwise it may be challenged, just as non-emotive verbal assessments can be questioned. So in the accounts analysis attention will be given, not only to the propositional content of the blame or account, but also to how a folk logic is implicated or presumed.

Social Constructionism and Conversation Analysis

Social constructionism and conversation analysis can be usefully integrated, in my view, for investigating phenomena like affect discourse and social accountability. These two perspectives can be complementary because social constructionism offers the conceptual insight of affect as a socially constituted appraisal based on a group's folk logic, while conversation analysis offers a thoroughly empirical methodology for examining social interaction.

To my knowledge conversation analysis has virtually ignored the notion of affect,[3] but it has contributed much to social accountability and accounts (see chapter 3). Conversation analysis has focused on accounts sequences, how accounts are made relevant as a response, and simultaneously, how accounts make relevant one's understanding and assessment of the problematic event in question. Here I want to extend this project by examining the sequential organization of affect discourse in accountability practices. That is, how is affect used and what does it make relevant or consequential in social accountability episodes?

Affect can be kept to oneself or concealed from others. Instead of being verbally conveyed or nonverbally displayed, affect can be hidden. An actor may mask anger so as not to cause a scene. So conversationalists may be seen to have the option whether or not verbally to identify their own or another's emotions. The identifying or labeling of one's own or another's emotion is, to adopt Jefferson's (1987) distinction, to 'expose' it rather than 'embedding' it in the interaction without comment. Jefferson's analysis of 'corrections' found that when persons exposed an interlocutor's spoken error, such as by questioning a mispronounced word or incorrect name, interlocutors explicitly attended to correcting or repairing it (1987). In short, they made the spoken error or mistake accountable. But when persons corrected an interlocutor's error in an 'embedded' fashion, such as by pronouncing the word properly in the course of their response, this did not make the error a focus – something to be accounted for. So I want to apply Jefferson's distinction to emotion because we see similar social organizational structures at work. Exposing negative affect (one's own or that of another) is a way to make relevant a problematic event. A problematic makes relevant an account about it. To avow or ascribe negative affect is to make it an object deserving an account – a state-of-affairs to be (hopefully) remedied.

Caveat   Having made the case that affect can be an important feature of social accountability, a caveat and qualification are called for. The claim is not being made that affect will be relevant in all cases of social accountability. There is a range of ways for accomplishing accusations, accounts, and evaluations – from *affective neutrality* to *strong affect display*. What I am purporting to do here is draw attention to some of the more clear-cut forms of affect discourse because even these cases have been neglected in the literature.

The Discourse of Affect in Social Accountability Practices

Emotion is taken here, not as an inner, hidden cause or motivational factor, but as a social discourse of appraisal. The emotions become interactional in at least three ways: through a verbal avowal of one's own emotion, a verbal ascription of another's emotion, or a nonverbal affect display (which may or may not accompany speech). Each of these three forms of affect can be captured in tape recordings of interaction.[4]

Avowals of Affect
Avowals, or first-person statements, of negative affect can serve social accountability purposes. By avowing negative emotions, the actor implicates his/her involvement and affective response to the event as a way to critically assess others or show constraints on him/herself. Such avowals expose the actor's positioning in the problematic situation.

In the following transcript K avows a negative emotion (arrow 1) as a procedure to invoke the social accountability of B's actions.

> **1**
> ¹→ *K*: You get me so mad.
>   *B*: Why?
> ²→ *K*: You flirt too and you know it
>   (1.5)
>   *K*: I've had millions of reports of people
>   saying
>   [ ]
>   *B*:   No you just told me
>   [   ]
>   *K*:   Stop it stop it! You're not listening to me=
>   *B*: =I'm listening to you
>   [   ]
> ³→ *K*:   You're not listening to me. You can accuse me
> ³→   but I can't accuse you.

K's avowal of being 'mad' (arrow 1) works as what may be called a shorthand formulation of a problematic event. Such shorthand formulations may require further explanation to be understood by the recipient. This affect avowal becomes interactionally unpacked through B's soliciting an explanation. K responds (arrow 2) with a critical ascription of B's behavior ('flirt') which may be heard to constitute the grounds for her anger. Also, notice a few turns later, K retrospectively labels her prior utterances as accusations (arrows 3). This meta-communicative identification provides further grounds for hearing K's avowal of affect as a criticism of B.

Avowals of emotion serve as *shorthand formulations* of the event to implicate blame or criticism of another. Avowals of negative affect make relevant a matrix of issues regarding the conditions for the actor's appraisal – the *reasons*, *causes*, *intensity*, and *justifiability* for the emotion. In other words, affect avowals raise questions such as: What are the events and circumstances which give rise to the actor's affective responses? Are such responses justified? So in the telling of one's negative affect, and thereby projecting social accountability to others, one simultaneously invokes issues of appropriateness and appraisal concerning the circumstances of the emotion.

In the following cases we see an avowal of emotion used to (a) *initiate* the telling of a problematic or an account, and (b) this is taken by the recipient as a shorthand formulation requiring further explanation.

    2 (Detail)
→ *K*: You get me so mad.
    B: Why?
    K: You flirt too and you know it

    3
→ *K*: I'm getting really mad
    B: Why?
    K: Because I don't

    4
→ *S*: So I'm a little a:: (2.2) <u>bummed</u> let's just say
        (3.1)
    W: Why::?
    S: Why you know why

    5
→ *K*: Because it upset me at the time
    B: Why?
    K: I have no right to be upset now

    6
→ *B*: I told ya, it takes the jealousy away and
        the pressure off

K: What kind a pressure you talking about?
B: Just pres– (1.5) uh

7
D: ↑ We:ll (0.3) .hhhhhhhh hhhh I just don't
→   know what to do:: I get choked up over things like this.
M: Yeah.
→ D: I: get choked up over >things like this<
     I can't– anybody that di:es that I barely even
     kno:w and .hhhh I me:an especially fts
     somebody who I'm gonna be looking a:t

8
→ S: It was a bad day. I just ah
T: Why?
S: I just blew a math test before it, so I didn't
     really feel like speaking.

Notice that the avowals of emotion (arrows) in the above fragments are presented as unexplained; no reason or cause for the affect is offered initially. Such inferentially rich avowals of emotion require an explanation for it to complete its point to the recipient – to ascertain what act the speaker uses it to perform. In these cases the avowal of negative affect is heard as a shorthand gloss of a complex of possibly critical assessments, negative feelings and misalignments which are taken by the recipient as in need of further explanation. Such avowals of affect, then, make relevant or project a question, request, or prompt from the recipient to unpack the problematic. For without such a cooperative response the problematic would remain (at least for the moment) unelaborated. So, then, a three-part sequence may be identified: affect avowal–prompt–initiation of explanation. This sequence works to interactionally unpack the grounds for the negative affect and its attendant ascriptions of culpability or defense.

Folk logic of the 'passions'   In addition to interactional accounts sequencing, consider the folk logic invoked through affect avowals. Avowals of affect implicate a folk logic of the passions – as that which happens to us beyond control, and thereby, prevents or inhibits adequate performance. Such avowals work to construct excuses or excuse components.

   9   (FO1aHARD.1)
↳ *Mother*:   pt .hhhhhh hhh it's gun be hard to do: I
              kno:w.
              (0.6)

Daughter:	↑ We:ll (0.3) .hhhhhhhh hhhh
²→	I just don't know what to do::
^{3a}→	I get choked up over things like this.
Mother:	Yeah.
^{3b}→ *Daughter*:	I: get <u>choked up</u> over >things like this<
	I can't– anybody that <u>di</u>:es that I barely even
	kno:w and .hhhh I me:an esp<u>e</u>cially fts
	somebody who I'm gonna be <u>look</u>ing a:t

Here the daughter presents a problematic situation through an avowal of feeling 'get[ting] choked up' (arrows 3a, 3b). This avowal begins to explain her prior claim – not 'know[ing] what to do' (arrow 2). Also, it further specifies the problematic glossed by the mother's ascription of it being 'hard to do' (arrow 1).

Avowals of affect which invoke a folk logic of the passions – being overcome by a feeling or emotion – serve as excuses in that the actor disavows full responsibility due to the uncontrollable affect.

> **10** (Background: participants are a college student and a graduate teaching assistant (GTA) in the latter's office)
>
> *GTA*: How did you feel about your last speech? Were you happy with how it went?
>
> *Student*: Yeah, not really. It was a bad day. I just ah
>
> *GTA*: Why?
>
> *Student*: I just blew a math test before it, so I didn't really feel like speaking.

In this fragment, the student draws on past feelings to account. This avowal of feeling is formulated using a classic excuse structure: these unintended feelings constrain or inhibit his performance as a way to mitigate the teacher's evaluation. Notice how this folk logic invokes time along with the negative affect: he failed the math test 'just . . . before' his speech, so his saddened or depressed affect did not have adequate time to subside, and allow for a competent performance.

While avowals of being 'overcome by affect' can be drawn upon in forming accounts, their adequacy as excuses also can be challenged by recipients.

> **11** (Coulter, 1990: 185)
>
> ¹→ *Mary*: –(as if I'm sick) (   ) I'm de<u>pressed</u>
>
> *John*: (I mean) uh-uh I don't feel like a custodian
>
> (1.5)
>
> ya know
>
> *Mary*: Yee:eah?
>
> *John*: But I'm not gonna see someone come up with a
>
> ²→ weak excuse like I'm depressed I'm gonna sleep away, no way, I wouldn't let my best <u>friend</u> do that

In this fragment, Mary avows being 'de<u>pressed</u>' (arrow 1) to partially excuse her behavior of sleeping during the afternoon. However, John formulates her affect avowal as an excuse, albeit a 'weak excuse' (arrow 2), which he refuses to accept as sufficient. While affect avowals do invoke a folk logic of passions, their implications for right conduct can be contested. So the relation of affect avowals to social accountability cuts both ways: not only can affect avowals serve social accountability purposes, but also one can be held accountable for one's affect avowals. In short, affect avowals are discursive practices for calling others to account, for offering an account, and self-reflexively a performance for which one is socially accountable.

Summary   In this section it has been shown how avowals of affect work to formulate a complaint or account. Such affect avowals serve as shorthand formulations of the problematic to implicate a matrix of related issues, background circumstances, and justifiability conditions. This explains why affect avowals as shorthand formulations make relevant a recipient's prompts, questions, or requests for elaboration. A three-part sequence can be identified, affect avowal–prompt–initiation of explanation. In making affect relevant, the actor invokes a folk logic of emotion as a constraint or inhibitor on the actor's performance. Of course, this implied folk logic can be challenged by recipients, which shows the discursive character of human conduct and the necessity of accounting for it.

Ascriptions of Affect
In this second section the focus shifts from avowals of one's own affect to the ascription of affect to others. That is, examine ascriptions of 'you' or second-person statements of affect in social accountability practices (Shotter, 1989). Emotions imply certain appraisals about appropriate or right action, so persons may be held accountable by interlocutors for their displays of emotions.

Similar to an individual's avowal of an emotion, ascribing an emotion of another is a way to make relevant something out of the ordinary. Ascribing affect can be used to prompt an account (arrows).

> **12**   (FO1aHARD.1)
> → *Mother*:   Well you don't sound like
> →   you're too excited about it
> *Daughter*:   .h Well no: I think it's fine I just don't want to get my hopes
>   up real high and have it turn out to be some old gu:y that's
>   gonna try to hi:re (0.4) you know for nothin'

In ascribing a lack of excitement of the daughter, the mother is proposing a certain critical appraisal that the daughter is implicitly making. The mother can be seen to be prompting the daughter to agree or disagree with her ascription and further explain her appraisal of the situation. Instead of directly asking her, the mother makes this ascription which makes relevant an explanation. The daughter's account makes her position understandable through her folk logic of reasonable 'hopes' for the situation.

Ascribing negative affect to another is a way to criticize or question another's behavior, and thereby, to call that person to account.

13
 B: So then what are you upset about
 K: I'm not
 B: Then why did you say that?
→¹ *K*: Because it upset me at the time
 B: Why?
→² *K*: I have no right to be upset now

This fragment begins with B ascribing negative affect to K (being 'upset'). This ascription implicates that K has no good reason to be 'upset.' To expose, and thereby, make relevant another's negative emotional state raises a problematic condition about another – as something to be explained.

The fact that B can question the conditions for K's negative emotion shows how affect avowals and displays are open to intersubjective standards for what counts as justified emotion. Quite simply, if B can successfully challenge K's reason for negative emotion, then K may have no grounds for avowing that emotion. K denies being 'upset,' but concedes to B's prompting by the account that she was upset 'at the time' of the incident (arrow 1). Notice that K's continued accounting (arrow 2) implicates a kind of rule that she has no right or justifiable reason 'to be upset now.' As observed previously, if an emotion cannot be justified, this constitutes grounds for changing, or at least disavowing, that emotion. Affect is discursive in that it implies a folk logic for justifiable claims to emotion. Like other judgments a person can make, affect displays can lead others to call for the grounds to support such displays.

Ascribing negative affect to another person commonly results in the accused denying or disagreeing with that ascription. This is not surprising given that ascription of negative affect is often taken as a criticism. Accounts commonly accompany the denial or disagreement as a way to explain. For instance:

14
 F: Oh <u>come on</u> don't be pissed.
 M: I'm not pissed I– just know (.) I (.) <u>know</u> I just have ↓ the feeling
  that we're not gonna get to Boston.
  (0.4)

M: Together.

15
B: So then what are you upset about
K: I'm not
B: Then why did you say that?
K: Because it upset me at the time

16 (FO1aHARD.1)
M: Well you don't sound like you're too exc̲ited about it
D: .h Well no: I think it's fi̲ne I just don't want to get my ho̲pes up

This pattern may be glossed as an *ascription of negative affect–accounted for denial* sequence.

The distinctive feature of this two-part sequence is the initial ascription of negative affect. Such ascriptions of negative affect of another are commonly taken as criticisms due to a folk logic of privileged access to one's own emotional states. The emotions are believed to be directly known by the subject. To ascribe negative affect of another presumes a certain level of intimate knowledge of that person.

Even though persons may deny other's ascriptions of affect of them (as seen in transcripts 14–16), others may not be convinced by such denials and continue to make ascriptions of affect. This re-ascription of affect appears in the following transcript:

17
→¹ *F*: = >I know but– you know really don't be pissed
        I mean I have to get< (.) ↓ my hair cut
        ↑ >not– not that that's so< important
    M: You're right that's not important
→² *F*: But I have a lot of things to do=
→²   =I have to bring my car in I have
→²   ((staccato)) a lo̲t of things to do,
→³   I know you're ↓ pi̲ssed but?
         (0.9)
    F: *I have to do it*

This transcript may be glossed as F offering accounts for canceling plans, M challenging the accounts, and F more forcefully reasserting her reasons. Consider the re-ascription of affect, 'pissed' (arrow 3) and the interactional work it is designed to achieve. F's account reasserts her position while simultaneously responding to M's prior critical evaluation. F presents her reasons (arrows 2) as a prelude to her repeated ascription of affect (arrow 3), which she contrasts to what she has to do. This contrast is sequentially organized in a standard excuse format: a statement of the problematic condition (M as 'pissed') is presented in the initial position, followed by 'but' to mark a contrast to her constraints. F's re-ascription of affect, 'I know you're ↓ pissed' (arrow 3), responds both to M's immediately prior critical assessment of her as well as contradicting his earlier denial of being 'pissed' (see transcript 14).

Also, notice that F prefaces her response with the affect ascription used as a disclaimer, 'you know really don't be pissed,' (arrow 1) to mitigate her reason. So these three affect ascriptions of M as 'pissed' each do different interactional work – at once responding to M's critical assessments and simultaneously projecting her desired reading of events. The ascription of negative affect can serve multiple accountability moves.

Summary   To ascribe negative affect of another person is to make that affect accountable. An actor's emotions can be seen to be, for example, excessive, unjustifiable, or their cause unknown. Persons can be questioned, challenged, or criticized for their affect avowals and displays. When persons cannot convincingly account for their emotions, they may even alter their emotions in accordance with what can be justified. As seen above, in response to a questioning ascription of affect, an actor conceded that she had 'no right to be upset' suggesting that she has no justifiable grounds for her feeling. In terms of sequential organization, the ascription of negative affect makes accounts relevant from the actor to defend or explain the critical appraisal implicated by the interlocutor's ascription. Actors may deny the affect that others ascribe to them, but others may refuse to accept these denials and reassert their ascriptions. The ascription (or re-ascription) of affect is not a neutral description of an interlocutor's condition, but can be employed to blame, complain, or defend in the course of presenting one's preferred version of events.

Affect Display
Emotions may not only be verbally avowed or ascribed to others, but also may be expressed nonverbally or vocally. As already noted, usually accounts are conceived in the literature as verbal texts or speech acts with little attention paid to the affective or the nonverbal dimensions of accounts. This lingual or textual emphasis perhaps is to be expected given that the dominant image of accounts is of verbal explanations. But when accounts are examined in naturalistic contexts, nonverbal and paralingual components become crucial to understanding persons' meanings and actions.[5]

The kinds of nonverbal components which can be used to display affect include: *paralinguistic* and *prosodic cues* (intonation, speech rate, volume), *vocalizations* ('uhm,' out breathes), *silences* (pauses, gaps), and *body positioning* (eye contact, posture). These seeming minutiae can be very powerful in displaying affect (for example, anger, exasperation) and are crucial in the assessments and alignments displayed in accountability practices. Vocal cues can work to mark utterances as problematic – as displaying negative affect in order to critically assess another's deeds or position.

> **18**   (Background context: F has been telling M that she has to go home during fall break to attend to an insurance policy)
> *M*:   ((with rising intonation)) I'm not gonna take– be able to take ↑ you to Bos:ton Fran:
> *F*:   >I understand we'll<– ↓ we'll go another ti:me: =
> ¹→ *M*:   = >Wh↑at other time?<
>   (1.5)
> *F*:   >In the sp↑ring I'm gonna have my car up here<
>   (1.2)
> *F*:   I'll bring it up after ah:
>   [
> ²→ *M*:   Something will come up hhhhh
> ³→ *F*:   Oh come on don't be pissed.

This fragment begins with M formulating an unwanted, emerging problematic condition of having to cancel their plans for Boston.[6] F readily accepts the change of plans and adds the formulaic remedy, ' ↓ we'll go another ti:me.' M immediately latches a response (arrow 1) on to F's postponement which is produced with a more rapid pace, emphatic vocal quality and rising intonation. Notice that these vocal cues render M's response hearable as an affect display of something like frustration, disappointment, or even challenge. Without attending to the production of this utterance through its vocal cues, it could easily be heard as simply a request for information. The general point here is that marked vocal cues work to display negative affect and signal to others how to interpret what is being said and implicated.

What has traditionally been considered 'micro' phenomena can display negative affect and intensify the problematic claims of the utterance (arrow 2). Here M dismisses F's remedy (arrow 2) by claiming that this new plan too will have to be changed. M's critical evaluation overlaps with F's proposal and prevents her from finishing. M's assessment concludes with a strong outbreath – hearable as a display of exasperation or anger with F. This complaint is most consequential for its concluding display of negative affect, which F makes relevant in her next turn through an ascription of M's affect (arrow 3). So these so-called 'micro' phenomena are far from insignificant, but comprise the very particulars by which this talk-in-interaction is achieved (Schegloff, 1987).

Affect display is commonly found in the production of *repeated* blames, criticisms, and accounts (Labov and Fanshel, 1977). The vocal cues used to display such negative affect serve to intensify or underscore an actor's positioning. For instance in the following transcript F repeats her solution for the problematic change of plans for their trip to Boston.

> 19 (Continuation of transcript 18 with a few lines omitted)
> F: We will go another time (.) Mike I promise we will go to boston together=
> → M: =<u>Fran</u>? (0.6) I'll put money on it ↓ right now, that we will <u>not</u> go ↓ to Boston.
> → F: WE WILL GO TO BOSTON! (.) WE WILL– BECAUSE WE CAN'T GO
> →   NOW WE HAVE (.) <u>spring</u>:ti:me to go
>   (2.6)
> F: I wanted to go just as bad as you did Mike

Here F repeats her prior 'solution' to the problematic of changing plans by proposing a future trip. M dismisses her solution, indeed in the form of a wager to dramatize his not being convinced by F's solution (arrow 1). This dismissal is achieved by M latching his response on to the end of her utterance (arrow 1) and underscoring his rejection with emphatic and downward shifts in intonation. M's critical assessment is produced with a more angry or aggravated affect display in contrast to his prior rejection of F's solution (see transcript 18, arrow 2) which displayed an affect of seeming disappointment or frustration. As negative assessments or rejections are *repeated*, actors commonly draw on *marked affect displays* as a technique to convey commitment to their positioning.

To counter M's dismissal, F replies with a marked increase in volume to assert her position and then justify it with an emphatic statement (by intonation and word stretch) of when they could go (arrows 2). The folk logic suggested by F's affect display of a loud voice is to shout down or emphatically counter M's assessment and thereby demonstrate her commitment to what she is saying.[7]

Affect display produced through marked vocal cues is most commonly found in doing blames or critical assessments, but it also can serve to underscore a position in accounting. In the following case (transcript 20) we see M denying F's criticism of being 'pissed' and substituting an alternative statement of his knowledge or feeling to account for his condition.

> 20 (Continuation of transcript 18)
> F: Oh <u>come on don't</u> be pissed.
> M: I'm not pissed

→   I– I just know (.) I (.) <u>know</u> I just have
→   the feeling that we're not gonna get to Boston.
    (0.4)
  M: Together.
  F: You're going to go there anyway right

M's denial plus explanatory account is marked by self-corrections, false starts, pauses and repetitions (see arrows). These cues can be heard to display M's frustration or disappointment, and seem to contradict his denial of negative affect.

To demonstrate the significance of affect display in accounting, consider the following case of a marked change in affect in the course of W's account (arrows).

21
  S: >Didn't didn't< didn't you last week say to me (.) ya know (1.3)
     that's– something like to the effect of that's what you're going to
     have to do::?
     (1.2)
  S: I mean >didn't you say something like that<?
  W: Yeah
  S: It's an important time
→ *W*: <u>Yes:</u>
     (1.5)
¹→ *W*: <u>It is Sam but not like</u>
     (1.2)
²→ *W*: I mean– *I don't know*

As an initial gloss of this fragment, W responds to S with a qualified agreement, but interrupts the initiation of her account and concludes with a display of something like exasperation. Notice how W's agreement plus account-initiation is produced emphatically (arrows 1), but then is self-interrupted and left uncompleted (arrow 2). W's intonation changes from *emphatic* to *halting* and finally to *quietly* or *softly*. The emphasis given to her initial agreement seems responsive to S's repeated formulation; repetition intensifies the implicated criticism, so to reciprocate requires marked vocal quality.

The intonation shift in W's response works as what Scott and Lyman (1968) call a 'meta-account' in that it circumvents, at least for the moment, giving an account. The rhetoric of falling silent implicates a being overcome by emotion. Interactionally this marked change in affect display indicates a change in the actor's alignment or footing with the interlocutor.

The contextual cues which display the actor's affect convey a power or immediacy which cannot be captured through verbal accounts alone. Actors can draw on *multiple levels of expression* in doing social accountability.

22   (Continuation of transcript 21, a few lines omitted)
S: Like you're going to go looking for somebody else?
     (1.4)
W: .hh
     (9.4)
W: I mean (1.7) first of all it's very: (0.8) difficult
     (2.0) to really– I mean
     (3.2)
W: It's too: ear:ly to talk about (.) *this kind of thing*

Here W's affect display is produced by an audible outbreath and between-turn gap of nearly ten seconds. As in transcript 21, W's accounts contain self-interruptions, within-turn pauses, and an intonational contour changing from emphatic to softly. These paralingual and prosodic features underscore what she is saying about the difficulty of the issue and it being premature to discuss it. Further, such affect displays not only underscore what is said but *demonstrate* her difficulty and assessment in the very act of answering. This shows the above point that actors can account by multiple levels of expression.

Summary   Here it can be seen how various paralingual and prosodic cues work to display affect in the course of social accountability practices. These nonverbal components (emphatic intonational contour, audible outbreath, word stretch, increased volume) work as cues to frame how to take what is being said – as serious, intensified, unintended, and so on. Also, such components display actors' emotions, such as exasperation, disappointment, or anger. Nonverbal affect displays present or demonstrate the actor's positioning and interactional alignments. These affect displays are interactionally consequential, as seen through recipient's uptake and responses in the form of blames and accounts. Actors can use *multiple* levels of expression to convey their assessments and alignments with others. Nonverbal components can be employed to convey messages which would be too threatening to say verbally, such as implied meanings involving challenge, deference, dominance, and the like.[8]

Conclusion

The main project of this chapter has been to show the importance of the emotions as a cultural resource in doing social accountability. The three forms of affect discourse – avowals, ascriptions, and displays – can discursively present the actor's critical assessments and evaluations of action. Avowals of affect and vocal affect displays formulate the event as problematic in shorthand ways. The recipient may not know or fully appreciate the reasons, circumstances, or background conditions for the actor's avowal or vocal display of affect, such as anger. So this adumbrative problem-telling works to project a pursuit of further elaboration for the negative affect. The presentation of the problematic, while initiated by the affect avowal or display as a shorthand, is responsive to the uptake by recipient. This results in the three-part sequence, affect avowal–prompt–explanation initiation. The actor's further explanation of emotions commonly becomes more pointed as an accusation or complaint in the third part.

The unpacking of the shorthand formulation of affect avowal or nonverbal display supports the contention from conversation analysis that presenting a problematic event through affect avowals or displays is an 'interactional accomplishment' – a presentation which is responsive to the moment-by-moment contingencies of interaction (Schegloff, 1982). This interactional accomplishment notion extends the social constructionist view of affect as appraisal. That is, use of affect implicates the actor's negative appraisal of events, but such appraisals are couched in shorthand verbal formulations or vocal cues. These negative appraisals require further expansion to be understood, as well as the recipient's cooperative uptake and responses.

This notion of appraisal is evident also in an actor's ascription of negative affect to others. To ascribe negative affect of another person is to make that affect accountable. A display of emotions can be said to be unjustified, overdone, or inexplicable. The ascription of negative affect is not a neutral description of another's affective state, but can work to call another to account and challenge other's positioning.

In terms of sequential organization, ascriptions of another's negative affect makes accounts relevant to defend against such critical evaluations. This relevance is evident in the two-part exchange, 'ascription of negative affect–accounted for denial.' The fact that persons can be questioned, challenged, or criticized by interlocutors for their affect displays or avowals supports the contention that emotion is discursive – accountable to socio-cultural rules and conventions of expression and justifiability. If actors cannot justifiably account for their emotions, they may even alter their emotions in accordance with what can be justified.

The uses of affect implicate the actor's folk logic in social accountability practices. Actors draw on a discourse of affect to convey, implicate, or display their alignment or positioning. As we have seen, the emotions work in accounting episodes in a variety of ways: to suggest or hint at, to emphasize or intensify, to project other's attentions, to challenge, to reassert, to show commitment, and so on. I have attempted to integrate these neglected uses of affect into the analysis of social accountability.

Notes

1. The distinction between feelings and emotion, and the distinctions among the various kinds of emotions will not be worked out here because of my primary interest in how affect is used in social accountability.

2. The notion of a folk logic of affect has been developed by Coulter (1989) along similar lines by what he calls the 'constitutive logic of emotion' (I quote this passage at length):

> [A] more fruitful enterprise for a social-constructionist sociology of emotion is to focus upon the study of the constitutive logic of actual avowals, ascriptions and other uses of affect predicates in social interaction. A properly social-constructionist approach should not concentrate upon the 'emoting agent' alone but on the field of social conduct within which any such agent is/can be intermeshed. This constitutive logic, which alone articulates the domain of culturally-normative possibilities for affect, need not be construed as a cognitive apparatus or interpretive codebook somehow invoked by or stored in the 'mind' of a given agent which 'causes' his experiential condition(s). Rather, it should be understood for what it is: *an explication of a logic for the intelligibility of phenomena* – in this case, of emotions. (Coulter, 1989: 46-7; emphasis added)

3. Heath (1988) and Goodwin and Goodwin (1987) are two notable exceptions to this gap in the literature. Goodwin and Goodwin (1987: 9) remark on the importance of affect: 'Affect displays are not only pervasive in the production of assessments, but also quite central to their organization.'

4. A problem for the analyst is how to identify the emotions as exhibited in and through these nonverbal or vocal cues. There is no one-to-one relationship between a particular nonverbal or vocal component and emotion. Closely related is the problem of transcription of nonverbal components, particularly paralinguistic and prosodic cues. As Labov and Fanshel (1977) observe, transcription of these vocal aspects of discourse is at best an art rather than an exact science. A partial solution to these difficulties is that these nonverbal cues are usually 'concentrated' and tend to 'reinforce each other' (Labov and Fanshel, 1977: 46). Interlocutors interpret nonverbal displays as relevant to some contextual antecedent (Sanders, 1985: 214). In addition, the analyst can use these nonverbal cues in conjunction with other interactional features: the co-occurring talk, the temporal and sequential interaction, the uptake by recipients, and the situated context. These various parts can be used in constructing an interpretation of the whole. Despite these methodological difficulties with transcription and interpretation, the nonverbal affect dimensions of accounts have been neglected for too long. Accounts analysis which fails to incorporate these nonverbal components misses crucial methods which persons use to do social accountability. My point here is that accounts need to be oriented to, not as an isolated speech act, but as a move sequentially and hierarchically connected with other verbal and nonverbal moves which comprise a discourse of affect.

5. This point about the social accountability of intonation is captured eloquently by Bakhtin:

    Intonation is the supple and most sensitive conduit of the social relations that exist between interlocutors in a given situation. . . . Intonation is the sound expression of social evaluation. (cited in Todorov, 1984: 46; emphasis in original)

6. This data fits Drew's (1984) observation that one way to cancel plans is to cite your constraints or difficult circumstances, and rely on your interlocutor to draw the conclusion. The transcript here begins with M drawing the conclusion of having to cancel.

7. It has been suggested that the lingual representation of emotion should take the form of adjectives or adverbs to indicate their 'intensity,' 'manner,' or 'degree' (Averill, 1991; Perinbanayagm, 1991).

8. The nonverbal channels, particularly vocal intonation, can allow actors to express critical assessments and negative affect, but simultaneously be able to deny intent verbally, if called to account: 'Speakers need a form of communication which is *deniable*. It is advantageous for them to express hostility, challenge the competence of others, or express friendliness and affection in a way that can be denied if they are explicitly held to account for it' (Labov and Fanshel, 1977: 46; emphasis in original).

The Social Accountability of Zen Understanding: Teacher–Student Interviews in a North American Zen Monastery

with Thomas L. Isbell

> Sometimes the dialogue which you read in *koans* or the dialogue that takes place in the interview room doesn't make sense, it's not intended to make sense because it's not a rational, linear sequential thing, this *Bodhidharma*, whatever you think it is it's not. It's not an idea, it's not a concept, it's alive and it's working. How to see that, how to express that is what the dynamics of interview, of *Dharma* talk are about.

This explanation from a Zen teacher to his students embodies the well-known precept that Zen knowledge cannot be conveyed rationally or verbally.[1] Language use is not everywhere valued as a vehicle for conveying knowledge. This point is depicted in recent studies of Quakers (Bauman, 1983), Trappist monks (Jaksa and Stech, 1978), and North American Zen Buddhists (Preston, 1988). In Zen, silent meditation, or *zazen*, is a central practice for training the body/mind for enlightenment. However, Zen practitioners are not continually silent. Talk occurs during teacher–student interviews, though this talk is of a very distinctive variety. During these interviews, the teacher often calls upon the students to express their understanding of Zen. This call creates conflicting demands on the student; on the one hand, speech is proscribed as a way of knowledge, but on the other hand, the teacher requests the student to convey understanding. The ability to communicate one's understanding of Zen is a basic problem for practitioners, especially for the newer students.

The project here is to examine Zen teacher–student interviews as a situation of social accountability. The focus is on two of the most distinctive ways of communicating in these interviews, *koan* (*ko-an*) practice and the demonstration of understanding. Zen beliefs about the epistemology of language create an interesting problem for participants; students are called upon to communicate their understanding of Zen, but verbal explanations and discursive talk are not valued as modes of expression. How do practitioners interactionally 'solve' this problematic? How do practitioners communicate their

Zen understanding? These questions are approached by analyzing the discourse of teacher–student interviews, in particular, the teacher's use of the *koan* as a challenge, and how these answers are interactionally achieved, negotiated, and evaluated. In short, how Zen understanding is socially accountable in the performance of *Dharma* combat.

Dharma *Combat as Communication Event*

There are two kinds of teacher–student interviews, one done privately, called *dokusan*, and the other performed in front of the entire community, called *Dharma* combat or *shosan*. The latter kind of interview is the focus of this study. The talk between teacher and student during *Dharma* combat reveals *unique* ways of speaking due to the radically distinctive epistemology of Zen. Instead of the Western emphasis on analysis of an object domain and its representation through language (or other symbol systems) as a way to knowing, the Zen tradition rejects analysis, and representation through language. However,

> Zen does not shun or despise language. It only requires that language be used in a very peculiar way. . . . The Master constantly urges the student to open the mouth and say something. . . . Asking the student to say something constitutes an integral part of the educational process of Zen. For the moment he opens the mouth and 'brings a decisive phrase', the student discloses to the eyes of the Master the exact degree of his spiritual maturity. (Izutsu, 1982: 97–8)

While it is impossible to explain Zen, a commentator describes the communication of Zen understanding as a 'pre-reflective' form of expression: '[S]tatements in (teacher–student interviews) are authentic or inauthentic not in reference to the proposition spoken but in reference to the speaker's state of mind. What is judged is the quality of the state of without-thinking, the source of the utterance, not the truth of the proposition or the content of the statement' (Kasulis, 1981: 119–20). So to appreciate the ways of communicating in the Zen speech community, look to the distinctive uses of language they employ to accomplish their social practices.

There is an extensive philosophical, historical, and experiential literature on Zen Buddhism, but to my knowledge, there are no empirical studies of language use and social interaction. *Dharma* combat offers an interesting communication event for analysis because it involves distinctive ways of speaking. Two of the most unique features of *Dharma* combat will be examined: the *uses of the koan* and the *showing of one's understanding*.

Koan *Practice*

Koan study is unique to the practice of Zen. No other religion uses a device parallel to the *koan*. The *koan*, however, does not directly contain religious instruction; it is indirect, often at first sight intractable. It is presented by the teacher as a problem to be solved, yet it is no ordinary sort of problem. A solution to a *koan* depends upon the teacher, the student, and the student's stage of development.

As to the unique method of study that is used to realize a *koan*, it is not based upon study as we usually use that word. The aim is to 'become one with the *koan*,' to embed the *koan* in one's mind, not as an idea but as an object of focus. During meditation, the student repeats the *koan*, or a phrase from the *koan*, slowly over and over. The meaning of the words fall away with constant repetition and the identity of words is blurred by the very slowness of the repetition. The inward voicing features syllables rather than thoughts: 'One must not be looking for an answer but looking at the *koan*' (Grimstone, 1977: 17). When an answer comes, as if of its own accord, then the student takes the answer to the teacher for validation.

The *koan* is used by the teacher during *Dharma* combat as a confrontation or 'a challenge demanding a response' (DeMartino, 1983: 16) in order 'to judge the student's understanding' (Rosemont, 1970: 114). *Koans* have been characterized as a verbal paradox or puzzle or problem (Kubose, 1973). The *koan* is used to 'shock' the student out of ordinary consciousness (Izutsu, 1982) and take the student 'beyond logic to where there is no "why" and no "because"' (Shimano, 1988: 73). 'Part of *koan* study is to try to sharpen the student's ability to communicate in a *lively* way what the meaning of Zen is all about' (Glassman, 1983: 11).

In much of the Zen literature, the master presents the *koan* to the student, or visiting monk, who then offers an answer which shows (or fails to show) enlightenment. These accounts of the exchange over the *koans* represent case studies or idealized moments in Zen history. Many *koans* are records of the conversations between teachers and students of the past. Some relate moments when a master or student achieved enlightenment.

But the use of *koans* during *Dharma* combat as a living, contemporary practice needs to be seen as *accomplished* in and through Zen practitioners' social interaction. That is, the *koan* as a linguistic document has no intrinsic significance which can be specified independently of its use (Wittgenstein, 1953). The *koan* becomes *re-created* as a challenge only because of how it is used and oriented to within Zen practice. Clearly, *koans* could be used as part of other practices, such as a historical study of Zen, a literary form, or even as part of a joke. So the *koan* is examined for its use in the contemporary practice of *Dharma* combat: how it is interactionally oriented to, formulated, responded to, and used to evaluate. These various uses of the *koan* constitute some of the ways that *Dharma* combat works as a confrontation or test of understanding.

Demonstration of Understanding

To become communicatively competent at *Dharma* combat, practitioners need to know how to present their understanding of Zen in culturally appropriate ways. Knowing how to communicate one's understanding is of central importance for practitioners of *Dharma* combat. Showing or demonstrating one's understanding of the *koan* are more valued forms of expression than discursively talking about it. Zen knowledge cannot be verbally explained; it cannot be propositionally formulated. However, errors or mistakes in expression are readily identified by the teacher. The most frequent error of expression is to take an intellectual or rationalistic approach. Demonstrating one's understanding, on the one hand, and intellectualizing about it, on the other, are contrastive modes of knowing and expression.

Methodology

This study attempts to extend the ethnographic work of Preston (1988) on North American Zen practice. Preston's research concentrated on the central role of meditation in training the body/mind and on associated Zen rituals. *Dharma* combat fits into Zen training as a way to test the understanding gained from meditation. But the focus here is more circumscribed in scope than Preston's work in that the analysis is limited to the communication event of *Dharma* combat to describe the distinctive cultural forms of speech and expression. Our principle interest is in the two most distinctive practices that comprise *Dharma* combat, the uses of the *koan* and the demonstration of understanding. Mastering these practices constitutes two fundamental ways of displaying communication competence in the Zen community. As already mentioned, *Dharma* combat provides a testing function for Zen practitioners. This testing function also serves as a way to rank members within the Zen community. *Dharma* combat provides an educational function by allowing the newer students to observe the interview between the teacher and senior students.

An audiotape recording of a *Dharma* combat is used to draw up transcripts of the interviews to do an analysis of the social interaction.

From a conversation analytic constructionist perspective, the practices of the *koan* and demonstration of understanding are interactionally achieved between student and teacher. The project here attempts to identify the moves made through language use, or nonverbal means, and how such moves are oriented to and responded to by participants as displayed in and through their talk.

Analytically we begin by focusing on the teacher's responses to the student's answer to the *koan*. The teacher's responses initially occur in the third turn of the interactional sequence of the interview following the teacher's presentation of the *koan* (or question) and the student's answer. The exchange is not terminated with the teacher's third turn, but regularly unfolds over several more turns. The point of beginning with this third turn is that it can be seen as an analytical resource to ascertain the teacher's recognition and evaluation of the student's prior answer, and as the teacher's projection of further activities for the student. In brief, this third turn allows us to analytically look backwards and forwards in the interaction.

A caveat: no pretense is made to capture the deep, intuitive levels of Zen meaning and experience. The analysis is limited to the level of analytical descriptions of participants' language use and social interaction, and the practices that are accomplished in and through these. How the community's distinctive communicative forms and patterns are used, displayed, and oriented to by the practitioners.

The following research questions will be addressed: (1) How is the *koan* used, oriented to, and responded to by participants? In particular, how does the teacher display an evaluation of the students' answers to the *koan*? (2) How do practitioners express their understandings of Zen given the constraints in ways of communicating? How are students and teacher alike called upon to demonstrate their understanding?

Materials
The *Dharma* combat that is examined here occurred at a Zen Buddhist monastery in the Northeastern United States. An audiotape recording of a *Dharma* combat is used for analysis. This Zen center routinely tape-records its *Dharma* lectures and *Dharma* combats for its library. All of the participants are native English-language speakers.

The Place of Dharma *Combat in Zen Practice*
Before turning to the interaction in *Dharma* combat, it may be useful to begin by situating *Dharma* combat within the context of a scheduled pattern of activities practiced in this Zen monastery. The

last week of each month is set aside for *sesshin*, or retreat, during which all other activities are suspended for full-time practice. *Sesshin* usually involves fifteen to twenty practitioners. Students begin the day with dawn *zazen* or silent meditation. The students sit in rows in the *zendo*, or meditation room, so they can give each other support and so that their practice can be easily monitored. *Zazen* is the principle practice of *sesshin*, accounting for eight to ten hours of the day. Morning *zazen* is followed by a brief liturgical service and *oriyoki*, an elaborate meal ritual. Throughout the day during *zazen* and other forms of practice, the concentration on the suspension of inner monologues is to be maintained.

During *sesshin* students go to interview with the teacher. Two or three interviews a day is normal at this monastery. During interview there are no formal constraints on communication – the student may say anything to the teacher. The teacher guides and encourages the student's practice. When the practice of *zazen* is sufficient, the student is given a *koan*. The *koan* is usually the transcript of an earlier Zen dialogue. The purpose of the *koan* study is to experience the realization in the original, historical case study and to demonstrate that experiential understanding in some direct way. When the student successfully demonstrates mastery of the first *koan*, then the teacher approves and presents a second *koan* for study. There are some 700 *koans* to be realized in this program of study. If the student is unable to demonstrate mastery of the *koan*, then the teacher will offer guidance and support, or answer questions. After interview the student returns to the *zendo* to resume *zazen*.

Koan study is further assisted by daily formal lectures, or *Dharma* talks, which usually provide the historical background in which the original dialogue or incident took place, characterizations of the actors involved, alternative translations to the translation with which the students are working, or point out how the particular *koan* in question can be misleading.

Dharma combat is much like an interview except that it is a public event and all participants are confronted with the same *koan*, which usually has been posted the night before. At the monastery studied, *Dharma* combat is offered once a year at the conclusion of the Spring training season. During *Dharma* combat the teacher interviews with community members in an open forum. After a short talk in which the *koan* is offered as a challenge, the student approaches the teacher and offers a response. This is a community event of great importance; it is highly valued for its tradition, pedagogical merit, and drama. Decisive directions in the historical development of Zen pivot upon such moments of *Dharma* combat between equal adversaries, such high moments of combat are called *mondos*.

The purpose of *koan* practice and *zazen* create pressures which structure *Dharma* combat. As students become more practiced the results show in *Dharma* combat. Novices at *Dharma* combat can be recognized by extraneous talking. The speech of the more advanced student will be heavily packed but sparse: gesture is highly valued as it is less abstract than discursive dialogue. Advanced students will be moved by the teacher from discussion *about* the *koan* to a direct demonstration of their realization of the *koan*. This becomes the art of *Dharma* combat – *to be* the *koan*.

The Use of the *Koan* as a Test of Understanding

One of the most distinctive features of *Dharma* combat is the use of the *koan* as an organizing device for the teacher–student exchange. How is the *koan* used by the Zen teacher in the practice of *Dharma* combat? What interactional functions does the *koan* serve, that is, how is the *koan* presented, oriented to and responded to by participants?

Presentation of the Koan

The teacher presents the *koan* to the Zen community during his opening talk.

	1	(Zen teacher's opening talk)
1.	The question that I'd like to put forward today is from Master
2.	Mumon . . . Master Mumon presents us: (2.3) with what he calls
3.	the Zen warnings:: (4.5) what he says is: (1.0) to observe the
4.	regulations: (0.5) and keep to the rules: (1.8) is tying
5.	oneself without a rope (2.6) to act freely and unrestrainedly
6.	just as one wishes: (1.3) is to do what heretics and demons would
7.	do (3.1) to recognize the mind and purify it (2.2) is the false
8.	Zen of silent sitting (2.8) to give reign to oneself and ignore
9.	the interrelating conditions: (1.4) is to fall into the abyss:
10.	(3.0) to be alert (1.4) and never ambiguous: is to wear chains
11.	and an iron yoke, (2.2) to think of good and evil (0.9)
12.	belongs to heaven and hell (2.2) to have a buddha view (1.0) and
13.	a *Dharma* view (1.4) is to be confined in two iron mountains:
14.	(4.8) they who realize it as soon as the thought arises::
15.	(1.4) is one who exhausts: energy (2.4) to sit blankly
16.	in quietism is the practice of the dead (2.3) if one
17.	procedes (0.4) that is goes forward (2.2) they will go
18.	astray from the principle (1.8) if one retreats: (1.8) they
19.	go against the truth, (1.4) if one neither progresses nor
20.	retreats: (2.6) they are a dead person (.) *breathing* (2.0)

21.   now tell me (1.6) what will you do (6.5)
22.   he says that the rules: to follow them (1.0) is tying oneself
23.   without a rope (2.1) to act free (1.0) without restraint
24.   (2.1) is what heretics and demons would do (1.6) what will
25.   you do? (3.2) to purify the mi:nd (0.9) to bring it peace
26.   (1.6) quiet (2.2) is the false Zen of silent sitting (3.3) to
27.   ignore cause and effect? is like falling into a great abyss:
28.   (2.9) good and evil belong to heaven and hell (3.5) if you go
29.   foward (.) you miss it (1.9) if you go backward (1.1) you
30.   miss it (1.2) if you go neither forward or backward (.) you
31.   miss it (2.8) *what will you do?* (1.6) how will you practice:
32.   your Zen? (2.5) what have you reali:zed? (1.9) how will you
33.   practice your life? (5.4) you see in our practice there's no
34.   guru (1.4) no guide no teaching no teachers: (3.0) we don't
35.   have the priest or the rabbi or a holy one to intercede (1.7)
36.   each one of us has to do it ourselves (3.3) there's nothing
37.   to transcend and there's no one to transcend (2.3) *then how
38.   will you practice?* (2.5) how do you live the Zen life (0.9)
39.   of bou:ndlessness (2.2) without speech without silence without
40.   action or non-action how do you manifes:t (1.1) the Bodhidharma
41.   in your life (2.4) speak (2.4) come up (2.0) say

In his presentation, the teacher reads the question to the audience (lines 3–21), and then formulates its gist in his own words (lines 22–33). He concludes the opening talk by a call to the students to come forward and express their understanding of Zen (lines 37–41). This call to the students underscores the importance of communication for Zen practice.

Following the teacher's presentation of the *koan*, some of the students self-select to give their answer. In the eleven teacher–student exchanges that comprise this *Dharma* combat, the student initiates by coming forward from the audience to sit before the teacher and speaking. The teacher, in turn, responds to the student's initiation.

The Koan *as a Communication Problem*

The confrontational character of *Dharma* combat creates what might be glossed as a *communication problem* for some of the students. *Koans* cannot be answered in a discursive manner, yet students are called upon to present their understanding of the *koan*. One way to ascertain the adequacy of the students' understanding of the *koan* is to examine how their answers are responded to and evaluated by the teacher. That is, how does the teacher display a recognition and evaluation of the student's answer in his response?

In the following exchange the student's answer to the *koan* is challenged in various ways.

> **2** (Eighth teacher–student encounter)
> *S*: The thing is not to be ti::ed
> (2.9)
> *S*: Do I (0.9) follow the ru::les >or< (2.4) follow (1.9) my free spirit?
> do I retreat? or go ahea:d (1.4) I do <u>all</u> of those things
> (2.1)
> *S*: The thing is not to be ti:ed to either way
> (2.5)
> →¹ *T*: How? ((clears throat)) *how to do that?*
> (5.7)
> *S*: Ther– there's no choice? (1.2) it's done
> (2.1)
> →² *T*: Why do you practi::ce?
> (14.8)
> *S*: I practice
> (9.9)
> *S*: I know it I can't say it
> →³ *T*: How do you practi:ce
> (16.6)
> *S*: I practice be:ing (0.9) I practice being here
> (3.5)
> →⁴ *T*: Hm that's what he talks about when says being lost in
> →⁴ silent elimination (1.7) turning off the world focusing or:
> →⁴ absorbing one<u>self</u> (1.7) is the <u>false</u> Zen (2.4) *silent
> →⁴ sitting*=>quietism<
> (9.0)
> →⁵ *T*: *So how? (to do this)*
> (9.6)
> *S*: I practice everything (2.8) I practice the silence I practice the
> struggling the fighting
> (6.3)
> *T*: Hm (.) you're on the right track? but it's still (0.9) a kind of an
> intellectual (.) thing that you're saying you know it's (like) (1.5)
> right out of a textbook (1.5) or a *Dharma* talk (2.4) so look at– look
> into (0.8) <u>how:</u> to present that ali:ve (.) not with dead words but
> ali::ve (1.8) how to practice our lives (1.2) how we manifest the
> Bodhidharma
> (3.8)
> *T*: Thank you

What has been glossed as a communication problem is evident, not only from the inherent difficulty of the *koan*, but also by the student being unable to answer the teacher's questions and by the teacher's critical evaluations of the student's answer. As a response to the student's initial answer to the *koan*, the teacher asks the student a series of questions (arrows 1–3). The student is unable to offer a satisfactory reply, so the teacher formulates the student's answer in terms of the problem of the *koan* – as reflecting 'quietism' (arrows 4). Bringing the talk back to the *koan* allows the teacher to invoke the authority of the *koan* to achieve his assessment. In critically assessing the student's answer in terms of the *koan* as 'quietism,' the teacher turns this problem back to the student – to further challenge her with the question (arrow 5). So the *koan* is not only used to *initiate* the exchange, but also is used to *evaluate* and *further challenge* the student's answer. In addition, the teacher's challenge is designed to encourage students to further pursue their Zen practice by formulating their answer in terms of the *koan* and leaving them with other unanswered questions.

The teacher's reinstating of the *koan* in response to the student's answer is also seen in the following exchange.

3   (Ninth teacher–student encounter)
→¹ S: Shosanshi I'm cold
         (2.4)
   T: Hm so am I=
→² S: =((laughter)) You've been through this already (1.3) uhm
         (1.4)
→³ S: I practice because I practice
         (1.1)
→⁴ T: Hm how? how do you practice:: how do you <u>do</u>: (1.2) if all
→⁴   these things that Mumon said are true (2.1) almost no matter
→⁴   what you do? (2.1) it's the wrong thing (1.0) if you go forward
→⁴   you go astray if you go ba:ck   (you miss it)
                    [   ]
   S: How do you go forward?
         (1.4)
   T: When he says go forward he means if you advance:: (1.5) in your
         practice if you if you uh (.) <u>work to attain the way</u> (.) you miss it
         (2.8) if you move away? move back you miss it (0.9) if you neither
         move backwards or forwards you miss it . . .

The teacher returns to the *koan* in his turn at talk following the student's second answer (arrows 4). The teacher formulates the student's answer about 'practice' in terms of the *koan*. Unlike the prior exchange, transcript 2, the teacher invokes the *koan* without a prior questioning of the student's answer. The return to the *koan* immediately after the student's second answer seems to display the teacher's negative assessment of the answer.

A noticeable feature of this exchange is that the student offers an answer (arrow 1), then withdraws it based on the teacher's response, and then offers another answer (arrow 3). The student's initial answer about being 'cold' was offered by a different student in an earlier exchange. Given the Zen precept 'to make understanding your own' (see transcript 1, lines 33–6), this answer is marked as repeated or copied. This problematic is recognizably displayed by the student's laughter and self-deprecatory comment (arrow 2). The student, then, attempts a different answer.

Throughout this *Dharma* combat, the *koan* is generally oriented to as a 'barrier' or problem for the students, but in one case, the authority of the *koan* is itself questioned by a student.

> **4** (Seventh teacher–student encounter)
> S: I thought that Mumon was ah (1.3) supposed to clarify our minds so why does he (.) hh– come up with all that bullshit hhh
> T: It's no:t bullshit it's uhm they're real questions:
> S: I know but when ya concen– when ya try to figure it out? (.) it's lost
>   (1.8)
> S: *So*=
> → T: =So what is it that he's trying to show us::
>   (2.1)
> T: by doing that?
>   (2.6)
> S: To dro:p it hh in my opinion .h (0.7) and just <u>go</u> on with washing the dishes or *whatever*
> T: When ya go on you (.) move away from it he says
>   (5.2)
> → T: If you retreat? (1.8) you miss it (1.4) and if you <u>don't</u>
> →   <u>move</u> =if you neither go forward or retreat (2.3) you're a
> →   <u>dead man</u> (2.6) *so how do we practi:ce*
>   (5.2)
> T: That's a really important question . . .

The teacher defends the *koan* as 'real questions.' Instead of invoking the *koan* to evaluate an answer, the teacher here must show the *koan* as a 'real' or genuine question worth confronting. To accomplish this, the teacher again formulates the problem of the *koan* (arrows 2). Initially he questions the student about the *koan* (arrow 1), but then moves to formulate the problem of the *koan* and justify it himself (arrows 2).

By way of summary, it is clear that *Dharma* combat involves more than simply the two-part exchange of the presentation of the *koan* and the student's answer as has been portrayed in some historical writings on Zen. In the transcripts examined so far, the teacher responds to the student's answer by further questioning, formulating the student's answer in terms of the *koan*, and evaluative comments. As analysts, these responses can be used as a resource to see the teacher's assessment of the student's understanding. These responses constitute some of the ways the teacher uses the *koan* to challenge and enliven the student's understanding. At the same time, the teacher's responses attempt to move the student toward a Zen form of expression.

The Demonstration of One's Understanding

In the teacher's concluding talk of this *Dharma* combat, he draws a *contrast* between intellectualizing about one's understanding and Zen expression: 'It's not an idea, it's not a concept, it's alive and it's working. How to see that, how to express that is what the dynamics of . . . *Dharma* talk are' (epigram). This is a common theme in the Zen literature – a Zen understanding cannot be rationally or intellectually conveyed. So the student faces the communication problem of putting into words that which cannot be said. The most distinctive forms of Zen expression in *Dharma* combat are the *koan*, and what might be glossed as the demonstration of understanding.

This contrast between ideas and Zen expression is evident in the following exchange.

> 5   (Tenth teacher–student encounter)
> *T*:   . . . we really need to <u>see</u> what it is that we're doing
>   (3.5)
> *T*:   We really need to see (.) it's true, nothing to atta<u>i:n</u>
>   (2.5)
> *T*:   everything's: perfect and complete as it is:
>   (2.5)
> *T*:   until we realize it (.) it's just an idea
>   (3.2)
> *T*:   doing what you're doing while you're doing it (.) is an idea
>   (3.2)
> → *T*:   How do we make that al<u>i:ve</u> (2.1) how do we <u>manifest</u>
> →   that in our very <u>existence</u>
>   (6.2)
> *S*:   *I don't know*
> *T*:   Well find out . . .

In this fragment the teacher critically evaluates the student's answer by calling it 'an idea.' Also, in transcript 2, a student's answer was criticized as 'intellectual.' The mistrust of 'words and ideas' as a way of understanding constitutes a central proscription for Zen ways of speaking.

In critically evaluating the students' answers, the teacher also exhorts or directs them toward a Zen mode of expression. For instance, in transcript 2 after his negative evaluation, the teacher calls upon the student 'to present that ali:ve (.) not with dead words but ali::ve.' This contrast between words and Zen expression is used to evaluate and exhort the student in transcript 5 (see arrows).

These critical evaluations and calls for Zen expression constitute what has been called the student's communication problem – students need to know how to express their understanding so 'it's alive and working.' Demonstration is a gloss for what the teacher calls expression that is 'alive' (see transcripts 2, 5, and the epigram). The demonstration of understanding and the proscription against intellectualizing each spring from the same root – the impossibility of putting Zen understanding into ordinary language.

The call for demonstration of understanding seems to be the most difficult challenge in *Dharma* combat. The teacher does not command a demonstration from every one of the students who come up to give answers. In the eleven encounters, the teacher calls for a demonstration four times. To call for a demonstration seems to mark these students as more advanced in their practice.

6   (Eleventh teacher–student encounter)
S: Mumon is a <u>fool</u> (1.8) why does he separate himself (1.2) does not he see: the moon? in the sky? (0.8) doesn't he see the grass growing from the earth
    (5.2)
T: That's a good capping phrase as ah hhh Roshi would say
    (1.2)
T: That's a good (.) way of capping it (1.3) but <u>ho:w</u> do <u>you</u> see it
    (1.8)
S: I see it
    (1.2)
→ T: <u>Show me</u> (0.7) <u>what you see</u>
    (3.6)
T: Is this the *Bodhidharma* that you practi:ce
    (1.2)
S: Yes=
→ T: =Why do you <u>point outside yourself</u>
→ S: That is not outside myself
→ T: <u>It is</u>
→ S: <u>It isn't</u>
    (1.2)
    Hhhhhhhhhhh ((mild audience laughter))
      [   ]
T: Thank you for your answer

The teacher favorably evaluates the student's initial answer, and then challenges the student further by commanding a demonstration of her understanding (arrow 1).

The advanced understanding of this student is displayed, not only by her ability to perform a demonstration, but also by her defense against the teacher's further challenge (arrows 2). This moment of successful defense against the teacher's challenge is also seen by the audience's appreciative response cries and laughter. She is the only student who is able to defend her understanding against the teacher's challenge throughout the encounter. The fact that she is the final participant to engage in *Dharma* combat may reflect her advanced status.

In another case, the teacher directs attention away from the student's verbal answer to a call for demonstration.

> 7   (Second teacher–student encounter)
> S: . . . I'm gonna realize heaven and hell (0.7) good and <u>evil</u>
>   (2.3)
> S: I'm gonna cherish: those two iron mountains
>   (14.2)
> S: A dead man <u>breathing</u>
>   (3.2)
> $\xrightarrow{1}$ S: What do you think he's going to do?
>   (1.4)
> T: What I want to know is? without falling into speech or
> $\xrightarrow{2}$ <u>s</u>ilence (0.8) how do you do this?
>   (5.5)
> S: Shosanshi
> $\xrightarrow{3}$ T: *(   ) show me now*
>   (8.0)
> S: *Thank you*
>   (16.0)
> T: Thank you for your answer

The student initiates the exchange by offering an extended answer to the question (only a portion of it is presented here). The student tags a question onto the end of his answer (arrow 1), but the teacher does not respond to this question; instead he asks the student 'how do you do this' (arrow 2). In other words, how to 'manifest' the answer or make it 'alive,' what we have glossed as demonstration. The teacher commands the student to 'show me now' (arrow 3). The student, then, gestures as a way to demonstrate his understanding.

The call for demonstration is used as a way to challenge the student and also to aid the students in their progression of Zen practice. In the following fragment, the teacher attempts to move the student toward a more valued form of expression.

8   (Fifth teacher–student encounter)

T: . . . when we're completely enmeshed in delusion: (.) and pai:n
         (2.8) >um< *how <u>do we realize ourselves</u>*
         (3.8)

S: Ya just <u>di:e</u> right there with it all?
         (1.4)

T: *Hm* how <u>do you die</u>
         (5.3)

S: Heh heh heh heh (.) You just (.) wait until that stuff burns: you
         right up

→¹ *T*:   *Hm* without <u>words:</u>
         (11.3)

→² *T*:   Without using an object

→³ *S*:   Heh heh heh (.) that's where you stuck me last time
         ((audience laughter))
         (2.5)

T: Hm without using an object
         (6.7)

T: Do you understand
         (5.9)

S: Nope

T: Now work on <u>that</u>=

S: =<u>Heh heh</u> heh heh

T: Thank you

S: Thank you

The teacher calls for a demonstration rather than the verbal presentation of the student's understanding (arrow 1). The teacher further challenges the student to demonstrate 'without using an object' (arrow 2). The student explicitly displays his inability to demonstrate in response to the subsequent challenge, 'that's where you stuck me last time' (arrow 3).

While the call for demonstration marks students as more advanced in their practice, students are not always able to give an appropriate demonstration. In the following exchange, the student is unable to offer any demonstration at all.

9   (Ninth teacher–student encounter)

T: . . . so how– how to do it
         (0.9)

S: In everything in everything
         (1.0)

S: If >you're if you're one< with:
         (7.2)

S: if you're one with that moment

    T: What is that (.) to be one with that moment
         (6.3)
    T: When you're re:ally: <u>be</u> the thing itself what is that?
         (4.6)
    T: That's <u>emptiness</u>: (1.3) <u>sunyata</u> (0.8) body and mind <u>fall</u> away
         (1.5)

→¹ *T*:   *So show me emptiness:* (1.0) right now
→²   (5.0)
→³ *T*:   You're working on the right *koan* to find out=
    S: =HA Ha ha
    T: Keep going
    S: .Hh Thank you

In this transcript the teacher calls upon the student to demonstrate or 'show . . . emptiness' (arrow 1). But the student is unable to do the demonstration as marked by the five second gap (arrow 2) and the teacher's exhortation to keep 'working' at it (arrow 3).

The students' failure to demonstrate in transcripts 8 and 9 displays the communication problem for students of how to 'show' their understanding so 'it's alive and working.'

Questions Prior to the Call for Demonstration

The teacher precedes the call to demonstrate by some preparatory work to ascertain the student's understanding. As seen, the teacher does not call for a demonstration from each of the students. In the four previous transcripts [6–9], the teacher's call for demonstration is preceded by a how question(s) in his prior turn or turns (see arrows).

   10 (Eleventh teacher–student encounter)
→ *T*:   . . . but <u>ho:w</u> do <u>you</u> see it
         (1.8)
    S: I see it
         (1.2)
    T: <u>Show me</u> (0.7) <u>what you see</u>

   11 (Second teacher–student encounter)
→ *T*:   . . . how do you do this?
         (5.5)
    S: Shosanshi
    T: *(   ) show me now*

   12 (Fifth teacher–student encounter)
→ *T*:   *how <u>do we realize ourselves</u>*
         (3.8)
    S: Ya just <u>di:e</u> right there with it all?
         (1.4)

→ T: *Hm* how <u>do you die</u>
        (5.3)
   S: Heh heh heh heh (.) You just (.) wait until that stuff burns: you
        right up
   T: *Hm* with<u>out words:</u>
        (11.3)
   T: Without using an object

   13   (Ninth teacher–student encounter)
→ T: . . . so how– how to do it
        (0.9)
   S: In everything in everything (1.0) if >you're if you're one< with
        (7.2)
   S: if you're one with that moment
   T: What is that . . . that's <u>emptiness</u>: (1.3) <u>sunyata</u> (0.8) body and
        mind <u>fall</u> away
        (1.5)
   T: *So show me emptiness:* (1.0) right now

The call for demonstration of understanding occurs in a sequential
environment of how-questions. How-questions may be used for
preparatory work by eliciting a process-like reply from the student –
how to *do* understanding, rather than verbally describing understanding. Of course, not all how-questions lead to a call for
demonstration (see: transcript 5, arrow; transcript 3, arrow 4;
transcript 2, arrows 1 and 3). But all calls for demonstration are
preceded by how-questions.

This form of questioning may be identified as a call-for-
demonstration sequence:

Teacher: How-question
Student: Discursive answer
Teacher: Call for demonstration

Such questioning strategies show the teacher's attempt to move the
student toward a more advanced form of expression. This sequence
seems to indicate the student's reluctance or unwillingness to initiate
a demonstration without an explicit call from the teacher.

Teacher's Demonstration of Understanding
Dharma combat as an activity is a confrontation for *both* student *and*
teacher. Thus far the focus has been on the teacher's challenge to the
student; at certain points the teacher is called upon by the student to
demonstrate understanding.

In the following transcript, the teacher tells a narrative about the
value of 'not-knowing' (only a portion of which is reproduced). Upon

the completion of the narrative, the student calls upon the teacher to 'show' his understanding (arrow 1).

14   (Sixth teacher–student encounter)

T: . . . Bodhidharma said I don't <u>know</u> (3.6) *but ah* fortunately (.) Emperor Wu didn't get it (1.6) <u>Bodhidharma</u> in disgust <u>turned</u> (1.7) left (0.6) <u>sat</u> for nine years: in a cave facing a wall (2.9)

T: ((whispered)) <u>I don't know</u> (3.6)

→¹ S: Shosanshi show me this don't know mind (3.5)

→² T: Huh sun ri:ses: (1.1) in the east sets in the we:st (5.0)

→³ S: When your head scratch– when your head itches you just
→³   scratch it

T: Sometimes they don't ((audience laughter))=

T: =Sitting in the zendo you scratch your head you get yelled at . . .

In response to the student's request and challenge (arrow 1), the teacher does not discursively explain the 'don't know mind;' instead he offers, from a Western perspective, what appears to be an irrelevant answer (arrow 2). From a Zen perspective, this answer need not adhere to conversational maxims (Grice, 1975) or make sense logically or discursively. This utterance may be glossed as the teacher's showing of the 'don't know mind.'

The student's attempt to match or imitate the teacher's answer in form (arrows 3) displays the student's recognition of the teacher's utterance as a demonstration of understanding. To put this another way, analysts can use the student's response (arrows 3) as his interpretation of the teacher's prior utterance. The student would not attempt to provide a structurally similar type of idiomatic answer, unless the student saw the teacher as presenting a demonstration.

The following transcript is the shortest exchange we have from this *Dharma* combat.

15   (Third teacher–student encounter)

S: If the buddha (1.0) banged on the <u>door</u> (1.1) or on the <u>floor</u> (1.5) or on the wall:s during the service (2.0) would ya turn him away:? (0.9) if he refused to observe the rule of silence? (1.0) or would ya hit him over the head with the rule book (1.6) or <u>what</u> (1.3)

T: ((slaps floor four times loudly))

S: ((leaves))

The student here initiates the encounter by asking a puzzle-like question. The teacher does not respond verbally to this puzzle, but rather slaps the floor four times. The student then leaves the encounter. The student's action of leaving may be seen as a response indicating his recognition of the teacher's demonstration and its completion.

In the following fragment, the teacher demonstrates an answer in response to a student's question.

> **16** (Fifth teacher–student encounter)
> S: How's your pract– ((clears throat)) how's your practice progressing
> Dido
> (1.3)
> → T: Ahh:: URGH:: MMMM::nn:: HAAaa::
> (2.8)
> S: Can't seem to get anywhere?
> (4.9)
> T: *Do you understa:nd?*
> (1.5)
> S: *No*
> (4.5)
> T: How does your practice go . . .

The teacher provides a demonstration of understanding (arrow) in response to the student's question. The student takes the teacher's apparent groaning conventionally as indicating difficulty as displayed by the student's follow-up question. But the teacher breaks out of this discursive talk by asking the student if he understands the significance of his answer.

In above encounters, the teacher's demonstration is in response to a request (transcript 14) or a question (transcript 16) from the student, but the teacher's demonstration simultaneously works as a challenge to the student. In each case, the student's response to the teacher's demonstration is negatively assessed. Demonstration is the valued form of expression, but it is apparently difficult for students to respond – to know what to do next. Students need to know how to produce a demonstration of understanding. As such, the teacher's demonstration of understanding furthers the communication problem for the student.

Discussion

The programs of the ethnography of communication and conversation analysis call for a comparison of ways of speaking across contexts. Other religions also use tests of understanding, such as

Talmudic disputation[2] and Taoist verbal confrontation. For instance, the Taoists at the Settled Heart commune in Colorado use various forms of verbal confrontation, 'ranging from softly spoken insults to full-fledged, face-to-face yelling matches replete with obscenities' (Crawford, 1986: 68). While this is clearly more vociferous than Zen, there is a parallel to the use of the *koan* in that each form is a confrontation designed to shock the student out of ordinary consciousness.

In comparison to middle-class North American English conversation, the *Dharma* combat discourse reveals noticeably more silences, that is, between-turn gaps and within-turn pauses. These silences are readily apparent from even a casual inspection of the transcripts presented above. These pauses and gaps display the importance or the carefulness the participants give to the activity. Such silences result from participants using their meditative states in answering and responding. These pauses and gaps function to minimize the possibility of overlaps and interruptions. This economy of speech to silence seems to provide a way for the participants to display orientation to the importance of the event and the respect they have for each other.

The above description of *Dharma* combat can be compared with schoolroom discourse: teacher–student exchanges in the classroom. Classroom talk and *Dharma* combat are more formal than ordinary conversation in that there are fewer speech overlaps and more silences (McHoul, 1978). In each context there occurs the pattern of the teacher putting a question to the students, a student offering an answer, and then the teacher evaluating this answer. This characteristic pattern has been described by the three-part sequence: (a) teacher's question, (b) student's answer, and (c) teacher's comment on answer (Sinclair and Coulthard, 1975). Analysts observe that part (c), or the third turn, imbrues such interaction with its pedagogic character (Heritage, 1984: 288–9). In this third turn the teacher may make various moves: assess the answer, question the student further, formulate the answer in terms of the original question, or challenge the student's understanding. In both communication contexts the third turn, or responses to the student's answer, can be used as a resource to ascertain the teacher's understanding and evaluation of the answer.

The distinguishing feature of Zen discourse comes in the members' understandings which are displayed in and through their communicative practices. In each context the characteristic three-part sequence is initiated by the teacher's question, but the question or *koan* in *Dharma* combat is of a radically different nature. As seen above, participants in *Dharma* combat face the problem of how to communicate an answer to a question, the *koan*, which cannot be suitably answered by discursive reasoning and Western canons of rationality. The impossibility of expressing such understandings in ordinary language moves the Zen practitioner toward different modes of expression, away from discursive talk and toward a demonstration of understanding. Consequently, some student answers and teacher responses do not make sense within a discursive discourse mode.

When the more advanced practitioners are asked *about* their knowledge of Zen, they claim ignorance or not to know. Preston (1988) also observed this disavowal of knowledge; to paraphrase his observation, 'Those who know, say they don't know.' Such disavowals seemed to come primarily from the more advanced practitioners and from the teacher (see transcript 14). At the same time, these advanced practitioners are more able to demonstrate their understanding. This verbal disavowal of knowledge by more advanced practitioners reflects the Zen preference for demonstrating one's understanding over discursive answers.

Another point of comparison is to the description of *Dharma* combat as practiced in other cultures, such as Japan. Izutsu (1982) characterizes *Dharma* combat by its terse and succinct manner of confrontation:

> The dialogue is . . . mostly of extreme concision and brevity. It is a real verbal fight. And the fight is over almost instantaneously, just like a contrast fought with real swords by two masters of Japanese swordsmanship. There is no room for a *dialektiké*. The Zen dialogue does not last long like a Platonic dialogue. . . . Rather, the Zen dialogue aims at grasping the ultimate and eternal Truth in a momentary flash of words. (Izutsu, 1982: 96)

This description of a brief, terse exchange between teacher and student does *not* fit the above North American case of *Dharma* combat. In only one or two instances could the above description be supported by the data (see transcripts 6 and 15).

By way of speculation about the divergence of the North American case from Izutsu's (1982) description of the terseness of Zen dialogue, two explanations seem plausible. First, Izutsu's description may be an idealized statement, a case of noteworthy historical significance between advanced Zen practitioners. What gets written of in Zen texts is the exemplary rather than the ordinary instance. Second, as Zen has spread throughout the world from China to Japan and Korea and now to the West, it has gone through various transitions due to its cultural base (Kraft, 1988). North American Zen practitioners may be more voluble than their Japanese counterparts. Even though Western and Zen epistemologies are radically different, North Americans come to Zen with cultural ways of learning acquired through verbal explanations and reasoning (Kapleau, 1988). This seems to be especially true in the dialogue with the newer, less advanced students; their exchanges with the teacher are more lengthy, literal, and discursive than the more advanced students'. The acquisition of communication competence at Zen practice requires more succinct and demonstrative ways of communicating.

By way of summary, two of the most distinctive features of the Zen practice of *Dharma* combat have been examined: the uses of the *koan* and the call for demonstration. *Dharma* combat is designed to challenge or confront participants with the problem of expressing one's understanding within the Zen constraints about thinking and ordinary language. For the newer student, in particular, this call for expression combined with the Zen constraints pose a communication problem. The *koan* and call for demonstration are not merely exotic or baffling forms of expression, but are the very activities through which the group's ways of knowing are interactionally conveyed and displayed, that is, rendered socially accountable.

Notes

1. This chapter is a slightly revised version of Buttny and Isbell (1991). In its original conception, this was not a study of social accountability. But I believe the analysis and findings can be usefully read from a social accountability perspective, so I include it here with some minor changes.
2. My thanks to Stuart Sigman for pointing this out to me.

8

Social Accountability Practices during a Welfare Interview: Diverging Accounts, Repeated Problems, and Ascriptions of Responsibility

Application interviews offer important communication contexts for examining social accountability due to the importance participants place on language-use and self-presentation.[1] Talk during interviews is highly goal directed, however participants often do not share mutual goals or equal means of attaining those goals. Interviewers function as gatekeepers for the direction and allocation of institutional resources and positions (Erickson and Schultz, 1982). There are well-known positional differences between participants (interviewer and interviewee) and the corresponding rights and obligations attached to each role. While these role differences are very real, they must be *interactionally accomplished through talk*: 'The study of language as interactional discourse demonstrates that these parameters are not constants that can be taken for granted but are communicatively produced' (Gumperz and Cook-Gumperz, 1982: 1; also see Cicourel, 1972). While decisions made in application interviews are constrained by external factors, such as economic and political realities, internal factors, such as talk-in-interaction, which constitute the interview are also crucial in understanding decisions and how they are justified.

In this chapter the social accountability practices of a welfare interview are examined: the clients' and caseworker's ways of justifying, evaluating, and challenging evaluations. One of the most striking features of this case is the recurring or repetitive character of the accountability discourse. The main attention will be given to the participants' procedures and methods for presenting and evaluating problems, and how these are used as justifications or challenges.

Welfare Interviews as a Language Game

Perhaps the most distinguishing characteristic of welfare interviews is the practice of applicants giving accounts of their problematic circumstances before a caseworker who evaluates whether the case merits assistance. Given the increasing bureaucratization of social aid programs, these interviews are structured by various standardized procedures: application forms, supporting documents, submitting to an interview, being investigated and the like. To qualify for assistance the applicant must meet certain institutional standards. Decision-making procedures are guided by various institutional rules and procedures. Caseworkers routinely expect applicants to have self-interested motives and to present their accounts of problematic circumstances so as to support their application (Zimmerman, 1974).

The practice of a professionally trained caseworker applying institutional criteria to a case to determine eligibility suggests an air of objectivity in decision making. However, researchers are beginning to demonstrate that such decision-making procedures of examining documents and records, listening to applicants' accounts, and conducting investigations are not entirely unambiguous and objective (Buckholdt and Gubrium, 1983). Decision making involves not only explicit institutional rules and procedures, but also tacit conventions and criteria based on cultural assumptions of the situation, appropriate ways of structuring information, and preferred ways of speaking. Those ignorant of such conventions and criteria are put at a disadvantage in attempting to attain their goals. Typically evaluators must decide 'for all practical purposes' that a 'fact' has been established or that a general rule applies in a particular situation (Zimmerman, 1970).

The decisions made in a welfare interview are, in principle, subject to public accountability according to 'objective' standards of evaluation. Thus caseworkers find it necessary to have accounts ready at hand to justify their decisions according to institutional standards. However, for the applicant successfully to challenge the caseworker's evaluation requires a specialized knowledge and rhetorical sophistication based on institutional assumptions (Gumperz and Cook-Gumperz, 1982).

These doubts about the objectivity of institutional decision making suggest the importance of understanding the procedures and rules which caseworkers actually use in the allocation and denial of assistance. Equally important is understanding the strategies which applicants use in presenting their case during the interview. Given that the discourse of welfare interviews is goal directed, and that participants may have diverging goals, but unequal participation rights in attainment of these goals (Rees, 1975), how do participants attempt to achieve their respective ends?

A welfare interview may be viewed as a particular kind of 'language game' (Wittgenstein, 1953) in which participants make various 'moves' (Goffman, 1981; Owen, 1981) in the attempt to realize their ends. The notion of a move may be characterized as an interactional unit to 'refer to any full stretch of talk . . . which has a distinctive unitary bearing on some set or other of the circumstances in which participants find themselves (some "game" or other in the peculiar sense employed by Wittgenstein)' (Goffman, 1981: 24). In the present case, moves include the acts of social accountability: requesting information, giving advice, directing to other channels, justifying decisions, describing personal circumstances, challenging decisions, explaining background information, and the like. A move may be used in conjunction with other moves in a strategic attempt to achieve desired ends.

The project here is to examine the social accountability practices of a welfare interview. In particular, when the caseworker and client have differing evaluations of the case, what are the participants' strategies for achieving their respective ends? What moves are made to accomplish these strategies? How are these moves contingent upon the other's moves and strategies? The organization of how problems are told is an important feature in this interview. The focus is on the moves participants make in formulating, using and evaluating problems as part of their social accountability strategies in the attempt to achieve their ends.

Materials

A film of a naturally occurring interview in a state welfare agency in the Northeastern US provides the materials. This filmed interview is a portion of a training film for welfare caseworkers. This film is an unedited portion from Frederick Wiseman's documentary, *Welfare* (1975).

There are three participants in this filmed interview: a caseworker, an applicant and the applicant's daughter. All the participants are female; the caseworker is white, or of European ancestry, and the applicant and her daughter are African-Americans. The applicant's daughter does most of the talking with the caseworker – she will be identified by the more convenient term, 'client.'

    1   (Welfare interview transcript)
1. *Caseworker*:   He's legally responsible to take care of the children.
2. *Client*:   We know that.
3. *Caseworker*:   And her as long as she's married.
                            [ ]   [ ]
4. *Client*:   Yes   Yes (   )
5. *Caseworker*:   But she went to court=
6. *Client*:   =He didn't show up

7. *Caseworker*: It has to be in the court's hands as long as he's
getting income and then he's not using it while
he's in the hospital. It's for the children (.)
that's the way
[

8. *Client*:   What's the alternatives? What, is she gonna
take checks from him if he doesn't want to give them to
her? (.) What's the alternative? She's been to court,
yesterday, yesterday.

9. *Caseworker*: Now wait a minute, what'd the court say?

10. *Client*: He didn't show up, they sent out a warrant for him.

11. *Caseworker*: Well he'll show up.

12. *Client*: But what do you want her to do if he doesn't show up?
And he's got the checks and he won't give them to her.

13. *Caseworker*: The only thing that I can suggest is that you talk
to the application supervisor and if you feel that
you've been treated unfairly
[

14. *Client*:   Of course we feel– why do
you think we're back here now?

15. *Caseworker*: She'll arrange a fair hearing
[ ]

16. *Client*:   And in the meantime what they
gonna do if they stay here, starve to death? (.) He's in
the hospital, she's sick, she's got diabetes, she's got
arthritis, she's got heart trouble (.) What is she supposed to do while waiting for a fair hearing? (.) Since
November I've been walking around, running around
with this woman.

17. *Caseworker*: You know you're making it sound like it's my fault.

18. *Client*: It's not my fault either– it's not his fault, he's in the
hospital– it's not her fault, she's sick. Whose fault is it?

19. *Caseworker*: I'm telling you what they're telling me.

20. *Client*: Who is responsible for her (.) if her husband is
sick, he's in the hospital, and she's
[ ]

21. *Caseworker*:   He's still on disability
payments.

22. *Client*: Can she take the checks from him?

23. *Caseworker*: He's legally responsible for her support.

24. *Client*: That's why she's taking him to court because he isn't
meeting his responsibilities.

25. *Caseworker*: It's in the hands of the courts
[

26. *Client*:   The court sent her here. I
have a letter from the court telling her to come here.

((Client hands the letter to the caseworker and caseworker reads the letter))

27. *Caseworker*: Now this was before the case was rejected.
The case was rejected on the twenty-fourth and this was given to her

[

28. *Client*: The same day I came here– when you rejected her she had this letter.

29. *Applicant*: They told me to go there, Social Security, that's where I went.

30. *Client*: She went to Social Security, they sent her back here. They gonna take care of her?

31. *Caseworker*: Well Social Security is evaluating her application– that's a different thing

[

32. *Client*: Okay, but meanwhile who's responsible for her?

33. *Caseworker*: Her husband.

34. *Client*: He's in the hospital as you very well know.

35. *Caseworker*: Well I understand he's in the hospital

[ ]

36. *Client*: Now what is she supposed to do?

37. *Caseworker*: The checks are coming

[ ]

38. *Client*: Hold onto the checks that don't belong to her? They belong to him.

39. *Caseworker*: He has a responsibility

[ ]

40. *Client*: He don't want to give them to her. We're going into a vicious cycle again and I'm getting tired of it.

41. *Caseworker*: Well as I said before you have to apply for a fair hearing.

42. *Client*: Oh and how long is a fair hearing going to take? And what's she going to do in the meanwhile while she's waiting for her fair hearing? (.) She's been coming here since November.

43. *Caseworker*: It's her responsibility to try to get

[ ]

44. *Client*: What do you think she's trying to do? (.) Why do you think she's going to court? (.) You're sending me around in a vicious cycle– I'm trying to tell you her hands are tied.

45. *Caseworker*: I'm not sending you

[ ]

46.	*Client*:	He's sick, she is sick– who is going to take care of her?
47.	*Caseworker*:	I'm not sending you anywhere.
48.	*Client*:	You told me to wait for a fair hearing– what's she going to do in the meanwhile?
49.	*Caseworker*:	Well you have to ask the application's supervisor to re-entertain the application.
50.	*Client*:	What do you think I'm here for now. Why am I talking to you now for this?
51.	*Caseworker*:	You don't need to shout.
52.	*Client*:	Well I'm gonna do some more shouting if you don't stop this. Ever since November (.) You talk about shouting– I've been trying to take care of this woman– what do you want from me? (.) Sending us around to all these places and sending us around in circles.
53.	*Applicant*:	Where are you supposed to go?
54.	*Client*:	That's what I want to know, she said go to court– she went to court. Go to Social Security– they sent her back here (.) They're up there sitting on their behinds upstairs, that's why that can't do nothin' for nobody (.) Have you sit here all damn day– sending you all around to the courts and the courts sending you here.

The Social Accountability for Problems in a Welfare Interview

This interview involves a dispute between the caseworker and client over the applicant's qualification for assistance. To give an overall gloss of the episode, the applicant's case has been previously rejected (line 27). Since this initial rejection, the applicant has pursued other means of support, such as applying to Social Security (line 29) and taking her husband to court for support payments. However, the Social Security Agency and the courts are delayed in deciding the applicant's case, consequently the applicant is presently without a means of support so she has returned to reapply for welfare assistance.

Evaluation and Challenge
Consider how the formulation of problems are used and evaluated. The caseworker initially evaluates the client's case as being in the court's jurisdiction (line 7). This evaluation is marked as necessary as indicated by the verb choice 'It has to be in the court's hands,' as well as by the justification of citing the husband's legal responsibilities. Here the caseworker draws on the institutional procedure that the courts take precedence over the welfare agency. This procedure is not verbally explained, but is the underlying assumption of the

caseworker's move. In other words, without this institutional procedure of the court's taking precedence, the caseworker could not accomplish this justification.

The caseworker is simultaneously making two moves here – in evaluating that the case is in the court's hands, she implicates that the client's application is being denied. The client's response (line 8) shows that she recognizes the implicated denial even though it is never explicitly said. This recognition is displayed by the client citing various problems with the caseworker's evaluation. The client's utterances are marked as problems in that they describe negative circumstances which will result from the caseworker's evaluation. These negative circumstances include the husband's not wanting to give her the checks, and already having been to court but the case being delayed. The client uses these problems as obstacles to the caseworker's evaluation. As obstacles, these problems respond to the caseworker's evaluation by challenging its appropriateness.

The client prefaces the presentation of these problems with the question, 'What's the alternatives?' (line 8). The implication the client wants the caseworker to draw is that the client has no other alternative for support except to receive welfare assistance. These moves of presenting problems-as-obstacles to the caseworker's evaluation to implicate the need for welfare assistance constitutes one of the client's discursive strategies.

At line 13 the caseworker displays recognition of the client's problems with the courts by suggesting that she arrange a fair hearing through the applications supervisor. This proposal allows the caseworker to continue to reject the application while simultaneously responding with a solution to the client's problems. These moves display that the caseworker does not accept the client's implied claim that there are no other options available except welfare assistance. Instead, the caseworker offers an option, consistent with bureaucratic procedures, which allows her to maintain the initial evaluation of the case.

The caseworker's moves are to direct the client to follow institutional channels: the case is the court's decision (line 7); or arrange a fair hearing through the applications supervisor (lines 13–15). The caseworker's moves may be seen to be based on the maxim, follow institutional procedures. This maxim is not explicitly stated, but is the underlying assumption behind the above-mentioned moves. Drawing on this maxim allows the caseworker to justify her evaluation by reference to institutional criteria, and to deny the client's reapplication. This combination of moves based on this follow-institutional-procedures maxim constitutes the caseworker's principle rhetorical strategy. This strategy appears throughout the interview.

In line 12 the client again challenges the caseworker's solution by *repeating the problems* of the husband's not appearing in court as well as not wanting to give her the checks. These problems were mentioned previously (lines 6, 8, and 10). The client prefaces the presentation of problems-as-obstacles with the question, 'But what do you want her to do if' these problems are not solved (line 12). This formulation is structurally similar to the preface to the problems at line 8, 'What's the alternatives.' These prefacing questions combined with the device, problems-as-obstacles, are used to implicate that there is nothing the client can do to solve these problems (line 12) or there are no alternatives left except welfare assistance (line 8). That is, the client's discourse strategy is to block the caseworker's evaluation and implicate that there are no other courses of action available to solve her problems other than assistance from welfare. The client uses these problems-as-obstacles throughout the interview as a response to the caseworker's negative evaluation.

Negotiation The participants' diverging ends and corresponding rhetorical strategies comprise the central tension of the interview: the conflict between the caseworker's maxim, follow institutional procedures, and the applicant's claim that all channels have been tried so her only alternative is welfare assistance.

Given the diverging perspectives on this case, how do the participants attempt to manage this divergence? Returning to the above fragment, it can be seen that the caseworker responds to the client's problems (line 9) by asking what appears to be an informational question. Note though that this question is oriented to 'what'd the courts say' (that is, the caseworker's preferred outcome), rather than to the client's problematic circumstances. That is, the question is not to the main point of the client's prior turn, but to an ancillary episode which the caseworker makes relevant. So the caseworker's question, in addition to unpacking the gloss, simultaneously attempts to regulate the discourse in the direction of the caseworker's proposal.

The client (line 10) answers this question in a way consistent with her accountability strategy. She answers by repeating the problem cited in her previous turn – the husband's failure to appear in court (line 8). So while the caseworker's question attempts to regulate the discourse in accordance with her strategy, the client is able to answer by continuing to cite problems-as-obstacles. The caseworker responds (line 11) by providing a 'solution' to the client's problem which works simultaneously to regulate the discourse toward the court's procedures. As seen previously the client (line 12) does not accept the caseworker's solution and continues to identify problems-as-obstacles.

A welfare interview as a language game may be seen as comprised of the two basic parts: (1) application or request for assistance, and (2) caseworker's evaluation which complies with or denies the request. In applying for assistance the client presents accounts of problematic circumstances. These descriptions of problematic circumstances have a different sequential implicativeness than (2), that is, problems make conditionally relevant a range of response types such as solutions. There seems to be a mixing of sequence types: on the one hand, *application–evaluation*, and on the other, *problem–solution*. In responding to the client, the caseworker may face the competing demands of administering institutional procedures and helping the client.

These competing demands may be seen, for instance, in the caseworker's response at line 13. The caseworker displays that she is oriented to the competing demands of providing a solution to the client's problems as well as applying institutional criteria to evaluate the client's application. In short, the caseworker's response may be seen as both a solution and an evaluation. It is a solution in that it suggests a course of action for the client to receive assistance. And it is simultaneously an evaluation in that it continues to deny the client's original application while directing the client to the appropriate bureaucratic channel. Or, it may be more parsimonious to say that the caseworker's solution is constrained by the institutional evaluation. The point here is that it is too simplistic to gloss the caseworker as merely applying institutional criteria to evaluate the client's case. The caseworker is responding to the sometime competing demands of the client's lifeworld and following institutional criteria (Mishler, 1984).

Recurring Problems and Evaluations

Towards the end of the interview the client metacommunicates, 'We're going into a vicious cycle again and I'm getting tired of it' (line 40). The client's remark, 'a vicious cycle,' seems an accurate formulation of the talk given the participants' diverging accounts. The client's utterance here not only describes the interview, but also criticizes it.

One of the most striking discourse features of this interview is the recurring statement of problems by the client and proposed solutions by the caseworker, but without any agreement. As already seen, the caseworker evaluates the case as needing to follow institutional procedures, while the client responds by claiming that all these procedures have been tried, but without success, so her only option is to receive welfare assistance. This recurrence of problems and solutions could be identified as a pattern and written as a redundancy rule from a systems perspective. But the analytic concern here is to see how these moves are produced and accomplished by the participants in the attempt to achieve their respective ends.

The recurrence or repetition of the discourse is accomplished by the client's challenge of the caseworker's evaluation. The client cannot simply reject the caseworker's evaluation. Rather the client's challenge is used to recycle the basic evaluation sequence. This is accomplished by making the problems relevant such that the caseworker's evaluation and solution do not alleviate them.

Most of this interview involves the caseworker's negative evaluation of the application and the client's challenging this assessment. The client does the challenging by presenting problems with the caseworker's assessment. By challenging the caseworker's evaluation the client does the work of recycling the basic sequence of the interview and making relevant her problems. Presumably the client could have accepted the caseworker's evaluation which would have led to the termination of the interview. But in challenging the negative evaluation by presenting problems, the client accomplishes the conditional relevance of those problems as needing to be addressed.

In recycling the sequence, the participants, of course, do not return to the beginning of the process. Rather, given the client's discourse strategy of presenting problems-as-obstacles, the client attempts to implicate a positive evaluation, that is, the necessity of receiving assistance. But the caseworker's use of the maxim, follow institutional procedures, allows her to channel the client's problems and adhere to her original evaluation.

The problem of waiting   Consider the client's use of the problem of waiting. The problems with waiting are cited on four occasions by the client (lines 16, 32, 42, and 48). How is the problem of waiting used as a move for rhetorical purposes, and what does it tell us about the language game? What responses does it bring about? And how is it resolved, if at all?

The problem of waiting first appears in the following fragment.

2   (Fragment)
15.   *Caseworker*:   She'll arrange a fair hearing
                                              [ ]
16.   *Client*:   And in the meantime what they
         gonna do if they stay here, starve to death? (.) He's in
         the hospital, she's sick, she's got diabetes, she's got
         arthritis, she's got heart trouble (.) What is she sup-
         posed to do while waiting for a fair hearing? (.) Since
         November I've been walking around, running around
         with this woman.

Waiting is used as a problem by the client in line 16 as a response to the caseworker's solution to 'arrange a fair hearing' (line 15). Having to wait is displayed as a problem for the client due to her immediate needs and poor health. Not only is waiting a problem, but it is also used as grounds for challenging the caseworker's solution. The problem of waiting constitutes part of the client's accounting – it challenges the prior solution thereby attempting to recycle the evaluation process in order to implicate the necessity for receiving welfare assistance. That is, the client implies the positive case of receiving assistance by making the negative case of obstacles to the caseworker's solution.

The problem of waiting appears on a second occasion as a response to the caseworker's solution 'to apply for a fair hearing.'

3   (Fragment)
41.   *Caseworker*:   Well as I said before you have to apply for a fair
                          hearing.
42.   *Client*:   Oh and how long is a fair hearing going to take? And
                          what's she going to do in the meanwhile while she's
                          waiting for a fair hearing? (.) She's been coming here
                          since November.
43.   *Caseworker*:   It's her responsibility to try to get

The caseworker's solution (line 41) again draws on the maxim, follow institutional procedures. This solution is presented as a directive '. . . you have to apply for a fair hearing.' In contrast, this solution was initially proposed as an option (lines 13–15) '. . . I can suggest that you talk to the application supervisor and if you feel . . .' The caseworker's solution here is shorter and more direct which is characteristic of repeated utterances. The caseworker marks the utterance as repeated by the preface 'Well as I said before . . .'

The client again responds (line 42) by challenging the caseworker's solution. The client's initial question, 'Oh and how long is a fair hearing going to take?', is not presented as a question-to-be-answered, but rather to implicate the problem with this solution. Note that the caseworker does not answer this question (though in a different sequential environment it would make a sensible query). The client makes the problems-as-obstacles explicit. In formulating the problem (line 42) she uses similar devices to those she used at line 16, 'what's she going to do in the meanwhile while waiting for a fair hearing' and '. . . since November.' Using these problems for a second time displays that the client does not feel that they were satisfactorily answered by the caseworker. The client's strategy turns on the assumption that problems that cannot be solved by the client or by the caseworker's proposals demand a solution from welfare.

The problem of waiting appears for a third time in the following fragment:

4   (Fragment)
48.   *Client*:   You told me to wait for a fair hearing– what's she going to do in the meanwhile?
49.   *Caseworker*: Well you have to ask the application's supervisor to re-entertain the application.
50.   *Client*:   What do you think I'm here for now. Why am I talking to you now for this?

In the first two instances the problem of waiting is used as a response to the caseworker's solution to see the applications supervisor and arrange a fair hearing. Here (line 48) the client formulates the caseworker's prior solution, 'You told me to wait for a fair hearing,' and the client's corresponding problem with that solution, 'what's she going to do in the meanwhile?' This formulation of the problem displays that the client feels that the caseworker has not solved the problem of waiting. It also indicates the key assumption of her accountability strategy – problematic circumstances that cannot be readily solved require assistance from welfare.

The caseworker avoids answering this problem, but rather refers the client to the applications supervisor (line 49). The caseworker's response displays that she does not accept the client's underlying assumption. Instead, the caseworker directs the client in how to re-entertain the application.

This answer is clearly not what the client was asking about as seen by the client's response of asking what is this interview about (line 50) and marked by her shouting (lines 51–2). The participants not only have diverging ends and accountability strategies, but also do not appear to agree on the very nature of what the interview is about. This exchange indicates to the client that she has been talking to the wrong caseworker to have her application reconsidered.

Responsibility   The ascription of responsibility occurs throughout the interview. Initially it will be examined as a response to the problems with waiting.

5   (Fragment)
17.   *Caseworker*: You know you're making it sound like it's my fault.
18.   *Client*:   It's not my fault either– it's not his fault, he's in the hospital– it's not her fault, she's sick. Whose fault is it?
19.   *Caseworker*: I'm telling you what they're telling me.
20.   *Client*:   Who is responsible for her (.) if her husband is sick, he's in the hospital, and she's
                                                                            [   ]
21.   *Caseworker*:   He's still on disability payments.

The caseworker responds (line 17) to the client's problem of waiting (fragment 2, line 16) with, what we may call, a denial of personal intent. The implicit contrast here is between her personal responsibility and the constraints she is under as a caseworker. At line 19 she draws upon her position as a caseworker to justify her actions. That is, by citing the membership category (Sacks, 1972) of caseworker, she denies that her decision is based on her personal feelings toward the client, but on job related responsibilities such as directives from superiors. The caseworker's justification displays that she takes the client's prior turn as a blame or ascription of fault. Her response is to deny personal accountability and attribute it to her superiors in the welfare system.

The client responds to the caseworker's denial of fault by making relevant the issue of fault in a broader sense (line 18). The client accomplishes this by drawing on the conversational recourses (Harré, 1977) of the prior two turns. The client uses the caseworker's term, 'fault,' to deny fault for herself as well as for her father and mother. Also, the client draws on a listing device used in line 16 (for example, a listing of ailments) to formulate a list of denials of fault at line 18. The client concludes by asking 'Whose fault is it?' given the above denials of fault. In response (line 19) the caseworker draws upon her institutional constraints. The client (line 20) moves from the denials of fault to the related notion of responsibility, 'Who is responsible for her.' This move is crucial for the production of the client's strategy – it is based on the assumption that if no one is responsible for these problems, her only option left is receiving welfare assistance.

The ascription of responsibility is used by both caseworker and client throughout the interview. Initially the caseworker labeled the client's husband as 'legally responsible' (line 1). The client later raised the question, 'Who is responsible for her' (line 20) given that it was not her fault for her circumstances. The client raises this question again orienting it to the problem of waiting for a decision to be made:

6   (Fragment)
31.   *Caseworker*: Well Social Security is evaluating her application–
                           that's a different thing
                                           [ ]
32.   *Client*:   Okay, but meanwhile who's respon-
                           sible for her?
33.   *Caseworker*: Her husband.

The client's move of raising the question of responsibility constitutes a version of her accountability strategy: the client is not responsible for her circumstances (line 18) and her husband 'isn't meeting his responsibilities' (line 24), so by implication the state has to be responsible for her. The caseworker, however, does not accept this implication and contradicts the client's claim by ascribing responsibility to the husband (line 33). The caseworker accomplishes this ascription of responsibility by again drawing on the maxim, follow institutional procedures.

This sequence (fragment 6) reflects the conflicting moves and strategies. As already mentioned, the client's move is to show that no one is responsible for her problematic circumstances, so by implication the welfare agency must be responsible. On the other hand, the caseworker subsumes the case under the maxim, follow institutional procedures, so the courts can obligate the husband to meet his responsibilities. The caseworker uses the ascription of responsibility throughout the interview as part of her social accountability strategy. For instance, following the client's problem of waiting, the caseworker ascribes responsibility to the client to arrange a hearing (lines 41–3). So in labeling the husband as 'legally responsible' (lines 1 and 16) and the client as responsible for arranging a fair hearing (lines 43 and 49), the caseworker is able to invoke institutional procedures, and thereby disavow the power to act on the case.

The ascription of responsibility seems to be an especially strong label for participants due to its implications for action. A marked asymmetry in the participants' respective uses of responsibility is that the caseworker directly ascribes responsibility to the husband and the client, while the client only raises it as a question with the implicated answer of the state is responsible. In addition, the caseworker can draw upon case files and her knowledge of institutional procedures to justify her ascriptions of responsibility. The client, in contrast, can only make an argument based on personal need and problematic circumstances. Here we see an asymmetry of specialized, bureaucratic knowledge and how it affects the discursive options in the production of moves for accountability strategies.

Conclusion

A caveat: racial differences of the client and caseworker are not used in the above analysis. The rationale for this is the attempt to focus on the talk itself and bracket categories of persons. The relevance of being an American of African or European heritage should be marked or displayed in their ways of speaking, not assumed as an a priori category (Heritage, 1984). By way of preliminary analysis, there is some indication for marked differences by race consistent with Kochman's work on diverging communication styles between middle-class white culture and inner-city black culture (Kochman, 1981: 12–15). For instance, the white caseworker appears to 'talk down' to the client in repeating institutional procedures and ascribing responsibility (Erickson, 1979), and the black client displays a more expressive communicative style in showing disagreement (Kochman, 1981).

It might be argued that the language game of a welfare interview reflects contemporary culture. One of the most noticeable features of the discourse of this interview is the advocacy of the client in challenging the caseworker's decision. The client is unwilling to accept the authority of caseworker as the final word. Given the bureaucratization of welfare agencies (indicative of the growing segmentation of everyday life), the caseworker cannot simply give aid to the applicant because she is needy, rather she must qualify for assistance according to standardized criteria. The language game of the welfare interview is based on a form of life of individual entitlements for the poor, rather than on its historical roots in charity. Thus, the accountability strategies can be drawn from a 'vocabulary of motives' (Mills, 1940; Burke, 1969) which uses problems, not to evoke charity, but to challenge the justification of the caseworker's decision.

Note

1. This chapter is a slightly revised version of Buttny and Campbell (1990). The approach used here reflects an early effort of mine at doing discourse analysis. While I would not write this in the same way today, I include it here because it does contain 'a few gems.' Also, a welfare interview is an inherently interesting situation of social accountability, and the interactional patterns seen here seem to reflect the recurring problems of bureaucratic settings.

9

Accounts and Accountability Practices in News Interviews

> All stories and accounts, no matter how much their style might protest
> innocence, contain a mythic level – that is they have a job to do, a
> perspective to promote, a kind of world to affirm or deny. Seemingly
> neutral accounts of activities deliver, by dint of their grammatical and
> rhetorical structures, implicit arguments, either legitimations for en-
> trenched authority or polemical critiques which seek to demystify or
> disestablish existing structures of power and domination. (Shapiro,
> 1984: 2)

A common setting for the soliciting of and giving of accounts is
broadcast news interviews. Live news interviews on television and
radio have developed into one of the primary forums for access to and
questioning of politicians, public figures and newsmakers. Given the
often-times controversial nature of the issues of the day, these
interviewees may be asked challenging questions by journalists about
their positions, actions or policies. Indeed, these challenging questions may be heard by both interviewee and overhearing audience
alike as thinly-veiled criticisms or implicating blame. In response,
politicians commonly present various kinds of accounts to defend,
explain or neutralize the critical evaluation implicated by the
question. Political figures may need to account, not only for their own
individual actions or conduct, but also for their administration and its
policies. Like few other communication contexts, the accounts
offered in news interviews may be scrutinized and evaluated by
millions of audience members.

While accounts and accountability are ubiquitous features of news
interviews they have received little analytic attention in the accounts
literature. So in this chapter I turn to how criticism-accounts
sequences can be interactionally achieved within the question–
answer format of broadcast news interviews.

News Interviews as Social Interaction

Broadcast interviews between public figures and journalists need to
be seen as a distinctive form of social interaction for the production of
news. Until recently the interactional dynamics of the interview

format have been ignored or considered unproblematical due to an assumption that social interaction is a mere conduit for information to be transmitted from newsmaker to interviewer and audience (Clayman and Whalen, 1988/89: 241). However, as will be shown, this assumption of communication as 'neutral conduit of information' has been largely discredited.

The approach to be taken here is that the news interview is a social accomplishment between interviewer and interviewee designed for the production of the news for viewing/listening audiences (Heritage et al., 1988). News interviews are cooperatively achieved between participants on a turn-by-turn, move-by-move basis. In the course of participants' turns at talk, the news interview gets recreated and achieved as a distinctive form of discourse (Greatbatch, 1988). The news interview is simultaneously a conventionally recognized format as well as locally achieved through the talk by participants. I begin with a brief review of the conversation analytic literature on news interviews as a prelude to my principle concern with social account-ability and accounts in this context.

A number of points may be made to characterize the news interview as a distinctive form of social interaction. First, most obviously, the news interview format consists of interviewer's questions and interviewee's answers. Participant's orientation to the question–answer interview format is displayed by the fact that the interviewee typically withholds replying until a question is forth-coming, even though the interviewer may preface the question with oppositional statements or points of contention (Greatbatch, 1988). Interviewer and interviewee alike are not constrained solely to questions and answers. Interviewers frequently engage in other communicative acts in the course of their speaking turn, such as opposing descriptions, evaluative statements, or critical attributions. The interviewee's response, in turn, may give answers which address more points or other issues than were raised in the interviewer's question. Participants' (at least minimal) orientation to questions and answers reflects their collaborative cooperation within the institutional ground rules of the news interview context (Heritage and Greatbatch, 1991).

Other ground rules include the expectation that journalists adopt a 'neutral' posture in their questioning, as opposed to expressing their own opinions or advocating a position (Clayman, 1988). Tradition-ally, the press is expected to perform 'a watchdog function' toward government, and consequently, journalists can ask hard questions of interviewees. However, journalists do more than simply ask ques-tions. In the speaking turn in which a question is posed, the journalist may make a number of other moves, such as proffer critical or evaluative statements, cite conflicting facts or evidence, attribute adversary positions to other experts, or embed challenging assumptions within the question. Journalists can be challenging and critical, while at the same time maintaining a neutral position, by combining evaluative statements with questions thereby designed for the interviewee's comment. By attaching evaluative or critical statements to questions, or attributing opposing points-of-view to others for comment, the journalist can challenge or criticize the interviewee while displaying a neutral stance (Clayman, 1988). Through these procedures the journalist is able to raise criticisms and solicit accounts, while accountably adhering to norms of neutrality, and thereby, avoiding the charge of bias.

While the news interviewer is held accountable to being neutral, the interviewee is held accountable to addressing the question posed by the interviewer. Interviewee's responses that avoid addressing the journalist's question face the possibility of sanction in the interviewer's follow-up questions. For instance, the interviewer may raise the question again or rephrase it, or may even call attention to the respondent's evasive answers. Interviewees can avoid this sanction by giving at least minimal responses to the question in combination with moving to their desired issue or point in their speaking turn. This movement has been described as 'agenda-shifting procedures' (Greatbatch, 1986a). Greatbatch shows that the most successful ways for the interviewee to avoid sanctions are by 'pre-answer agenda shifting' (that is, raising another issue prior to addressing the question in the answer) and by 'post-answer agenda shifting' (that is, moving to a different issue after addressing the question in the answer). Such procedures allow the interviewee to manage the constraints of the interview format while enabling the interviewee to address their own concerns in the course of offering an answer.

News interviews consist of talk designed for mass audiences (Heritage, 1985). As a consequence, the speaking turns taken by participants in news interviews are generally longer than the turn-taking found in ordinary conversation (Heritage et al., 1988: 87). Journalists may need to provide audience members with background information in the course of presenting a question. Another consequence of news interviews as 'talk for overhearing audiences' is that the interviewer usually avoids responding to an interviewee's answer with 'news receipts' (such as, 'oh,' 'really') or 'backchannel' actions (such as, 'mm hm,' 'yeah') which are commonly found in ordinary conversation (Heritage, 1985; Greatbatch, 1988). The interviewer's withholding of news receipts and backchannel responses suggests that the audience is the primary recipient of the interviewee's answer.

Interviewers frequently follow the answers they receive from the interviewee by moving on to their next question. However, the interviewer may not want to move to the next question, but rather probe or seek clarification of the interviewee's prior answer. One way to accomplish this is to 'formulate' the gist of what the interviewee has just said (Heritage, 1985). The interviewer's formulation 'selectively re-presents' certain aspects of the interviewee's answer in a summary fashion to underscore these points for the audiences. Formulations serve to hold interviewees accountable for their answers by seeking a confirmation/denial of the formulation along with further explanation.

Politicians, of course, are notoriously skillful at evasiveness (Harris, 1991) or avoiding giving answers to difficult questions (Clayman, in press). Journalists can pursue such evasions through the use of follow-up, or supplemental, questions as a way to hold interviewees accountable for addressing the question (Greatbatch, 1986b, 1988). So the interviewee faces *competing demands* in responding to challenging questions: the interviewee wants to present the issue in question in a favorable light, but at the same time, needs to address, at least minimally, the interviewer's question so as to avoid the criticism of evasiveness. Accounts often need to be given, but the interviewee does not want to appear as overly defensive or going beyond the bounds of credibility.

The conversation analytic approach has made important inroads in describing the social dynamics of the news interview, particularly how the news is an interactional achievement between interviewer and interviewee. But within this research program more attention needs to be given to the discursive practice of social accountability. How do interviewers do challenges, implicate criticism or invoke a problematic in the course of their questions; and how do interviewees accomplish accounts and related defenses, or avoid giving them, in the course of their answers?

Materials
Tape recordings of live news interviews were gathered from television and radio between November 1990 and January 1991. Given the previous finding (Harris, 1986) that politicians and policymakers usually receive more challenging questions from interviewers, thereby making accounts more likely, I limited my sample to this group of interviewees. The programs recorded for analysis were: *The MacNeil/Lehrer Newshour* (PBS), *Nightline* (ABC), *This Week with David Brinkley* (ABC), *All Things Considered* (NPR), and *As It Happens* (CBC). Over twenty hours of video- and audiotaped

recordings were collected. In these recordings those segments that contained accounts episodes were transcribed for analysis.

Accounting for Problematic Events during News Interviews

A central issue here will be to explain how the interviewee's answer works to account for the problematic raised or the criticism implicated in the interviewer's question. That is, how do participants make relevant and use various contextual materials (for example, facts, descriptions, positions, and the like) to construct a criticism or account in the course of raising questions or giving answers? How are accounts designed as responsive, or not, to the prior criticism? What do accounts make relevant from the problematic to address (explain, justify, excuse) in the course of the answer? How are criticisms and accounts interactionally constructed, and what do these constructions implicate about the interlocutor or make relevant about the problematic? The project here is not to code or do a frequency count of accounting techniques, but rather to do the more primary job of showing how they work interactionally, how they are sequentially structured and constructed in the discourse.

From examining the tape-recorded materials, four kinds of discursive practices emerge as ways of doing accounts in the broadcast news interview context: (1) justifying disagreement; (2) accounting for concessions; (3) formulation of the problematic to account for; and; (4) accounts for not answering the question.

Justifying Disagreement
Given the sometime adversarial character of news interviews, broadcast journalists may present contrary positions, interpretations, or facts in the course of asking questions as a way to challenge the interviewee. A familiar response to such challenges is to straightaway disagree with or deny the prior claims, and support this with justificatory accounts. For instance:

1   (*As It Happens*, CBC, with Joe Clarke, Canadian External Affairs Minister)
IR: Quick last question Mister Clarke could Saddam Hussein or those people around him take your letter to Secretary Baker as a tiny indication that the coalition is not holding
Clarke: No I don– I think quite the contrary I think what eh they should read from it is that eh that there is a common determination to maintain (.) ah the pressure upon Saddam Hussein to eh to negotiate including . . .

First of all, notice that Clarke's answer is responsive to the critical possibilities posed by the interviewer. Clarke begins by explicitly disagreeing with the possibility that Hussein and colleagues could take his letter in the way suggested. Disagreement tokens, such as 'no,' used at the beginning of the respondent's turn, serve to underscore the interviewee's positioning toward the interviewer's suggestion. However, many interviewees do disagreeing without an explicit 'no'; the disagreement becomes apparent in the course of the interviewee's explanation.

Clarke does not support or give evidence for his disagreement; instead he moves to offer his own interpretation of the letter as reflecting 'a common determination.' This descriptor, 'a common determination,' accomplishes a *marked contrast* to the interviewer's formulation, 'the coalition is not holding.' So Clarke's response does not attempt to rebut the interviewer's speculation, but instead offers his own *preferred interpretation* of how Saddam will see his letter, and thereby, attempts to mitigate criticism.

In disagreeing with a proposition put forward by the interviewer, the interviewee frequently accounts for the disagreement by *substituting a preferred way to see the event* in question. The substitution of interpretations is apparent in case 1 and it is also evident in the following transcript.

2   (*This Week with David Brinkley*), ABC, with Dick Cheney, US
    Secretary of Defense)

Donalson: Now let me ask you about the Baker initiative (.) if eh
            Saddam Hussein does not backdown:: and say well now
            that you're here in Baghdad thank you because I <u>do</u> want a
            face-saving way to withdraw from Kuwait and I can now
            talk to you about it and if in fact as the President says
            Secretary Baker has not gone to <u>cha:nge:</u> the President's
            very stiff no negotiating posture (.) why isn't it proper to
            see it as simply a diplomatic feint to help assuage concerns
            in the United States and among our <u>allies</u> before we go to
            war.

Cheney: I think I think the way to interpret (.) what the President's
            doing here is exactly what the President said? and that is to
            make it abundantly clear by ah communicating directly
            with the Iraqi government that the President is as he said
            on many occasions deadly serious (.) the only acceptable
            outcome is the full implementation of the UN resolution
            the withdrawal from Kuwait the restoration of the
            legitimate government of Kuwait and the release of all
            hostages tho::se indee:d are not eh subjects we can
            compromise on . . .

The interviewer, Sam Donalson, presents a scenario derived from the Baker initiative which projects *conflicting* or *inconsistent elements*. This apparent inconsistency provides a rationale for Donalson to suggest the Bush administration's hidden political strategy and solicit Cheney's comment. Donalson's reading of the strategic nature of the Baker initiative may be heard as critical in that it is ascribed as pretense ('simply a diplomatic feint to help assuage concerns in the United States and among our allies before we go to war') and Cheney's response takes it in just this way – as criticism.

Media critics have observed that political figures come to news interviews with well-rehearsed positions which they launch into without seeming to address the question asked by the journalist. Cheney's answer here *seems* to fit this observation of the well-rehearsed, pre-planned policy statement (especially beginning at 'to make it abundantly clear . . .' (arrow)). But even given the fact that interviewees' positions may be pre-planned and rehearsed, to be coherent they have to be sensitive to the moment-by-moment contingencies of the talk and at least minimally relevant to the interviewer's prior statements and questions. To put this another way, the interviewee needs to know how to insert the rehearsed position statement into the answer without drawing undue attention to that move. Notice how Cheney achieves the transition into his recitation of the administration's policy. He counters Donalson's critical reading by avowing that the 'correct' interpretation of the President's actions is what the President claims that he is doing, and then he moves into what seems to be a prepared policy statement. So in both transcripts 1 and 2 we see the interviewees present their preferred interpretation of events in contrast to the interviewer's version.

In transcript 2 the interviewer may be heard to cast doubt upon the administration's official position by *juxtaposing incompatible elements* in his construction of a scenario. This is done as a rationale for his challenging question. Similarly, in the following case the interviewer verbally establishes the background context as a prelude to her critical question.

3   (*This Week with David Brinkley*), ABC, with Mohammed Al-Mashatt, Iraq's Ambassador to the US, and the interviewer, Cokie Roberts)

Roberts: Mister >Ambassador you say the United States has< the power >to level Iraq< (.) so you could– your country could disappear (0.5) right <u>now</u>: you have people in the country who are <u>hurting</u> from the embar:go:, you're <u>not</u> getting the benefit of the Kuwaiti oil, because of the embargo,

→   WHY NOT JUST GET OUT OF KUWAIT END ALL THIS NOT HAVE
→   THE– THE DESTRUCTION of your country at hand?=

Al-Mashatt: =Because we will (0.8) I want you to know? that we do
not act under intimidation and a threa:t (0.8) what did we
do? to you? in order to have this fate have you ever
thought of it?

The interviewer, Cokie Roberts, constructs the background context
for her question through: (a) paraphrasing the interviewee's answer
to a prior interviewer's question ('you say the United States has<
the power >to level Iraq<'), (b) drawing out the possible consequences of (a) ('your country could disappear'), (c) citing apparent
facts ('right now: you have people in the country who are hurting
from the embar:go:'), and (d) causal relationshps ('you're not
getting the benefit of the Kuwaiti oil, because of the embargo').
This *establishing of the background context* serves as a *rationale* for
her proposal which is structured in a question format (arrows).
Further, this question implicates a criticism of the Iraqi policy. The
critical aspects of her question are heightened by Roberts' increased
vocal volume.

The interviewer's construction of the background context serves
not only as an information function for the overhearing audience, but
as a rationale for her question as well as making it difficult for the
interviewee simply to disagree with an opposing interpretation. The
interviewee, Al-Mashatt, immediately justifies his country's policy
by labelling the United States' actions as 'intimidation' and 'threat.'
Notice that this account does *not challenge the factual record*
presented by the interviewer, but disagrees by offering a different
interpretation of these events and possibilities ('we do not act under
intimidation and a threa:t'). This justificatory account invokes other
considerations, what may be glossed as a 'higher principle,' or matter
of 'face,' as a way to resist the implications of the criticism.

In transcripts 1 and 2 the interviewer offers a reading of political
events which may be heard as critical, and the interviewee disagrees
with that reading by presenting their own preferred interpretation.
Cheney supports his interpretation in transcript 2 by referring to the
credibility of the President's statements, while in transcript 1 Clarke
does not point to any external evidence or authority to support his
interpretation. By way of contrast consider how examples are used in
the following case to justify implicitly disagreeing with a prior
criticism.

4 (*MacNeil/Lehrer Newshour*), PBS, with Pete Williams, Pentagon
spokesman)

MacNeil: But let me just go back on Stan Cloud's point that this that
your motive is not just to protect the troops and prevent the
enemy from finding out about eh positions and plans but it is
to manage the coverage of this war

Williams: Well where where else if we stayed out of it where else
would editors have put reporters in the beginning of an air
war? where the pla↑nes take off ↓ aircraft carriers where
the cruise missiles takes off– take off battle ships where the
planes take off from air forces bases=I– we're trying to get
reporters to the scene of the action I don't know where else
in the beginning of an air campaign they would be

The interviewer, Robert MacNeil, refers to a co-interviewee's
ascription of motives to the Pentagon for plans to limit press coverage
of the war through the use of journalistic pools. Pete Williams
attempts to support his implicit disagreement by *listing examples* of
cases where reporters were on hand 'to see' the air war ('where the
pla↑nes take off ↓ aircraft carriers where the cruise missiles takes
off– take off battle ships where the planes take off from air forces
bases'). These counter-examples are presented as evidence to justify
disagreeing with the interviewer's formulation of the co-
interviewee's criticism. So Williams' answer may be heard to invoke
specific cases *designed to rebut* the critic's ascription of Pentagon
motives to restrict press coverage of the war.

By way of summary, some ways of 'doing criticism' include:
presenting readings of future events or political scenarios which
challenge the interviewee's position, or design a background context
of facts, descriptions, and prior statements to suggest an oppositional
viewpoint, or formulate others' criticisms as a way to call for an
account. The interviewee, in turn, can draw on techniques for 'doing
justification': substituting preferred interpretations, or invoking
another's credibility to support an interpretation, or resisting critical
implications of an undesired scenario by invoking higher principles,
or by attempting a refutation through counter-examples. Various
contextual materials can be drawn upon to implicate criticisms or to
justify disagreeing in the course of asking a question or answering.

Accounting for Concessions

Interviewees are sometimes faced with the prospect of having to
agree with or concede to a blameworthy event, fact, or possibility
brought forward by the interviewer. However, rarely is the matter
left at that; instead the interviewee proceeds to account for the
critical incident by placing it into a context to better explain,
defend, or mitigate the negative implication of the concession. For
instance:

5   (*MacNeil/Lehrer Newshour*), PBS, with Louis Sullivan, Secretary of
Health and Human Services, and Dr Tuckson, Director of the
March of Dimes)

Tuckson: . . . Dr Sullivan whose personal commitment to this I am completely comfortable with his staff put together a report some six eight months ago that described how we might be able to sa:ve at least ten thousand of the forty thousand babies that we lose in this country every year, that report has yet to be acted on by the superiors <u>above</u> Dr Sullivan, in the months that that report has taken hundreds of babies have died <u>unnecessarily</u> that is an absolute outrage

MacNeil: Let's ask <u>Dr</u> Sullivan about that, what's happened to that report Dr Sullivan?

Sullivan: Yes let me say that ah that report ah is still ah under review:: the reason ah it was not ahm issued earlier was the fact that there were some <u>really</u> very legitimate questions about the effectiveness of some of the proposals in that, so it was actually dela:yed to get more information.

The interviewer, MacNeil, asks Dr Sullivan about the co-interviewee, Dr Tuckson's criticism. Notice that Dr Tuckson provides a *strong formulation* of the problematic state-of-affairs, 'hundreds of babies have died <u>unnecessarily</u> that is an absolute outrage.' The force of the blame, however, is not directed at Dr Sullivan, but at Sullivan's superiors in the Bush administration.

Notice the *differing formulations* of the problematic: (a) Tuckson claims 'that report has yet to be acted on by the superiors *above* Dr Sullivan, in the months that that report has taken . . .' (b) while MacNeil makes relevant from Tuckson's comment, 'that report,' as an account-seeking device, and (c) Sullivan draws on an administrative discourse, 'that report ah is still ah under review::'. Tuckson's formulation ascribes implicit blame to the actors involved ('superiors above Dr Sullivan'), cites the length of the delay ('months'), and links this delay to the causal consequences of the death of hundreds of babies.

Dr Sullivan's response makes relevant his identity as a member of the administration by not distinguishing himself from his superiors. That is, he gives an account for the Bush administration, even though Tuckson explicitly exempted him from the criticism. Sullivan explains the administration's delay by citing concerns that there were 'some really very legitimate questions' about the report and the need for 'more information.' To offer an account for such a serious problematic condition ('hundreds of babies have died <u>unnecessarily</u>') requires a correspondingly strong defense. Sullivan explains the obstacle in issuing the plan as 'some <u>really</u> very legitimate questions,' what Pomerantz (1986) identifies as 'extreme case formulations.'

A commonplace way to concede to a criticism while explaining is by the formulaic, 'Yes, but [account].' The concession, 'yes' or its substitutes, occurs initially in the response (as in transcript 5, 'Yes let me say that ah that report ah is still ah under review:: . . .'). Given that the concession may be politically damaging, respondents may instead *embed* their concession within the answer, rather than exposing it initially in the response. An instance of an *embedded concession* is seen in the following.

6   (*This Week with David Brinkley*, ABC, with Dick Cheney, US
     Secretary of Defense)

Will: The ambassador to the UN from Iraq said this morning and
           others have said there's a <u>hidden</u>:? ↓ barely hidden any more
           US agenda=and that has to do with reducing the arsenal .hh
           and perhaps the prestige of Saddam Hussein before we leave.
           (.) ah: given that there does seem to be an additional US
           agenda independent of the UN points with regard
           particularly to nuclear weapons the Vice President has said it
           t– that's it's unacceptable that he continue .h developing
           nuclear weapons .h doesn't that <u>ra</u>dically reduce Hussein's
           incentive to get out of Kuwait because we still have (.) ah
           demands on him after he does that.

Cheney: Well I think <u>the</u>: the point would be that that eh assume for a
           moment that he complies that he does withdraw from Kuwait
           .h that eh we are still going to be faced with eh an <u>Iraq</u> that
           has enormous military capability and has demonstrated a
           desire to develop even more nuclear weapons ballistic
           missiles etcetera .hh and that it would be important to fashion
           in the international community a set of sanctions that were
           targeted specifically on those technologies that's he trying to
           acquire to develop that capability? it would be foolish for us
           to do anything less?

→   and whether– how that might affect his response it seems to
           me is (.) eh is problematical he has to know and I think the
           world knows that we are very concerned about that capability
           and we are prepared to find diplomatic ways to deal with it if
           possible but it has to be dealt with.

Notice that Secretary Cheney does not address George Will's question directly until he constructs a context in which to present the administration's strategy as intelligible. Once he does turn to Will's question (arrow) he concedes by the gloss that it is 'problematical,' but justifies it through the higher consideration of halting Saddam's military capability. The interviewee delays directly addressing the interviewer's question in order to *provide a context* through citing facts, possible scenarios, and strategies. This context, then, provides a backdrop to mitigate the potentially damaging implications of partially conceding to the problematic.

The practice of mitigating a concession to a problematic can also be achieved by implicating one's concession (as seen in transcript 7). However, this practice is vulnerable to the interviewer's supplemental questions (Greatbatch, 1986b) making the implicit explicit.

7 (*This Week with David Brinkley*, ABC, with Mohammed Al-Mashatt, Iraq's Ambassador to the US)

Will: Let me ask Sam's question again that– ah you said you
    don't want war grant that (0.8) you said we're not acting
    on our national interest that's your opinion ↓ do you
    have any doubt, (0.8) that if you get into a war with the
    United States, and its allies, that you will be beaten?
    (0.8)

Al-Mashatt: Well you are a super-po↑wer we are a small
    country but certainly you (.) you will be you will=
        [   ]

Will: Is that a yes?

Al-Mashatt: = be (0.6) humiliated and you– it will be the beginning of
    the <u>down</u>fall of <u>A</u>merica

The interviewer, George Will, frames the initiation of his interview as repeating a previously asked question, implying thereby that it was not answered. Prior to re-asking, Will paraphrases two of Al-Mashatt's earlier statements along with an assessment of each. The point of Will's paraphrase and assessments is to address, and get out of the way, what Al-Mashatt previously has said in order to move on to Will's agenda – the Iraqi perception that they will lose a war with the US. Ambassador Al-Mashatt's response concedes to this problematic, though avoiding an explicit yes or no. Will, in pursuit of an explicit concession, overlaps Al-Mashatt with 'is that a yes' as Al-Mashatt moves from his implicit concession to another statement initiated by 'but.' The fact that Will's overlap is positioned to overlap with the word following the discourse marker, 'but,' suggests Will's recognition of the familiar accounting format: '[concession], but [account].'

Formulation of the Problematic to Account For

Given the ongoing controversies of issues in the news, interviewees may anticipate and prepare for criticisms from the interviewer. A technique to manage criticism is for the interviewee to take pre-emptive actions[1] to formulate the problematic *prior to a question about it* and then *proceed to account for it*. Such formulating of the problematic allows the interviewee to display awareness of the issues, the concerns of opponents, and as a consequence, possibly preclude

the interviewer from raising that criticism. An anticipatory formulation of the problematic and account for it is seen in the following.

> **8** (*MacNeil/Lehrer Newshour*, PBS, with Pete Williams, Pentagon
> spokesman)
> *Williams*: . . . second thing eh the second I guess aspect of
> the operation over there right now: that's received
> →¹ some criticism is eh the fact that <u>right now</u> we
> deployed reporters out to where the combat's taking place
> →² in <u>poo</u>ls: (.) and the criticism before this all started was we
> wouldn't put the pools in place in time to see anything
> ha↑<u>ppen</u> (.) uh we've had pools in place on the ah aircraft
> carrier Kennedy the pools that were there: I heard one
> reporter say last night on CNN that they heard <u>ten</u> hours
> before the operation was going to start exactly what was
> going to happen=so they were there they could watch it all
> unfold (.) uh we had reporters on the battleship that fired
> the first cruise missiles so there were reporters there to see
> that we had pools of reporters in the airbases to watch the
> first airplanes take off . . .

Here Pete Williams formulates the criticism made of the Pentagon
policy regarding the restrictions of journalistic pools. Notice how
Williams' formulation is accomplished: he begins by offering the
frame for the problematic by the mitigated description, 'some
criticism' (arrow 1), and the contrastive, 'the criticism before this all
started was' (arrow 2), the implied contrast being between what was
said 'before' and what is really happening 'now.' This *contrast* is
achieved in Williams' account through listing *counter-examples* to the
criticism; that is, specific instances of reporters in pools being in place
to witness the action.

The following transcript contains another instance of the interviewee formulating the problematic and then accounting for it.

> **9** (*Nightline*, ABC, with Tariq Aziz, Iraq's Foreign Minister)
> *Aziz*: . . . the President and Secretary said that my impression is that
> they have ah (.) ah: mis– ah perception a wrong perception
> about the position of of Iraq? (.) they have both said that ah that
> Iraq eh might not be aware of of what's going <u>on</u>, eh that Iraq
> might not be aware of the meaning of the (   ) UN resolution
> that Iraq might not be aware of the meaning of the deployment
> of <u>forces</u> (.) in the– the region I would like to comment on that
> → that we:: kn<u>o</u>::w everything we know all: the facts and we
> → are prepared for all expectations so eh (.) the President is going
> to con<u>fine</u> this meeting with me by telling me those things I
> think that it's not going to be a very (.) useful eh meeting . . .

Here Minister Aziz initiates the formulation of the problematic by citing *who* is making the criticism, that is, 'the President and the Secretary.' This referencing of the authors of the criticism is also evident in Williams' formulation transcript 8 in which the press is implied to be making the 'criticism.' In addition to indicating its authors, Aziz moves to formulate the criticism or problematic. Like Williams in transcript 8, upon completion of the formulation, Aziz moves to a rebuttal of it through a justificatory account (arrows). So there appear to be four elements sequentially structured to do this accounting work: (1) reference the author(s) of the problematic/criticism, (2) formulate the problematic/criticism, (3) rebut the formulation along with (4) a justificatory account.

These pre-emptive accounting actions of formulating the problematic prior to being asked about it may be compared to Atkinson and Drew's (1979) finding that defendants in the courtroom at times offer justifications or excuses prior to being directly accused by counsel. Even more than the pre-emptive function, this allows the interviewee to frame the problematic event.

Interviewees' formulations of the problematic will be designed so that their account can defend, explain or answer the criticism. Complex problematic issues can be formulated, described, and accounted for in multiple ways. While this technique of anticipating a criticism through a formulation of the problematic and then accounting for it has the advantage of framing the issue, it is nonetheless open to further challenge from interviewer and co-interviewees alike.

Accounts for Not Answering the Question
It is not uncommon for interviewers to ask difficult questions which interviewees may not wish to answer. Given the broadcast interview format, interviewees seldom brush aside questions with a 'no comment' response. But there are various interactional solutions to this problematic for the interviewee, such as give a vague answer (Jucker, 1986) reformulate the question to be answered (Clayman, in press), or give minimal attention to the question and then shift to a desired agenda (Greatbatch, 1986a). Even given these answering strategies, in some cases the interviewee may be unwilling or unable to answer the question. In such cases, accounts may be used to explain or justify not answering the question.

In the following we see an instance of not wanting to answer:

10 (*As It Happens*, CBC, interviewing Joe Clarke, Canadian External Affairs Minister)

IR: One:: of the suggestions that I think you put raised in the letter correct me if I'm wrong? is that Saddam must be convinced that his survival is not ti:ed to withdrawal from Kuwait is that right?

> *Clarke*:   Yeah I don't want to get into the:: ehm (.) ah: what
> specifically was: was in the letter=
>   [
> *IR*:   >All right<
> *Clarke*:   =I don't think there's– there's a lot of ah point to that .h but
> I've made the point be<u>fore</u> that . . .

Here Joe Clarke declines to answer questions about the letter which he justifies by the account, 'I don't think there's– there's a lot of ah point to that.' Clarke then proceeds to provide a lengthy answer (not shown here) which addresses the interviewer's formulation of the issue of Saddam's survival and withdrawing from Kuwait. Consider Clarke's movement in his reply: he draws a contrast between 'what specifically was in the letter' (namely, that which he does not want to discuss) to 'I've made the point before' (which he is willing to discuss and indeed provides the entree into his lengthy answer about political strategy in dealing with Saddam).

Clarke's account itself is minimally informative. But notice that the interviewer accepts Clarke's refusal to address the letter *prior to* Clarke's account. The interviewer's ready acceptance of Clarke's declining reflects the interviewer's recognition of what might be called the taken-for-granted justified need for diplomatic secrecy.

In the following, the interviewee offers an account of being *unable* to answer the question (arrows).

> **11**   (*Nightline*, ABC, with Tariq Aziz, Iraq's Foreign Minister)
> *Koppel*:   Do you have idea how many foreign nationals we are talking
> about altogether speaking now only of those in Iraq not for
> the moment those in Kuwait
> (1.2)
> → *Aziz*:   Well ah: (.) unfortunately I certainly don't have
> →   the ah figure anymore (   )
> *Koppel*:   Maybe you could be a little bit more precise ah I'm sure you
> can understand the families and loved ones who are of those
> that are <u>waiting</u> <u>for</u>: ah (.) their families to come <u>out</u> of Iraq
> ah are concerned by what is <u>meant</u> when you say a few days,
> do you mean less than a week? less than two weeks
> (1.2)
> → *Aziz*:   Well I don't know I cannot say how many weeks but ah it
> →   won't be a long time they should not be worried eh: eh their
> loved ones will be eh ho:me very soon

Here Minister Aziz responds to Ted Koppel's query with excusing accounts for being unable to answer his questions. There is an important difference in the folk logic of inability in contrast to unwillingness in the accounting for not answering (Drew, 1984;

Heritage, 1988). It is the difference in portraying action between what the actor can (or cannot) do versus what the actor wants (or does not want) to do.

Notice that Koppel follows up to Aziz's initial account for not answering with a mild rebuke, 'Maybe you could be a little bit more precise.' Koppel's follow up may be heard as challenging Aziz's avowed inability to answer and implicating that this is really an unwillingness.

Other accounting techniques for not answering involve challenging the question, or a portion of it. For instance, in the following transcript the interviewee calls into question the interviewer's use of 'rhetoric.'

12 (*This Week with David Brinkley*, ABC, with Mohammed Al-
   Mashatt, Iraq's Ambassador to the US)
Donalson: Mister Ambassador we hear a lot of rhetoric these days
        from you:: and other Iraqi officials (0.7) about eh (.)
        preparations for the <u>mother of battles</u>, and that the
        <u>batt</u>lefields will be turned to ashes but you don't really
        think that Iraq can wi↑n a wa:r with the United States do
        you? and it may not even sur↑vive a war.
Al-Mashatt: .Hh Well first of all we don't want a war=I me:an this
        rhetoric=so-called rhetoric ca:me as a response to your
        threat and your ah assembling of massive <u>o</u>ffensive
        forces . . .

Compare Sam Donalson's formulation of background context, 'we hear a lot of rhetoric these days from you:: and other Iraqi officials,' to Al-Mashatt's reply, 'this rhetoric=so-called rhetoric.' To use the same descriptive term as one's interlocutor, and to preface it with the locution 'so-called,' is a technique to challenge or question the validity of that descriptor. More importantly, Al-Mashatt is not only challenging the description, 'rhetoric,' but is also claiming that the Iraqi actions came about 'as a response' to the US 'threat,' instead of initiating the present conflict.

In the following case, the term 'holy war' is contested. Notice that the interviewer prefaces holy war by the location 'so-called' (arrow). This allows the interviewer to raise a controversial issue and attribute to some unidentified others. The use of 'so-called' prior to a term *marks* it as controversial and possibly problematical.

13 (*As It Happens*, CBC, with Imam Gad, Canadian-Muslim religious
   leader)
IR: .Hhh Imam there's been a call by Saddam Hussein for a a
→   <u>jihad</u> a so-called <u>holy</u> war: has that had any impact on the
        Muslim community in Canada

Gad: Well ah first of all if I may make some simple remark that holy
war there is no such holy war either in Islam or Christianity it
should be either a just war or unjust war ah the holy war there's
only a holy pe::ace

In both transcripts 12 and 13 the move of challenging the descriptive
term is *positioned initially* in the interviewee's turn. This sequential
positioning of the challenge to the term allows the interviewee to
resist answering the question, at least in its original format, and
thereby shifts the ground of the accountability called for through the
question.

Conclusion

A most striking fact about the broadcast news interview context is
that an interviewee's answers and accounts are heard and evaluated
by a mass audience. Interviewees are very concerned with the
perception and effectiveness of their accounts. In practically no other
setting is a person's answers to questions and defenses against
criticisms observed by such a large audience and scrutinized so
closely. One consequence of the mass audience and interviewee's
preparation is that there are noticeably fewer excuses used to account
in this context. Of the transcripts presented in this chapter only two
are recognizably excuses (see transcript 5 and 11). Given the
interviewee's anticipation of questions and criticisms, ways can be
prepared to avoid conceding to criticisms. Respondents can use
various techniques to avoid conceding to blame, such as: pre-emptive
actions of formulating the problematic to account for, substituting a
preferred interpretation of events, citing counter-examples as rebuttal, challenging the interviewer's descriptive terms, and so on. Of
course to be coherent, prepared statements need to be fitted into the
on-going interaction – need to be made relevant to the contingencies
of the talk.

Our analysis has concentrated on the production and organization
of the criticisms implicated in the course of interviewers' questions
and the accounts offered in interviewees' answers. But in this final
section consider what happens in the slot or turn *following* an
interviewee's prepared account? Given the news-interview norm of
journalistic neutrality, the interviewer is constrained from overtly
evaluating the interviewee's answer as acceptable, believable, sufficient, or not. Following the interviewee's answer, the interviewer
may move on to the next question, thereby implicating an acceptance
of that answer. But when the interviewee's account appears insufficient or in need of further explanation, then the journalist may press
the issue with supplemental, or follow-up, questions (Greatbatch,

1986b). While journalists are constrained to the ground rules of asking questions, as already seen, this does not prevent them from citing conflicting facts, competing descriptions, or attributing claims to others which challenge or criticize the interviewee's position. So while the journalist's response to the interviewee's account needs to be fitted into a question format, this does not preclude the journalist from further assessing or challenging the interviewee.

One technique for challenging accounts is to formulate a portion of an answer in a critical light thereby making relevant a further account from the interviewee on that issue. In the following transcript the interviewer, Sam Donalson, uses this technique to follow up on an answer by Dick Cheney (examined previously, see transcript 2). Donalson begins with the locution, 'so you – you're really are saying,' as a way to mark that his formulation is a reading, so to speak, 'beneath the surface' of Cheney's answer. Notice that Donalson's formulation of the administration's political strategy would not be acceptable to Cheney; indeed, this formulation may be heard as ridicule or criticism.

14 (*This Week with David Brinkley*, ABC, with Dick Cheney, US Secretary of Defense)

Cheney:	. . . tho::se indee:d are not eh subjects we can compromise on we're not going to let him keep <u>part</u> of the hostages or keep part of Kuwait that would be unacceptable
	[ ]
Donalson:	So–
→¹	so you– you're really are saying to us that (1.4) the
→¹	White House feared that Saddam Hussein did not believe
→¹	George Bush long distance (.) but that if a Bush embassary
→¹	come– comes and says the same thing: he might believe
	him, (.) but the embassy is not empowered to negotiate? to
	change a jot or a tittle, of US foreign policy to suggest that
	maybe a de::al down the line could be made?
Cheney:	On those basic fundamental conditions (.) that eh the
→²	United Nations has endorsed and they're at the heart of
→²	US objectives in the area (.) uhm Jim will not be
→²	going to negotiate, we will be going specifically to
→²	make it clear that the President's deadly serious
→³ Donalson:	How do you make that clear=
Cheney:	=Well I think I think Secretary
	[ ]
Donalson:	( ) how does
→⁴	sitting across the table make it clear (.) by the
	fierce look in his ey::es=
	[ ]

Cheney:	I have
Donalson:	[By pounding the table? I mean how do you do it
	=[ ]
Cheney:	[I have
Cheney:	I have kno:wn: ah Jim Baker a: for many years I know him to be a man eh who's extremely persuasive we've just seen him put together a tremendous diplomatic victory in the United Nations Security Council vote, .h and I'm confident that he can conve:y in no uncertain terms to Saddam Hussein the President's wishes and desires

Cheney's answer (arrows 2) does not account for the critical point of Donalson's prior formulation (arrows 1) regarding Baker's message 'long distance' versus 'face-to-face.' Given that interviewers can raise more than one issue in the course of asking their question, the interviewee can have some selection in what to address.

Donalson pursues a response for his previously asked 'long distance versus face-to-face' issue through further supplemental questions. These follow-ups are pointed by forming the questions through using Cheney's prior words 'make it clear' into 'How do you make that clear' (arrow 3) and further 'how does sitting across the table make it clear' (arrow 4). Donalson continues by making ironic descriptions ('the fierce look in his eye::s' and 'By pounding the table?') about how face-to-face negotiation could be more successful in conveying the President's message. The use of irony in forming these questions serves to cast doubt on the positions Donalson ascribes to the administration thereby making relevant a correction or explanation from Cheney.

Cheney's response avoids discussion of the specifics of how face-to-face negotiation will succeed, but instead accounts by the general claim that Secretary Baker is 'extremely persuasive' and provides an example of his abilities to support this ascription. This offering a general answer to avoid specifics is a common accounting practice, also known as 'mystification' (Scott and Lyman, 1968).

Note

1. My thanks to an anonymous reviewer for suggesting this descriptive term.

10
Conclusion: Social Accountability Practices in Contexts

> Everything we do can be redone by talk. In the course of talk our actions can be redefined and in the process are transformed. (Marsh et al., 1978: 21)

This epigram captures the spirit of what I have been attempting to do in this work: to describe and explain the power of speech in accounting for actions. The notion of social accountability has been used to cover the various specific discursive practices of blaming, questioning, justifying, explaining, and evaluating conduct in different contexts. Given that the previous empirical chapters are studies in different contexts of social accountability, what can be said about how accounts and accountability practices are shaped by context? Different contexts provide points of comparison for understanding accountability practices. The necessity, formulation, and evaluation of accounts depends on the context. So the issue of context provides a frame to look back over the work of the prior chapters.

Conceiving of Context

Context is regarded as crucial for making sense of social interaction, yet it is a little understood concept. Often context is loosely conceived as those situational features which, so to speak, 'surround' the text (or talk), and can be used by the researcher for interpretation of the text. Context is often unreflectively deemed unproblematical: simply as a 'container' for social interaction, or operationalized as a variable among other variables to be included in the explanatory equation. Not uncommonly, context serves as a kind of 'utility factor' – as a way to include those features of the setting not explicitly inscribed in the present moment of the conversation, for example, categories of persons (social identities, status), their social relationship, knowledge (shared/not shared, articulated/taken-for-granted), social situation (formal/informal; everyday/institutional), physical situation (environmental conditions) and so on. A number of such contextual factors may influence the course of the social accountability episode: who gets accused and with what amount of force, the length and structure of the accounts, and how accounts are evaluated and by what category of person. Thus the problem of an indefinitely large number of contextual conditions which conceivably could affect the talk. But which of these contextual conditions are relevant to *this* particular situated context (Heritage, 1984; Schegloff, 1987; Mandelbaum, 1990/91)?

Social Identities

One avenue to approach context is to consider the people who populate the context – what social identities persons take on and display. The concept of social identity involves the categories of persons located within the contexts: from ordinary folks (family members, couples) to those identities associated with specialized training or institutional affiliation (therapist, caseworker, policy analyst). These social identities do not determine the course of action, but they can be seen as providing members with a broad, normative range of conversational and discursive resources, such as, who asks the questions and who gives the answers, who begins and ends the encounter, who offers advice and direction, who decides that eligibility requirements are satisfied, and so on. Social identity can be approached by considering the displays and alignments a person can *make relevant* and *draw on* by virtue of that identity. For instance, the discursive resources for institutional representatives are commonly based on specialized training and familiarity with bureaucratic procedures. While this asymmetry of specialized knowledge can create an asymmetry in evaluating accountability talk, this is not invariably so as seen in the welfare interview study.

The discursive options of different social identities may be seen as both *enabling* and *constraining* conditions of that context. Enabling in the sense that through communicative choices a person reflexively presents self, displays and continually updates social identity and alignments with others. Persons participate in *co-creating* and *reproducing* social identities, and thereby context, through their ways of speaking. Communication contexts get 'talked into being' by participants.

Discursive options are also constrained in that persons, by virtue of their social identities, are limited not only by choice but by background knowledge, social norms, and institutional legitimation. Of course, an individual's actions may go beyond the bounds of normative social identities, as when a therapist–client relationship evolves into lovers. In addition, the range of ways of speaking associated with a given social identity is not always well-defined. A matching of conduct to role description is too simplistic. The norms and shared rules for which persons can be held accountable do not apply to all actors in the same ways. What is problematic, who is culpable, and with what magnitude gets interactionally worked out in different contexts and in the course of questions, criticisms, and accounts. The enactment of social identity needs to be seen as an interactional negotiation of propriety realized in communication. In the couple therapy case, Jenny at one point uses therapy jargon which leads the therapist to tease her about psychoanalysis. The therapist's move may be seen as a gentle criticism designed to prevent the formation of a coalition between him and Jenny, thereby isolating her relational partner, Larry (Sluzki, 1990). The therapist maintains his therapeutic positioning by refusing to reciprocate with therapy jargon and siding with Jenny, but instead, attempts to position himself as neutral.

The point here is that conversational and discursive options are both enabled and constrained by the social identities adopted by participants in context. As seen in the couple therapy study, relational partners tell their problems to the therapist. Problem tellings are not neutral descriptions of their interpersonal relationships, but ways to present relationships which implicitly ascribe responsibility, criticize, or offer accounts. Given that the therapist is initially a virtual stranger, the clients must offer more background descriptions in their tellings to make their desired interpretations understandable and convincing. The clients, especially Jenny, orient to the therapist as an 'expert' or 'authority' of interpersonal relations. This orienting is displayed through the couple's following the therapist's questions and topic shifts, as well as deferring to his suggestions and conversational overlaps.

In the broadcast news interviews study, the interviewer accomplishes this identity through various discursive options: by the initiation and termination of the interview, by asking questions and supplemental questions, by displays of neutrality about controversial issues, and the like. When interviewers fail to enact these characteristic discourse patterns, they may be heard to be no longer doing an interview, but enter into some other communication event. For example, the George Bush–Dan Rather exchange during the 1988 US Presidential campaign may be seen as going beyond a conventional interview format into a conflict episode (Clayman and Whalen, 1988/89). There are a range of ways in which individuals can achieve 'doing being' (Wieder and Pratt, 1990) a recognizable social identity – a news interviewer, a Zen teacher, a welfare caseworker, a relational partner. Some identities are more constrained and narrower than others in the range of conversational and discursive options. But each *identity must be performed* – continually *updated* and *enacted* through communication.

As seen from conversation analysis, accounts become conditionally relevant as a response to prior questioning, but to respond one must make relevant what dimensions of the problematic to account for. In forming an account an actor can draw on various *contextual resources*: the interlocutor's or actor's formulation of the event, shared background knowledge, or unknown or unappreciated features to construct the actor's preferred version of events.

The making relevant features of the event to be accounted for reflexively projects the *actor's positioning vis-à-vis other* – as serious, ironic, conciliatory, and the like. Such framing moves are commonly expressed through nonverbal or paralingual cues. These cues also can serve as *displays of affect* in doing accountability – as angry, depressed, sad, aggravated and so on. As already shown, many accountability episodes become emotionally charged and actors use affect to do blaming and accounting. Affect displays, avowals, or ascriptions are powerful constituent features of self-presentation and claiming a person's positioning in a situated context.

An individual's performance not only reflects social identity, but also displays more specific features of that identity: as a tough or easy interviewer, as a cooperative or difficult interviewee. For instance in the news interview study, Sam Donalson's refusal to accept the administration's standard policy statement from Secretary of Defense, Dick Cheney, his raising contradictory evidence, his supplemental questions overlapping with Cheney's answers, in short, his pursuit of a straight answer to tough questions is reflexive of Donalson what may be glossed as an aggressive, or challenging interviewer. Contrast Donalson's performance with the news interviewer who routinely readily accepts a policymaker's answers and forgoes further supplemental questions. Notice how our hearing an interviewer as being tough or easy, aggressive or docile is at least in part due to the interviewee's accountability practices: attributing critical descriptions, raising conflicting evidence or points-of-view, asking tough questions, pursuing avoided questions, and the like.

The social identities persons enact reflect their recognition of the situated context. The context itself may be seen differently by different persons given their respective positionings. For instance, in the prior study of a welfare interview, the applicant draws on a rhetoric of personal need while the caseworker faces the strain of helping the applicant as well as following institutional procedures. By virtue of the positionings of their social identities, the applicant and caseworker see the interview context differently. This ratio of social identities to discursive options to context appears more cohesive in other cases. In the Zen study, the exchange between the advanced student and the teacher reflects a mutual recognition of the communication event of *Dharma* combat. Indeed, one of the main ways to recognize students as advanced is through their performance of giving a good answer and defending against the teacher's challenge. Compare to the less-advanced students whose answers were criticized as too intellectual or as imitations. The point here is that the relation between social identity and context is *reflexive* – each is evaluated in terms of the other and such enactments get realized in communication.

The Logics of Contexts

Contexts are comprised of a cast of characters taking on certain social identities which are expressed through their discourse options. But these discourse options reflect and enact, not only social identities, but also a logic of action – what has been called a folk logic.

Accountability practices invoke a cultural system of moral and practical beliefs, norms, and ideologies beyond the talk itself designed to warrant the actor's claims. This cultural system provides members with a logic for action, that is, the social rules and normative order concerning what is right, moral, or at least acceptable. This folk logic gets invoked through the actor's discursive practices of blames and accounts. Taking accounts *as practices* points to the speech actions, moves, and discourses through which the social significance of events are interactionally constructed through talk. Typically folk logic is not articulated in propositional form, rather it is implicit or at a taken-for-granted assumptive level. Through accountability practices, persons attempt to make relevant a folk logic to the situated context in order to warrant their particular claims to good character and relational alignments.

The analysis of folk logic can reveal context in two ways: by making explicit what is implicit, by specifying the implicated assumptions behind what is said. Secondly, by examining how the folk logics are made relevant to *this* situation – how the folk logic gets interactionally invoked, evaluated and negotiated. Contexts are constructed and recreated through the instantiation of certain logics of doing and being. For instance, *Dharma* combat gets recreated as a recognizable communication event, not simply due to Zen prescriptions and proscriptions, but because of participants' production of Zen ways of speaking. The Zen teacher's challenges, questioning, and critical assessments of students' answers work to uphold, and thereby reproduce, a Zen discourse. The same could be said about each of the contexts previously examined: persons display recognition of and orientation to context through the logic of their communicative actions.

Consider the not uncommon situation of two (or more) persons avowing competing accounts based on different folk logics for the 'same' event. How are these folk logics invoked through blames and accounts, and how are conflicting logics interactionally negotiated and evaluated? In the study of couple therapy, Jenny criticized Larry for a lack of openness in their relationship based on a folk logic of deficiency (that is, intimate relationships should be based on open and meaningful talk, but he does not share this with her). Jenny makes this folk logic relevant through descriptions of their problematic relationship which is portrayed as primarily due to Larry. He responds by partially conceding to this criticism, but also offering an account which draws on a folk logic of balance: he may not talk enough about problems, but she talks too much about them, so 'the balance between them is about right.' As this episode unfolds, the therapist accepts neither Jenny's nor Larry's accountings, but instead he attempts to reframe the couple's situation by proposing that they are involved in a relational 'ritual.' The therapist's assessments and ascriptions draw on the specialized logic of therapy.

In institutional contexts, codes, norms, procedures, rules of interpretation, and inference-making can become highly specialized and require years of training and expertise. Folk logic needs to be distinguished from these specialized logics. No attempt is being made to privilege the specialized logic, say of the therapist, over the couple's folk logics, but only to observe that these sometimes diverge and can be at odds. We need to examine how these logics are invoked through accountability practices in the situated context. The notion of practice provides a useful analytic device for examining how differing logics can be aligned/misaligned in situations, rather than assuming that the specialized logics invariably will be dominant. For instance, in the therapy episode, Jenny uses a folk logic of deficiency, Larry responds with a balance logic, and the therapist attempts to reframe both of these by a logic of relational ritual. Each of these logics represents an attempt by the participants to *construct* a way to interpret the couple's situation as well as implications for future actions. In the therapy episode examined in chapter 5, there is no clean resolution. Looking at the entire therapy consultation (see Sluzki, 1990), there is a negotiation of meanings through accountability practices and a further development of the respective logics, particularly on the part of the therapist.

A tension between a folk logic and a specialized logic is evident in the welfare interview study. The applicant draws on a folk logic of personal needs, while the caseworker invokes the logic of institutional procedures. While there is an asymmetry of specialized knowledge of bureaucratic rules, there is not a rigid suppression of the applicant's folk logic by the institutional logic. The applicant seems able to challenge the caseworker's claim to follow institutional procedures and justify her need for welfare assistance. My point is that negotiating and coordinating diverging logics is more complex than simply applying a general rule to a particular situation. Rules apply to different people in different ways. Using rules in the service of challenges, directives, explanations, and justifications constitutes an accountability practice for how such episodes get negotiated and aligned.

So, then, context may be conceived of as multiple levels of meanings which actors may draw on and make relevant in the course of accountability practices. Whatever aspect of context matters, it must be shown, displayed, or in some way publicly available to interlocutors. Context is not simply a container or another variable to be added to the equation, but a constituent feature of the social interaction.

Facts, Accounts, and Contexts

The social constructionist approach to accounts begins with the premise that human actions, social relations, and states-of-affairs are not invariably self-explanatory, or may be seen by others as problematic, so actors may need to tell their version of events – to account for them. Persons are self-interpreting creatures of their own and others' conduct. This social-construction-of-realities-through-accounts thesis is epitomized in the epigram of this chapter.

The accounts literature has been criticized in some quarters for overemphasizing the ability of accounts to transform or change the meanings of problematic events, especially for serious incidents (Shields, 1979). It is argued that as the severity of the problematic event increases, the efficacy of accounts decreases (Semin and Manstead, 1983). For larger misdeeds, accounts are evaluated, not merely as an expression of remorse or goodwill on the part of the offender, but as a representation of 'what really happened.' There may be external realities, constraints, or rules which limit the effectiveness of accounts. In institutional settings, such as court-rooms, a defendant's accounts are scrutinized and cross-examined. Prosecutors commonly bring forth evidence to challenge or cast doubt on a defendant's accounts. Such 'reality constraints' (Schlen-ker, 1980) appear to limit the capability of accounts to transform discrediting meanings and mitigate accusations.

There is some validity to this criticism of overestimating the power of accounts for change – the real world enters in to sober the exuberance of the actor's accounts. But this should not lead us to throw out the baby with the bathwater. The core conception of the social constructionist view of accounts remains: the social meanings and evaluations of human actions are not 'given' as brute facts, but are discursive, negotiable, socially accountable practices.

One way to read the above criticism is that it is based on the false dichotomy between 'the facts' of the case ('what really happened') and the actor's accounts. On this view, accounts are seen, at best, as mere excuses, pretexts, or rationalizations, and at worst, as fabrications.[1] While inauthentic accounts occur (all too often), on a more theoretically interesting level, the facts and accounts cannot be so readily distinguished (Edwards and Potter, 1992: 104–7). The facts do *not* 'speak for themselves' – they must be seen as part of some telling of events, narrative framework, or construction of a context to see the event. Reports or narratives are communicative activities commonly found in the course of accounts. The point here is that factual observations can be used as part of a reconstruction of events and provide part of the social accountability for the event.

The very notion of a fact itself can be problematic. If a fact is taken as an observation statement which corresponds to the state of the world, then this is not as transparent as it may seem, particularly in the domain of human action or 'social facts.' Even when persons agree on the facts of a case, this does not adjudicate what the appropriate course of action should be. Looking back at the prior accounts studies, persons can be seen to establish the facts of what happened through their accountability practices. In the welfare interview a number of facts are presented by the client: the wife has been to court, her husband did not appear in court and will not surrender the checks, her appeal for assistance has been rejected by social security, she is physically ill, and so on. The client and caseworker do not disagree over the facts, but over the consequences of those facts for future action. The client draws on those facts to justify welfare assistance, while the caseworker takes the facts of the case, at least provisionally, within the context of following institutional procedures.

In other cases the *significance* of the facts may be in dispute. In the study of news interviews, Cokie Roberts prefaces her question by listing a number of facts as a criticism of Iraq's policy. However, the Iraqi ambassador, Mohammed Al-Mashatt, does not disagree with those facts but with their significance. His account criticizes the US policy as 'intimidation and threat.' Agreement on the facts does not preclude disagreement over their significance, because the facts require some interpretative framework, some context, indeed some account to make sense of what is happening.

In still other cases the *occurrence* of the facts may be in dispute. In the couple therapy study, Larry reported that Jenny 'overdid the talk about problems.' She disagreed with this claim and attempted to establish that she does not 'overtalk about problems' through comparing herself to other people she knows in similar contexts. Looking back over the accounts studies, there are surprisingly very few instances of disagreement over 'what happened' – the occurrence of certain facts. The disagreements in these case studies come from how these facts are interpreted in terms of their significance and consequences, in short, how the facts are accounted for in context.

Another kind of case is one in which auditors can independently observe the facts of the case as well as hear the accounts offered by the participants. For example, recent courtcases played videotape recordings to the jury of the defendant in the act of committing a crime, the videotapes of the Rodney King incident in Los Angeles or Washington DC Mayor, Marion Barry, using cocaine. But even in such cases, ascriptions of what happened and how it happened are still necessary to identify and understand the event at issue (recall Hart's hypothetical example of the seven pleas that can be made for hitting another, chapter 1). It is a fact that police officers repeatedly kicked Rodney King while he was prone on the ground, and Marion Barry snorted cocaine, but the circumstances under which these actions were committed, as constructed by the defense, were seen by the jury as mitigating conditions for the defendant's responsibility. In other words, the defense created a context for the jury to see these videotaped events consistent with their accounts – the defendants were able to 'position' themselves so as to modify the incident (Cobb, 1992).[2]

The general point here is that the facts and accounts are not different in kind; they are each linguistic reconstructions of events. I am not arguing for relativism here and claiming that all accounts are of equal merit. But instead of looking to the epistemological status of factual statements versus accounts statements, attention should be given to how each of these statements are used, evaluated and interactionally negotiated. A hard and fast distinction between the facts and accounts will not hold, because the facts themselves can be contestable, and even when there is consensus, persons may disagree over their significance or implications for action. To be meaningful, the facts have to be interpreted within some context which gets created through a report, narrative, or account.

Conclusion

This work offers no grand theory of accounts, but instead focuses on the 'local' work, in Geertz's sense (1983) of constructing accounts in contexts. As argued in chapter 2, it seems fanciful to posit some underlying monistic principle to explain the multiplicity of ways of doing accounts. To study accounts as embodied in talk, at street level rather than from a distance, requires analytic concepts and methods attuned to what persons are doing with words, their discursive practices. In examining accounts talk, I have attempted the beginnings of a synthesis between conversation analysis and social constructionism. Accounting is taken as the discursive practice of invoking a folk logic, of offering an interpretation, a context for others to see a problematic event. How episodes of social accountability unfold and get interactionally resolved depends on interlocutors' moment-by-moment understandings, displays and assessments. The consequences of accounts talk in interpersonal relations can affect one's claims to good character or alignments with others, and in institutional contexts can affect one's success or competencies in specialized interviews.

To end, let me touch on a context of accounting implicit throughout this work (perhaps more precisely a meta-context), that of *writing accounts*. A few years back while completing an earlier review of the accounts literature (Buttny, 1993), some empiricist-minded colleagues sent me a pre-print of their own review of this 'same' accounts literature. What astounded me was that these two reviews, each completed around the same time, could not have been more different. My review emphasized the interpretative work from Goffman, Scott and Lyman, and recent work on rules theory and conversation analysis, while theirs read social psychological research as support for their own accounts model. Such disparity of findings, directions of importance, and even what to read, throws into bold relief how a corpus of literature gets shaped according to the writer's commitments and assumptions (Tracy, 1988). The writer does not merely report 'what we know,' but instead gives direction to a literature by interpreting its significance and framing it as part of a narrative.

This, of course, should come as no surprise given the recent upsurge in critical reflection on how social texts get written (Clifford and Marcus, 1986; Simons, 1989; Hunter, 1990; Brown, 1992). The various articles, book chapters, and monographs on accounts themselves need to be seen as rhetorical constructions, as an accounting for accounts. One wonders, what aspect(s) of accounts phenomena does the researcher make relevant and attend to, and what gets ignored or backgrounded? How are the accounts under study transformed from their use in a situated context to their final form in another situated context – the document that appears in print? What is the shape of the phenomena as re-presented in the scholarly text? The answer to these is largely driven by the researcher's theoretical and methodological commitments. So, the issue of reflexivity applies, not only to everyday actors in contexts of accountability, but also to the writer's accounting for accounts in print.

Notes

1. A former colleague once claimed that she never gives accounts such as excuses to her students. While I find such self-reports incredulous as an accurate description of her behavior, her avowals are more interesting as a commentary on our folk logic of appropriate discourse for classroom contexts. Excuses are commonly seen as inappropriate speech practices, especially for those of higher status positions.
2. For an insightful critical discourse analytic approach to the Rodney King case, see Cobb (1992).

Appendix

The transcription system used here is adapted from the Gail Jefferson system.

[   ]   Marks overlapping utterances. For example:

           A: Why don't you come up and see me sometimes.

                                                       [   ]
           B: I would like to.

=   Marks when there is no interval between adjacent utterances. For example:

           A: You don't have one this week?=
           B: =No

(0.0)   Intervals within and between utterances timed to tenths of a second. For example:

           S: Makes a big difference in what?
               (1.6)
           W: Well first things first

(.)   A short untimed pause within and between utterances. For example:

           M: I just know (.) I (.) I know I just have the feeling

:   Marks the extension of the sound or syllable it follows; the more colons the longer the sound stretch. For example:

           T: You are involved in a:: in a: very particular ritual.

?   Marks a rising inflection. For example:

           F: I know you're pissed but? (0.9) I have to do it.

–   Marks a halting, abrupt cutoff. For example:

           B: Just pres– (1.5) uh
           K: Pressure to be with somebody

↑   Marks a rising shift in intonation. For example:

           F: In the sp↑ring I'm gonna have my car up here

↓   Marks a falling shift in intonation. For example:

           F: I understand we'll– ↓we'll go another ti:me.

<u>word</u>	Emphasis is marked by underlining. For example:
	F: Oh <u>come on</u> don't be pissed.
WORD	Capital letters indicate that the passage is spoken louder than surrounding talk. For example:
	F: ( ) you know (.) SHE NEVER WROTE ME LAST YEAR SO you know
* *	Marks a passage that is quieter than surrounding talk. For example:
	W: It's too: ear:ly to talk about (.) *this kind of thing*
> <	Marks an utterance delivered at a quicker pace than surrounding talk. For example:
	W: Uhm again back to th– >you know what I said originally I think ya know< just this inability
hhh	Audible outbreaths including laughter. For example:
	H: I think the balance between us is (0.5) ah: about right hhhhh
	[ ]
	T: Um huh
.hhh	Audible inhalations. For example:
	S: Like you're going to go looking for someone else?
	(1.4)
	W: .hh
	(9.4)
	W: I mean (1.7) first of all it's very difficult
( )	Transcriptionist doubt. For example:
	M: (as if I'm sick) ( ) I'm de<u>pressed</u>
(( ))	Scenic details or description. For example:
	S: How's your pract– ((clears throat)) how's your practice progressing

References

Adams, J.C. (1985) An explication and presentation of an expanded typology of forensic stases for use in the study and practice of interpersonal conflict. In C.W. Kneupper (ed.), *Oldspeak/Newspeak: Rhetorical Transformations*, pp. 227–40. Arlington, TX: Rhetorical Society of America.

Addelson, K.P. (1990) Why philosophers should become sociologists (and vice versa). In H.S. Becker and M.M. McCall (eds), *Symbolic Interaction and Cultural Studies*, pp. 119–47. Chicago: University of Chicago Press.

Anscombe, E. (1960) *Intention*. Oxford: Basil Blackwell.

Antaki, C. (1987) Performed and unperformable: a guide to accounts of relationships. In R. Burnett, P. McGhee and D. Clarke (eds), *Accounting for Relationships: Explanation, Representation and Knowledge*, pp. 97–113. New York: Methuen.

Antaki, C. (1988) Explanations, communication and social cognition. In C. Antaki (ed.), *Analysing Everyday Explanation: A Casebook of Methods*, pp. 1–14. London: Sage.

Antaki, C. (1990) Explaining events or explaining oneself? In M.J. Cody and M.L. McLaughlin (eds), *The Psychology of Tactical Communication*, pp. 268–82. Philadelphia: Multilingual Matters.

Atkinson, J.M. and Drew, P. (1979) *Order in the Court: The Organization of Verbal Interaction in Judicial Settings*. Atlantic Highlands, NJ: Humanities Press.

Atkinson, P. (1988) Ethnomethodology: a critical review. *Annual Review of Sociology*, 14: 441–65.

Austin, J.L. (1961) A plea for excuses. In *Philosophical Papers*, 2nd edn, pp. 175–204. Oxford: Oxford University Press.

Austin, J.L. (1962) *How to do Things with Words*, 2nd edn, J.O. Urmson and M. Sbisá (eds). Cambridge, MA: Harvard University Press.

Averill, J.R. (1980) A constructivist view of emotion. In R. Plutchik and H. Kellerman (eds), *Emotion: Theory, Research, and Experience,* Vol. 1, pp. 305–39. New York: Academic Press.

Averill, J.R. (1991) Emotions as episodic dispositions, cognitive schemas, and transitory social roles: steps towards an integrated theory of emotion. In D. Ozer, J.M. Healy, and A.J. Stewart (eds), *Perspectives in Personality*, Vol. 3a, pp. 139–67. London: Jessica Kingsley Publishers.

Backman, C.W. (1977) Explorations in psycho–ethnics: the warranting of judgments. In R. Harré (ed.), *Life Sentences*. London: John Wiley.

Backman, C.W. (1985) Identity, self presentation, and the resolution of moral dilemmas: towards a social and psychological theory of moral behavior. In B.R. Schlenker (ed.), *The Self and Social Life*, pp. 251–89. New York: McGraw-Hill.

Bateson, G. (1972) *Steps to an Ecology of Mind*. New York: Ballantine Books.

Bauman, R. (1983) *Let your Words be Few: Symbolism of Speaking and Silence Among Seventeenth-century Quakers*. Cambridge: Cambridge University Press.

Beach, W.A. (1990) Orienting to the phenomenon. In J. Anderson (ed.), *Communication Yearbook 13*, pp. 216–44. Beverly Hills, CA: Sage.

Becker, A.L. (1988) Language in particular. In D. Tannen (ed.), *Linguistics in Context: Connecting Observation and Understanding*, pp. 17–36. Norwood, NJ: Ablex.

Bedford, E. (1962) Emotions. In V.C. Chappell (ed.), *The Philosophy of Mind*, pp. 110–26. Englewood Cliffs, NJ: Prentice Hall.

Berger, P.L. and Luckman, T. (1966) *The Social Construction of Reality*. Garden City, NJ: Doubleday.

Bernstein, R.J. (1976) *The Restructuring of Social and Political Theory*. New York: Harcourt Brace Jovanovich.

Bernstein, R.J. (1985) *Beyond Objectivism and Relativism*. Philadelphia: University of Pennsylvania Press.

Bilmes, J. (1988a) The concept of preference in conversation analysis. *Language in Society*, 17: 161–81.

Bilmes, J. (1988b) Category and rules in conversation analysis. *IPrA Papers in Pragmatics*, 2: 25–59.

Blatz, C.V. (1972) Accountability and answerability. *Journal for the Theory of Social Behaviour*, 2: 101–20.

Blum, A. and McHugh, P. (1971) The social ascription of motives. *American Sociological Review*, 36: 98–109.

Blumstein, P.W., Carssow, K.G., Hall, J., Hawkins, B., Hoffman, R., Ishem, E., Maurer, C.P., Spens, D., Taylor, J., and Zimmerman, D.L. (1974) The honoring of accounts. *American Sociological Review*, 39: 551–66.

Bochner, A.P. (1985) Perspectives on inquiry: representation, conversation, and reflection. In M.L. Knapp and G.R. Miller (eds), *Handbook of Interpersonal Communication*, pp. 27–58. Beverly Hills: Sage.

Bostrom, R. and Donohew, L. (1992) The case for empiricism: clarifying fundamental issues in communication theory. *Communication Monographs*, 59: 109–29.

Brown, H.I. (1977) *Perception, Theory, and Commitment*. Chicago: University of Chicago Press.

Brown, P. and Levinson, S.C. (1978) Universals in language usage: politeness phenomena. In E.N. Goody (ed.), *Questions and Politeness: Strategies in Social Interaction*, pp. 56–311. Cambridge: Cambridge University Press.

Brown, R.H. (1987) Personal identity and political economy. In *Society as Text: Essays on Rhetoric, Reason, and Reality*, pp. 28–63. Chicago: University of Chicago Press.

Brown, R.H. (ed.) (1992) *Writing the Social Text: Poetics and Politics in Social Science Discourse*. New York: Aldine de Gruyter.

Buckholdt, D. and Gubrium, J.F. (1983) Practicing accountability in human service institutions. *Urban Life*, 12: 249–68.

Burke, K. (1936) *Permanence and Change: An Anatomy of Purpose*. Berkeley: University of California Press.

Burke, K. (1966) *Language as Symbolic Action*. Berkeley: University of California Press.

Burke, K. (1969) *A Grammar of Motives*. Berkeley: University of California Press.

Buttny, R. (1985) Accounts as a reconstruction of an event's context. *Communication Monographs*, 52: 57–77.

Buttny, R. (1986) The ascription of meaning: a Wittgensteinian perspective. *Quarterly Journal of Speech*, 72: 261–73.

Buttny, R. (1987a) Sequence and practical reasoning in accounts episodes. *Communication Quarterly*, 35: 67–83.

Buttny, R. (1987b) Legitimation techniques for intermarriage: Accounts of motives for intermarriage from U.S. servicemen and Philippine women. *Communication Quarterly*, 35: 125–43.

Buttny, R. (1990) Blame-accounts sequences in therapy: the negotiation of relational meanings. *Semiotica*, 78: 219–48.

Buttny, R. (1993) Accounts and the accountability of social action. In B. Dervin and U. Hariharan (eds), *Progress in Communication Sciences*, Vol. 11, pp. 45–74. Norwood, NJ: Ablex.

Buttny, R. and Campbell, J.L. (1990) Discourse direction and power: diverging strategies during a welfare interview. In S. Thomas and W.A. Evans (eds), *Culture and Communication*, Vol. 4: *Language, Performance, Technology and Media*, pp. 69–82. Norwood, NJ: Ablex.

Buttny, R. and Cohen, J.R. (1991) The uses of goals in therapy. In K. Tracy (ed.), *Understanding Face-to-Face Interaction*, pp. 63–78. Hillsdale, NJ: Erlbaum.

Buttny, R. and Isbell, T.L. (1991) The problem of communicating Zen understanding: a microanalysis of teacher–student interviews in a North American Zen monastery. *Human Studies*, 14: 287–310.

Cappella, J.N. (1990) The method of proof by example in interaction analysis. *Communication Monographs*, 57: 236–40.

Cicourel, A.V. (1964) *Method and Measurement in Sociology*. New York: Free Press.

Cicourel, A.V. (1972) Basic and normative rules in the negotiation of status and role. In D. Sudnow (ed.), *Studies in Social Interaction*, pp. 229–58. New York: Free Press.

Clayman, S.E. (1988) Displaying neutrality in television news interviews. *Social Problems*, 35: 474–92.

Clayman, S.E. (in press) Reformulating the question: a device for answering/not answering questions in news interviews and press conferences. *Text*.

Clayman, S.E. and Whalen, J. (1988/89) When the medium becomes the message: the case of the Rather–Bush encounter. *Research on Language and Social Interaction*, 22: 241–72.

Clifford, J. and Marcus, G.E. (1986) *Writing Culture: The Poetics and Politics of Ethnography*. Berkeley: University of California Press.

Cobb, S. (1992) The social construction of intentions in narratives: power as position in discourse. Paper presented at the International Communication Association Convention, Miami.

Cody, M.J. and McLaughlin, M.L. (1985) Model for the sequential construction of accounting episodes: situational and interactional constraints on message selection and evaluation. In R.L. Street and J.N. Cappella (eds), *Sequence and Pattern in Communicative Behavior*, pp. 50–69. Baltimore: Edward Arnold.

Cody, M.J. and McLaughlin, M.L. (1988) Accounts on trial: oral arguments in traffic court. In C. Antaki (ed.), *Analysing Everyday Explanation: A Casebook of Methods*, pp. 113–26. London: Sage.

Cody, M.J. and McLaughlin, M.L. (1990) Interpersonal accounting. In H. Giles and P. Robinson (eds), *Handbook of Language and Social Psychology*, pp. 227–55. London: John Wiley.

Coulter, J. (1983) Contingent and *a priori* structures in sequential analysis. *Human Studies*, 6: 361–76.

Coulter, J. (1986) Affect and social context: emotion definition as a social task. In R. Harré (ed.), *The Social Construction of Emotions*, pp. 120–34. Oxford: Basil Blackwell.

Coulter, J. (1989) Cognitive 'penetrability' and the emotions. In D. D. Franks and E. D. McCarthy (eds), *The Sociology of the Emotions*, pp. 33–50. Greenwich, CT: JAI Press.

Coulter, J. (1990) Elementary properties of argument sequences. In G. Psathas (ed.), *Interaction Competence*, pp. 181–203. Washington DC: University Press of America.

Crawford, L. (1986) Reluctant communitarians: personal stories and commune behavior. *Communication Quarterly*, 34: 62–77.

Cronen, V.E., Pearce, W.B., and Snavely, L. (1979) A theory of rule structure and types of episodes, and a study of perceived enmeshment in unwanted repetitive patterns (URPs). In D. Nimmo (ed.), *Communication Yearbook III*, pp. 225–40. New Brunswick, NJ: Transaction Press.

Cupach, W.R. and Metts, S. (1990) Remedial processes in embarrassing predicaments. In J.A. Anderson (ed.), *Communication Yearbook 13*, pp. 323–52. Newbury Park, CA: Sage.

Davis, K. (1986) The process of problem (re)formulation in psychotherapy. *Sociology of Health and Illness*, 8: 44–74.

DeMartino, R. (1983) On Zen communication. *Communication*, 8: 13–28.

Dervin, B., Grossberg, L., O'Keefe, B.J., and Wartella, E. (eds) (1989) *Rethinking Communication*, Vol. 1: *Paradigm Issues*. Newbury Park, CA: Sage.

Draper, S.W. (1988) What's going on in everyday explanation? In C. Antaki (ed.), *Analysing Everyday Explanation: A Casebook of Methods*, pp. 15–31. London: Sage.

Drew, P. (1984) Speakers' reportings in invitation sequences. In J.M. Atkinson and J. Heritage (eds), *Structures of Social Action: Studies in Conversation Analysis*, pp. 129–51. Cambridge: Cambridge University Press.

Drew, P. (1987) Po-faced receipts of teases. *Linguistics*, 25: 219–53.

Duck, S. and Pond, K. (1989) Friends, Romans, countrymen, lend me your retrospections: rhetoric and reality in personal relationships. In C. Hendrick (ed.), *Review of Social Psychology and Personality*, Vol. 10: *Close Relationships*, pp. 3–27. Newbury Park, CA: Sage.

Duncan, H.D. (1962) *Communication and Social Order*. New York: Bedminister Press.

Edwards, D. and Potter, J. (1992) *Discursive Psychology*. London: Sage.

Erickson, F. (1979) Talking down: some cultural sources of miscommunication in intercultural interviews. In A. Wolfgang (ed.), *Nonverbal Behavior: Applications and Cultural Implications*, pp. 99–126. New York: Academic Press.

Erickson, F. and Schultz, J.J. (1982) *The Counselor as Gatekeeper: Social and Cultural Organization of Communication in Counseling Interviews*. New York: Academic Press.

Feinberg, J. (1970) Action and responsibility. In *Doing and Deserving*, pp. 119–51. Princeton, NJ: Princeton University Press.

Fisher, W.R. (1987) *Human Communication as Narration*. Columbia: University of South Carolina Press.

Gale, J.E. (1991) *Conversation Analysis of Therapeutic Discourse: Pursuit of a Therapeutic Agenda*. Norwood, NJ: Ablex.

Garfinkel, H. (1967) *Studies in Ethnomethodology*. Englewood Cliffs, NJ: Prentice Hall.

Geertz, C. (1973) Thick description: toward an interpretative theory of culture. In *The Interpretation of Cultures*, pp. 3–30. New York: Basic Books.

Geertz, C. (1983) Blurred genres: the reconfiguration of social thought. In *Local Knowledge: Further Essays in Interpretative Anthropology*, pp. 19–35. New York: Basic Books.

Geist, P.G. and Chandler, T. (1984) Account analysis of influence in group decision-making. *Communication Monographs*, 51: 67–78.

Gergen, K.J. (1982) *Toward Transformation in Social Knowledge*. New York: Springer-Verlag.

Gergen, K.J. (1985) The social constructionist movement in modern psychology. *American Psychologist*, 40: 266–75.

Gergen, K.J. and Gergen, M.M. (1983) Narratives of the self. In T.R. Sarbin and K.E. Scheibe (eds), *Studies in Social Identity*, pp. 254–73. New York: Praeger.

Gill, M.R., Newman, R., and Redlich, F.C. (1954) *The Initial Interview in Psychiatric Practice*. New York: International Universities Press.

Glassman, B.T. (1983) Zen and communication. *Communication*, 8: 1–12.

Goffman, E. (1959) *The Presentation of Self in Everyday Life*. New York: Anchor Books.

Goffman, E. (1967a) On facework: an analysis of ritual elements in social interaction. In *Interaction Ritual*, pp. 5–46. New York: Pantheon Books.

Goffman, E. (1967b) The nature of deference and demeanor. In *Interaction Ritual*, pp. 47–96. New York: Pantheon Books.

Goffman, E. (1967c) Embarrassment and social organization. In *Interaction Ritual*, pp. 97–112. New York: Pantheon Books.

Goffman, E. (1971) *Relations in Public: Microstudies of the Public Order*. New York: Harper & Row.

Goffman, E. (1974) *Frame Analysis*. New York: Harper & Row.

Goffman, E. (1981) *Forms of Talk*. Philadelphia: University of Pennsylvania Press.

Goodwin, C. (1986) Between and within: alternative and sequential treatments of continuers and assessments. *Human Studies*, 9: 205–18.

Goodwin, C. and Goodwin, M.H. (1987) Concurrent operations on talk: notes on the interactive organization of assessments. *IPrA Papers in Pragmatics*, 1: 1–54.

Greatbatch, D. (1986a) Aspects of topical organisation in news interviews: the use of agenda shifting procedures by interviewees. *Media, Culture, and Society*, 8: 441–55.

Greatbatch, D. (1986b) Some standard uses of supplementary questions in news interviews. In J. Wilson and B.K. Crow (eds), *Belfast Working Papers in Language and Linguistics*, Vol. 8, pp. 86–123. Jordanstown: University of Ulster.

Greatbatch, D. (1988) A turn-taking system for British news interviews. *Language in Society*, 17: 401–30.

Grice, H.P. (1975) Logic and conversation. In P. Cole and J. Morgan (eds), *Syntax and Semantics 3: Speech Acts*, pp. 41–58. New York: Academic Press.

Grimstone, A.V. (1977) Introduction. In K. Sekida *Two Zen Classics*. New York: Weatherhill.

Gumperz, J.J. and Cook-Gumperz, J. (1982) Introduction: language and the communication of social identity. In J.J. Gumperz (ed.), *Language and Social Identity*, pp. 1–21. New York: Cambridge University Press.

Hanson, N. (1960) *Patterns of Discovery*. Cambridge: Cambridge University Press.

Harré, R. (1977) The ethogenic approach: theory and practice. In L. Berkowitz (ed.), *Advances in Experimental Social Psychology*, Vol. 10, pp. 284–314. New York: Academic Press.

Harré, R. (1979) *Social Being*. Totowa, NJ: Littlefield, Adams.

Harré, R. (ed.) (1986) *The Social Construction of Emotions*. Oxford: Basil Blackwell.

Harré, R. (1991) *Physical Being*. Oxford: Basil Blackwell.

Harré, R. and Secord, P.F. (1973) *The Explanation of Social Behaviour*, Totowa, NJ: Littlefield, Adams.

Harris, S. (1986) Interviewer's questions in broadcast interviews. In J. Wilson and B.K. Crow (eds), *Belfast Working Papers in Language and Linguistics*, Vol. 8, pp. 50–85. Jordanstown: University of Ulster.

Harris, S. (1991) Evasive actions: how politicians respond to questions in political interviews. In P. Scannell (ed.), *Broadcast Talk*, pp. 76–99. London: Sage.

Hart, H.L.A. (1955) The ascription of responsibility and rights. In A.G.N. Flew (ed.), *Logic and Language*, pp. 145–66. Oxford: Basil Blackwell.

Harvey, J.H., Weber, A.L., and Orbuch, T.L. (1990) *Interpersonal Accounts: A Social Psychological Perspective*. Oxford: Basil Blackwell.

Heath, C. (1988) Embarrassment and interactional organisation. In P. Drew and A. Wootton (eds), *Erving Goffman: Exploring the Interaction Order*, pp. 136–160. Boston: Northeastern University Press.

Heritage, J. (1984) *Garfinkel and Ethnomethodology*. Cambridge: Polity.

Heritage, J. (1985) Analyzing news interviews: aspects of the production of talk for an overhearing audience. In T.A. van Dijk (ed.), *Handbook of Discourse Analysis*, Vol. 3: *Discourse and Dialogue*, pp. 95–117. New York: Academic Press.

Heritage, J. (1988) Explanations as accounts: a conversation analytic perspective. In C. Antaki (ed.), *Analysing Everyday Explanation: A Casebook of Methods*, pp. 127–44. London: Sage.

Heritage, J. and Greatbatch, D. (1991) On the institutional character of institutional talk: the case of news interviews. In D. Boden and D.H. Zimmerman (eds), *Talk and Social Structure*, pp. 93–137. Berkeley: University of California Press.

Heritage, J., Clayman, S.E., and Zimmerman, D.H. (1988) Discourse and message analysis: the micro-structure of mass media messages. In R. Hawkins, S. Pingree, and J. Weimann (eds), *Advancing Communication Science: Merging Mass and Interpersonal Processes*, pp. 77–109. Beverly Hills, CA: Sage.

Hewitt, J.P. (1984) *Self and Society: A Symbolic Interactionist Social Psychology*, 3rd ed. Boston: Allyn & Bacon.

Hochschild, A.R. (1979) Emotion work, feeling rules, and social structure. *American Journal of Sociology*, 85: 551–75.

Hopper, R., Koch, S., and Mandelbaum, J. (1986) Conversation analysis methods. In D.G. Ellis and W.A. Donahue (eds), *Contemporary Issues in Language and Discourse Processes*, pp. 169–86. Hillsdale, NJ: Erlbaum.

Hunter, A. (ed.) (1990) *The Rhetoric of Social Research*. New Brunswick, NJ: Rutgers University Press.

Izutsu, T. (1982) *Toward a Philosophy of Zen Buddhism*. Boulder, CO: Prajna Press.

Jackson, S. (1986) Building a case for claims about discourse structure. In D.G. Ellis and W.A. Donahue (eds), *Contemporary Issues in Language and Discourse Processes*, pp. 129–48. Hillsdale, NJ: Erlbaum.

Jacobs, S. (1990) On the especially nice fit between qualitative analysis and the known properties of conversation. *Communication Monographs*, 57: 241–49.

Jaksa, J.A. and Stech, E.L. (1978) Communication to enhance silence: the Trappist experience. *Journal of Communication*, 28: 14–18.

Jayyusi, L. (1984) *Categorization and Moral Order*. Boston: Routledge & Kegan Paul.

Jefferson, G. (1987) On exposed and embedded correction in conversation. In G. Button and J.R.E. Lee (eds), *Talk and Social Organisation*, pp. 86–100. Clevedon, UK: Multilingual Matters.

Jucker, A.H. (1986) *News Interviews: A Pragmalinguistic Analysis*. Philadelphia: John Benjamins.

Kaplan, A. (1964) *The Conduct of Inquiry: Methodology for Behavioral Science*. San Francisco: Chandler.

Kapleau, P. (1988) The private encounter with the master. In K. Kraft (ed.), *Zen: Tradition and Transition*, pp. 44–69. New York: Grove Press.

Kasulis, T.P. (1981) *Zen Action/Zen Person*. Honolulu: University Press of Hawaii.

Kochman, T. (1981) *Black and White Styles in Conflict*. Chicago: University of Chicago Press.

Kraft, K. (1988) Recent developments in North American Zen. In K. Kraft (ed.), *Zen: Tradition and Transition*, pp. 178–98. New York: Grove Press.

Kubose, G.M. (1973) *Zen Koans*. Chicago: Henry Regnery Company.

Labov, W. and Fanshel, D. (1977) *Therapeutic Discourse: Psychotherapy as Conversation*. New York: Academic Press.

Lannamann, John W. (1989) Communication theory applied to relational change: a case study in Milan systems family therapy. *Journal of Applied Communication Research*, 17: 71–91.

Levinson, S.C. (1983) *Pragmatics*. Cambridge: Cambridge University Press.

Lutfiyya, M.N. and Miller, D.E. (1986) Disjunctures and the process of interpersonal accounting. In *Studies in Symbolic Interaction, Supplement 2: The Iowa school*, part A, pp. 131–47. Greenwich, CT: JAI.

Lutz, C.A. (1987) *Unnatural Emotions*. Chicago: University of Chicago Press.

Lutz, C.A. (1990) Morality, domination and understandings of 'justifiable' anger among the Ifaluk. In G.R. Semin and K.J. Gergen (eds), *Everyday Understanding: Social and Scientific Implications*, pp. 204–26. London: Sage.

MacIntyre, A. (1984) *After Virtue*, 2nd edn. Notre Dame, IN: University of Notre Dame Press.

Mandelbaum, J. (1990/91) Beyond mundane reason: conversation analysis and context. *Research on Language and Social Interaction*, 24: 333–50.

Mangham, I.L. and Overington, M.A. (1990) Dramatism and the theatrical metaphor. In D. Brissett and C. Edgley (eds), *Life as Theater*, pp. 333–46. New York: Aldine de Gruyter.

Marsh, P., Rosser, E., and Harré, R. (1978) *The Rules of Disorder*. London: Routledge & Kegan Paul.

McHoul, A. (1978) The organization of turns at formal talk in the classroom. *Language in Society*, 7: 183–213.

McLaughlin, M.L., Cody, M.E., and O'Hair (1983) The management of failure events: some contextual determinants of accounting behavior. *Human Communication Research*, 9: 208–24.

McLaughlin, M.L., Cody, M.E., and Rosenstein, N.E. (1983) Account sequences in conversations between strangers. *Communication Monographs*, 50: 102–25.

Mellinger, Wayne Martin (1987) Talk, power and professionals: partial repeats as 'challenge' in the psychiatric interview. Paper presented at the Institute for Ethnomethodology and Conversation Analysis, North Andover, MA.

Mills, C.W. (1940) Situated actions and vocabularies of motive. *American Sociological Review*, 5: 904–13.

Mishler, E.G. (1984) *The Discourse of Medicine: Dialectics of Medical Interviews*. Norwood, NJ: Ablex.

Morris, G.H. (1985) The remedial episode as a negotiation of rules. In R.L. Street and J.N. Cappella (eds), *Sequence and Pattern in Communicative Behavior*, pp. 70–84. Baltimore: Edward Arnold.

Morris, G.H. (1988) Finding fault. *Journal of Language and Social Psychology*, 7: 1–25.

Morris, G.H. (1991) Alignment talk and social confrontation. In J. Anderson (ed.), *Communication Yearbook 14*, pp. 401–11. Newbury Park, CA: Sage.

Morris, G.H. and Hopper, R. (1980) Remediation and legislation in everyday talk: how communicators achieve consensus. *Quarterly Journal of Speech*, 66: 266–74.

Much, N.C. and Shweder, R.A. (1978) Speaking of rules: the analysis of culture in breach. In W. Damon (ed.), *New Directions for Child Development*, Vol. 2: *Moral Development*, pp. 19–39. San Francisco: Jossey-Bass.

Newell, S.E. and Stuttman, R.K. (1988) The social confrontation episode. *Communication Monographs*, 55: 266–85.

Nofsinger, R. (1991) *Everyday Conversation*. Newbury Park, CA: Sage.

Owen, M. (1981) Conversational units and the use of 'well . . .' In P. Werth (ed.), *Conversation and Discourse: Structure and Interpretation*, pp. 99–116. New York: St Martin's Press.

Owen, M. (1983) *Apologies and Remedial Interchanges: A Study of Language Use in Social Interaction*. New York: Mouton.

Pearce, W.B. and Cronen, V.E. (1980) *Communication, Action, and Meaning: The Creation of Social Realities*. New York: Praeger.

Perinbanayaģm, R.S. (1991) *Discursive Acts*. New York: Aldine de Gruyter.

Peters, R.S. (1958) *The concept of motivation*. London: Routledge & Kegan Paul.

Peyrot, Mark (1987) Circumspection in psycho-therapy: structures and strategies of client-counselor interaction. *Semiotica*, 65: 249–68.

Pittenger, R.E., Hockett, C.F., and Danehy, J.J. (1960) *The First Five Minutes*. Ithaca, NY: Paul Martineau.

Pomerantz, A. (1978) Attributions of responsibility: blamings. *Sociology*, 12: 115–21.

Pomerantz, A. (1984) Agreeing and disagreeing with assessments: some features of preferred/dispreferred turn shapes. In J.M. Atkinson and J. Heritage (eds), *Structures of Social Action: Studies in Conversation Analysis*, pp. 57–101. Cambridge: Cambridge University Press.

Pomerantz, A. (1986) Extreme case formulations: a way of legitimizing claims. *Human Studies*, 9: 219–29.

Pomerantz, A. (1990) Conversation analytic claims. *Communication Monographs*, 57: 231–5.

Potter, J. and Wetherell, M. (1987) *Discourse and Social Psychology: Beyond Attitudes and Behaviour*. London: Sage.

Preston, D.L. (1988) *The Social Organization of Zen Practice: Constructing Transcultural Reality*. Cambridge: Cambridge University Press.

Psathas, G. and Anderson, T. (1990) The 'practices' of transcription in conversation analysis. *Semiotica*, 78: 75–99.

Ragan, S.L. (1983) Alignment and conversational coherence. In R.T. Craig and K. Tracy (eds), *Conversational Coherence: Form, Structure and Strategy*, pp. 157–71. Beverly Hills, CA: Sage.

Rees, S. (1975) How misunderstanding occurs. In R. Bailey and M. Brake (eds), *Radical Social Work*, pp. 62–75. New York: Pantheon Books.

Reid, T. (1977[1788]) *Essays on the Active Powers of Man*. New York: Garland Publishers.

Rorty, R. (1979) *Philosophy and the Mirror of Nature*. Princeton, NJ: Princeton University Press.

Rosemont, H. (1970) The meaning is the use: *koan* and *mondo* as linguistic tools of the Zen masters. *Philosophy East and West*, 20: 109–19.

Rosenblum, K.E. (1987) When is a question an accusation? *Semiotica*, 65: 143–56.

Sabini, J. and Silver, M. (1982) *Moralities of Everyday Life*. Oxford: Oxford University Press.

Sacks, H. (1972) On the analyzability of stories by children. In J.J. Gumperz and D. Hymes (eds), *Directions in Sociolinguistics: The Ethnography of Communication*, pp. 325–45. New York: Holt, Rinehart & Winston.

Sacks, H. (1975) Everyone has to lie. In B. Blount and M. Sanches (eds), *Sociocultural Dimensions of Language Use*, pp. 57–80. New York: Academic Press.

Sacks, H. (1987 [1973]) On the preference for agreement and contiguity in sequences in conversation. In G. Button and J.R.E. Lee (eds), *Talk and Social Organisation*, pp. 54–69. Cleveland, UK: Multilingual Matters.

Sacks, H. (1989 [1964]) Lecture three: the correction–invitation device. *Human Studies*, 12: 247–52.

Sacks, H., Schegloff, E.A., and Jefferson, G. (1974) A simplest systematics for the organization of turn-taking for conversation. *Language*, 50: 696–735.

Sanders, R.E. (1985) The interpretation of nonverbals. *Semiotica*, 55: 195–216.

Sanders, R.E. (1991) Presentation at the Speech Communication Association Annual Convention, Atlanta.

Sarbin, T.R. (1986) The narrative as root metaphor for psychology. In T.R. Sarbin (ed.), *Narrative Psychology: The Storified Nature of Human Conduct*, pp. 3–21. New York: Praeger.

Scheff, T.J. (1990) *Microsociology: Discourse, Emotion, and Social Structure*. Chicago: University of Chicago Press.

Schegloff, E.A. (1982) Discourse as an interactional achievement: some uses of 'uh huh' and other things that come between sentences. In D. Tannen (ed.), *Georgetown University Roundtable on Languages and Linguistics*, pp. 71–93. Washington DC: Georgetown University Press.

Schegloff, E.A. (1987) Between micro and macro: contexts and other connections. In J.C. Alexander, B. Giesen, R. Much, and N.J. Smelser (eds), *The Micro–Macro Link*, pp. 207–34. Berkeley: University of California Press.

Schegloff, E.A. (1988) Goffman and the analysis of conversation. In P. Drew and A. Wootton (eds), *Erving Goffman: Exploring the Interaction Order*, pp. 89–135. Boston: Northeastern University Press.

Schegloff, E.A. (1991) Reflections on talk and social structure. In D. Boden and D.H. Zimmerman (eds), *Talk and Social Structure*, pp. 44–70. Berkeley: University of California Press.

Schegloff, E.A. and Sacks, H. (1973) Opening up closings. *Semiotica*, 7: 289–327.

Schlenker, B.R. (1980) *Impression Management*. Monterey, CA: Brooks/Cole.

Schönbach, P. (1980) A category system of account phases. *European Journal of Social Psychology*, 10: 195–200.

Schönbach, P. (1990) *Accounts Episodes: The Management or Escalation of Conflict*. Cambridge: Cambridge University Press.

Schutz, Alfred (1964) *Collected Papers II: Studies in Social Theory*. The Hague: Martinus Nijhoff.

Scott, M.B. and Lyman, S.M. (1968) Accounts. *American Sociological Review*, 33: 46–62.

Scott, M.B. and Lyman, S.M. (1970) Accounts, deviance, and social order. In J.D. Douglas (ed.), *Deviance and Respectability*, pp. 89–119. New York: Basic Books.

Semin, G.R. and Manstead, A.S.R. (1982) The social implications of embarrassment displays and restitution behaviour. *European Journal of Social Psychology*, 12: 367–77.

Semin, G.R. and Manstead, A.S.R. (1983) *The Accountability of Conduct: A Social Psychological Analysis*. New York: Academic Press.

Shapiro, M.J. (1984) Introduction. In M.J. Shapiro (ed.), *Language and Politics*. New York: New York University Press.

Shields, N.M. (1979) Accounts and other interpersonal strategies in a credibility detracting context. *Pacific Sociological Review*, 22: 255–72.

Shimano, E.T. (1988) Zen koans. In K. Kraft (ed.), *Zen: Tradition and Transition*, pp. 70–88. New York: Grove Press.

Shotter, J. (1981) Telling and reporting: prospective and retrospective uses of self-ascriptions. In C. Antaki (ed.), *The Psychology of Ordinary Explanations of Social Behaviour*, pp. 157–181. New York: Academic Press.

Shotter, J. (1984) *Social Accountability and Selfhood*. Oxford: Basil Blackwell.

Shotter, J. (1985) Social accountability and self specification. In K.J. Gergen and K.E. Davis (eds), *The Social Construction of the Person*, pp. 167–89. New York: Springer-Verlag.

Shotter, J. (1987) The social construction of an 'us': problems of accountability and narratology. In R. Burnett, P. McGhee, and D. Clarke (eds), *Accounting for Relationships: Explanation, Representation and Knowledge*, pp. 224–47. New York: Methuen.

Shotter, J. (1989) Social accountability and the social construction of 'you'. In J. Shotter and K.J. Gergen (eds), *Texts of Identity*, pp. 133–51. London: Sage.

Shweder, R.A. and Fiske, D.W. (1986) Introduction: uneasy social science. In D.W. Fiske and R.A. Shweder (eds), *Metatheory and Social Science: Pluralisms and Subjectivities*, pp. 1–18. Chicago: University of Chicago Press.

Sigman, S.J. (1987) *A Perspective on Social Communication*. Lexington, MA: Lexington Books.

Simons, H.W. (ed.) (1989) *Rhetoric in the Human Sciences*. London: Sage.

Sinclair, J. McH. and Coulthard, R. M. (1975) *Towards an Analysis of Discourse*. London: Oxford University Press.

Sluzki, C.E. (1975) The coalitionary process in initiating family therapy. *Family Process*, 14: 67–77.

Sluzki, C.E. (1978) Marital therapy from a systems theory perspective. In T.J. Paolino and B.S. McCrady (eds), *Marriage and Marital Therapy*, pp. 366–94. New York: Brunner/Mazel.

Sluzki, C.E. (1983) Process, structure and world views: toward an integrated view of systemic models in family therapy. *Family Process*, 22: 469–75.

Sluzki, C.E. (1990) Therapeutic conversations: systemic blueprints of a couple's interview. In R. Chasin (ed.), *Couple Therapy: Many Approaches to One Case*. New York: Guilford Press.

Stokes, R. and Hewitt, J.P. (1976) Aligning actions. *American Sociological Review*, 41: 838–49.

Synder, C.R. and Higgins, R.L. (1988) Excuses: their effective role in the negotiation of reality. *Psychological Bulletin*, 104: 23–5.

Synder, C.R., Higgins, R.L., and Stucky, R.J. (1983) *Excuses: Masquerades in Search of Grace*. New York: John Wiley.

Taylor, C. (1978) Interpretation and the sciences of man. In R. Beechler and A.R. Dreugson (eds), *The Philosophy of Society*, pp. 156–99. London: Methuen.

Tedeschi, J.T. and Reiss, M. (1981) Verbal strategies in impression management. In C. Antaki (ed.), *The Psychology of Ordinary Explanations of Social Behaviour*, pp. 271–309. New York: Academic Press.

Todorov, T. (1984) *Mikhail Bakhtin: The Dialogical Principle* (translated by Wlad Godzich). Minneapolis: University of Minnesota Press.

Tompkins, P.K. and Cheney, G. (1983) The use of accounts analysis: a study of organizational decision-making and identification. In L.L. Putnam and M.E. Pacanowsky (eds), *Communication and Organizations: An Interpretative Approach*, pp. 123–46. Beverly Hills, CA: Sage.

Toulmin, S. (1970) Reasons and causes. In R. Borger and F. Cioffi (eds), *Explanation in the Behavioural Sciences*, pp. 1–26. London: Cambridge University Press.

Tracy, K. (1988) A discourse analysis of four discourse studies. *Discourse Processes*, 11: 233–45.

Turner, R. (1976) Utterance positioning as an interactional resource. *Semiotica*, 17: 233–45.

Watson, D.R. (1978) Categorization, authorization and blame-negotiation. *Sociology*, 12: 105–13.

Watson, D.R. and Sharrock, W.W. (1991) Something on accounts. *Discourse Analysis Research Group Newsletter*, 7: 3–11.

Watson, D. R. (1992) The understanding of language use in everyday life: is there a common ground? In G. Watson and R. Seiler (eds), *Text in Context: Studies in Ethnomethodology*, pp. 1–19. Newbury Park, CA: Sage.

Watzlawick, P., Bavelas, J.B., and Jackson, D.D. (1967) *Pragmatics of Human Communication*. New York: W.W. Norton.

Weber, A.L., Harvey, J.H., and Stanley, M.L. (1987) The nature and motivations of accounts for failed relationships. In R. Burnett, P. McGhee, and D. Clarke (eds), *Accounting for Relationships: Explanation, Representation and Knowledge*, pp. 114–33. New York: Methuen.

Weiner, B., Amirkham, J., Folkes, V.S., and Verette, J.A. (1987) An attributional analysis of excuse giving: studies of a naive theory of emotion. *Journal of Personality and Social Psychology*, 52: 316–24.

White, G.M. (1991) Moral discourse and the rhetoric of emotions. In C.A. Lutz and L. Abu-Lughod (eds), *Language and the Politics of Emotion*, pp. 46–68. Cambridge: Cambridge University Press.

Wieder, D.L. and Pratt, S. (1990) On being a recognizable Indian among Indians. In D. Carbaugh (ed.), *Cultural Communication and Intercultural Contact*, pp. 45–64. Hillsdale, NJ: Erlbaum.

Wittgenstein, L. (1953) *Philosophical Investigations* (trans. G.E.M. Anscombe). New York: Macmillan.

Wodak, R. (1981) How do I put my problem? Problem presentation in therapy and interview. *Text*, 1: 191–213.

Wuthnow, R. (1987) *Meaning and Moral Order*. Berkeley: University of California Press.

Zimmerman, D.H. (1970) The practicalities of rule use. In J.D. Douglas (ed.), *Understanding Everyday Life*, pp. 221–38. Chicago: Aldine.

Zimmerman, D.H. (1974) Fact as a practical accomplishment. In R. Turner (ed.), *Ethnomethodology*. Baltimore: Penguin.

Zimmerman, D.H. (1988) On conversation: the conversation analytic perspective. In J. Anderson (ed.), *Communication Yearbook*, Vol. 11, pp. 304–26. Beverly Hills, CA: Sage.

Index